Georgia Bible Records

— *Supplement* —

1772-1940

Collected by
Jeannette Holland Austin

HERITAGE BOOKS
2008

HERITAGE BOOKS
AN IMPRINT OF HERITAGE BOOKS, INC.

Books, CDs, and more—Worldwide

For our listing of thousands of titles see our website at
www.HeritageBooks.com

Published 2008 by
HERITAGE BOOKS, INC.
Publishing Division
100 Railroad Ave. #104
Westminster, Maryland 21157

Copyright © 1977 Jeannette Holland Austin

All rights reserved. No part of this book may be reproduced or transmitted in any form or by any means, electronic or mechanical, including photocopying, recording or by any information storage and retrieval system without written permission from the author, except for the inclusion of brief quotations in a review.

International Standard Book Number: 978-1-58549-588-7

NOTE:

These bible records came mostly from the Georgia State Archives' folder collection; also from Leonardo Andrea Collection as well as my own personal collection.

If no name ("owner" of the bible) is provided, then it is a donated bible at the Georgia State Archives, Atlanta, Georgia. When it was provided, I added the year of donation adjacent to the name and address of owners. A current address for any of the owners is not available.

Jeannette Holland Austin

TABLE OF CONTENTS

ABERCROMBIE-HILL-WARNER of Meriwether Co., Ga. 44-46
ADAMS, WILLIAM TANNER of Washington Co., Ga 12-13
ANDREWS, MARK of Essex and Cumberland Co.'s, Va, and Ga 34-35
ASH, JOHN HERGAN of Savannah, Ga 26-27
ATKISSON, JOAB of Fluvanna Co., Va. And Oglethorpe Co., Ga. 21-23
AUSTIN, SOLOMON KIRKSY of Newton, Henry & DeKalb Co.'s, Ga. 59-60
AYCOCK-LACKEY of Augusta, Ga 18-21
BACCOS, THURMOND JOSEPH 23-24
BAILEY-MAY-COLLINS FAMILY 1-3
BANKS, RALPH of Columbus, Ga 24-26
BANKS, JAMES OLIVER of Banks Co., Ga 16-18
BARNETT, WILLIAM 27-28
BARNETT-GRIFFIN of Powhatan Co., Va. And Greene Co., Ga 38-39
BARRETT, WILLIAM GODWIN of Sumter Co., S. C. and Ga 13-15
BARWICK, NATHAN of Washington Co., Ga 11-12
BATES-WALLACE 52-53
BELL, SAMUEL 50-51
BIRD, HOMER V. of Hall Co., Ga 15-16
BIRDSEY of Fayetteville & Wilmington, NC, Ocala, FL, Macon, Ga 54-55
BLUE, F. A. 81-82
BLUE-MITCHELL-MCDUFFIE-WILLIFORD 46-47
BOND, JAMES G. 78-81
BOND, WILLIAM DUDLEY of Gwinnett Co., Ga 79
BOND, JOSEPH 77
BOOTH, THOMAS ATKINS of Hartwell, Hart Co., Ga 82-85
BOWDOIN, JOSHUA 85
BOWLING, THORNBERRY OF OGLETHORPE CO., GA. 86-87
BUIE, JAMES A. 89
BULL, JAMES A. 89-90
BULLOCK, WILLIAM of Franklin Co., Ga 129-130
BURCH, WILLIAM DAPESNEY of Hart, Towns and Habersham Co.'s, Ga. 99
BURCH, JOHN B. of Rabun Co., Ga 100
BURCH, THOMAS 98
BURGE, WOODY 101
BURKS, JAMES M. of Jasper, Washington, Houston, Bibb Co.'s, Ga 103-104
CALDWELL, DAVID of Pittsylvania Co., Va. And Jasper Co., Ga 32-34
CALDWELL, JOHN, formerly of Ireland; Ga 104-105
CALHOUN, JAMES of Washington and Baker Co.'s, Ga 159-160
CALLAWAY, JOSHUA S. 114-115
CALLAWAY, JOSEPH 115-116

CAMPBELL, ARCHIBALD 112-114
CANDLER, ASA GRIGGS of Atlanta, Ga 120-121
CANDLER, Charles Howard of Atlanta, Ga 116-120
CARLTON, JAMES, SR. of Greene Co., Ga 111-112
CARLTON, THOMAS of Wilkes Co., Ga 110-111
CARTER 71
CASSADAY, RICHARD W. 95-96
CHAMLEE, JOHN of Cherokee Co., Ga 99
CHAPEAU, OLIVER of Charleston, SC and Savannah, Ga 5-6
COBB, DAVID H. of Milton Co., Ga 106
COBB, SAMUEL of Franklin and Cherokee Co.'s, Ga 105-106
COBB, JAMES 155-156
COBB, JAMES H. 107
COLLEY, JOHN 127-128
COLLEY, JOHN 172-173
COLLINS, JOHN 28-29
COLQUITT, John Wesley of Pike Co., Ga 171
COLQUOHOUN, DUNCAN of Cheraw Dist., SC and Talbot Co., Ga 134
CONNER, WILSON of Craven Co., SC and Ga 145-146
COOK, JAMES of Clarke Co., Ga 183
COWAN, NATHANIEL HARRIS 141-144
COWAN, WILLIAM S. of Newton Co., Ga 182
DANCER, W. R. of Dougherty Co., Ga 180-181
DARSEY, HENRY W. of Bainbridge, Ga 187-188
DARSEY, JOSEPH 186-187
DAY, DAVID of Clarke Co., Ga 169-170
DELANY, JOHN MCMILLAN 140-141
DENHAM, WILLIAM THOMAS 170
DEVEREUX, CHARLES of Baldwin and Hancock Co.'s, Ga 174
DEWOLF, ANTHONY 168-169
DICKINSON, BENJAMIN SLATON of Prattville, AL and Atlanta, Ga 179-180
DICKSON, WILLIAM W. of Clayton Co., Ga 62-65
DICKSON, STEPHEN L. of Franklin Co., Ga. 60-62
DOZIER, ALBERT GREEN of Columbia Co., Ga 188-190
DOZIER, GREEN JONES of Columbia and Wilkes Co.'s, Ga 191
DOZIER, LEONARD III of SC and Elbert Co., Ga 136
DUGGAN, ARCHELEUS CONE of NC, Barnwell, SC & Warthen, Ga 147-148
EARP, CALEB of 96TH Dist., SC and Franklin Co., Ga 139-140
EATON, JOSEPH 167
EDWARDS, LITTLETON CLEAVELAND 167-168
ELKINS, THOMAS 175-176
EVANS, GEORGE BROWN 66
EVANS, DAVY OF LONDIN, S. C. AND GA 56-59

FEW, JOSEPH of Chester and Spartanburg Co.'s, SC, Warren Co., Ga 135
FISH, NATHAN OF JASPER CO. 128-129
FRANKLIN, JEREMIAH of NC, Franklin Co., Ga, Dallas Co., AL 158-159
GILBERT, J. D. 71
GORHAM, WILLIS 150-151
GREER, LEONARD FORSYTH of Monroe Co., Ga 162-163
HALSEY of Bibb Co., Ga 1
HARPER-BARNETT of Auburn, AL and Atlanta, Ga 35-38
HARRIS, SIDON H. of Burke and Madison Co's, Ga 160-161
HARRISON, JOHN 178
HEARN, JONATHAN of Sussex Co., Delaware and Putnam Co., Ga. 133
HEIDT, JOHN 102
HILL, WILLIAM, SR. 48-50
HILL, BENJAMIN F. 31-32
HOLLAND, HETTY JANE of Columbus Ga, and Russell Co., AL 29-30
HORNSBY, THOMAS JEFFERSON 54-55
HUNT, RICHARD H. 121-122
JORDAN, JOHN A. 97-98
JORDAN, JOHN W. 108
JORDAN, NEWTON M. of Washington Co., Ga 108-109
KEMP, JOHN, SR. of Wayne Co., Ga 130
KILGORE-TURK 76-77
LITTLE, AMANDA HOLLAND 4
MAJORS, of SC and Ga 136-137
MARTIN, CHARLES of Union Co., SC and Jasper Co., Ga 137-138
MARTIN, JAMES MARION of Jasper Co., Ga 138-139
MCDANIEL, JAMES 173-174
MCGEHEE, JOHN 157-159
MERCK, WILLIAM E. 164
MICHAEL, ANDERSON GREEN of Walton Co., Ga 151-152
MIKEL, DAVID of Walton Co., Ga 153
MITCHELL, W. W.109-110
MORGAN, ASA WARE 74
MORGAN, HIRAM of Greenville, Ga 73
MORGAN, WILLIAM 72
MORGAN of Berkshire Co., Massachusetts and Macon Co., Ga 39
NICHOLSON, ELIZABETH SOPHIA SPANN 163
OVERBY, NICHOLAS of Abbeville Co., SC and Stewart Co., GA 148
PEACOCK 3-4
PERKINS, ABRAHAM 67-68
POPE, JESSE of Warren Co., Ga 144
PORTER, OLIVER of Madison, Ga 124
ROLLINS, HARRY BRENT 99

ROSE, WILLIAM of Chattooga Co., Ga 123-124
SCAIPE, MARY CROSBY POOLE of Ga and LA 69
SCHUMPERT, FREDERICK of Newberry Co., SC and Hartwell, Ga 161
SEE, JOHN 72
SMITH, HYROM JACKSON 5
STEPHENS, GREENBERRY of Clayton Co., Ga 91-93
STEVENS, OBEDIAH 126
STOW-FERRELL of GA and AL 70
STRICKLAND, JAMES 164
SULLIVAN, DENNIS of Burke Co., Ga 131
TATUM, ABNER of Norfolk, VA, Granville, NC, 9th Dist., SC, Lincoln and Madison Co.'s, Ga 139
THOMAS, JOHN SHERWOOD of Baldwin Co., Ga 177
THOMAS, WILLIAM C. 51-52
THREADGILL, WILLIAM 149
TURK, JOHN NEWTON 74
TURK, WILLIAM 75
UPSHAW, JOHN 99-100
WALDEN, SAMUEL 132
WALKER, JOHN of Orangeburg Dist., SC and Washington Co., Ga 154
WALL, ROBERT E. of Wilkes Co., NC, Spartanburg, SC, and Walker Co., Ga 94-96
WALLER, JOHN of Maryland and Hancock Co., Ga 31
WALLER, JOHN of Hancock Co., Ga 31
WASHBURN, MICHAEL A. 141
WEST, A. J. of Ashville, NC and Gilmer Co., Ga 8

HALSEY BIBLE of Bibb Co.
GA DAR Collection

BIRTHS:

David Parkman Halsey 1/7/1857
Henry Freeman Halsey 4/13/1858
Lachlan McIntosh Halsey 12/28/1861
Alexander Campbell Halsey 1/30/1864
William Harris Halsey, son of Lachlan McIntosh Halsey and Anna Harris, Halsey, born 10/30/1888 in Bibb Co., Ga.

DEATHS:

S. Parkman Halsey died on Sunday, 9/4/1864
Eugenia Campbell Halsey died on Friday, 12/10/1875
Lachlan McIntosh Halsey died in Macon, Bibb Co., Saturday, 2/2/1895
William Harris Halsey, son of Lachlan McIntosh Halsey and Anna Harris Halsey, died in Elpaso, Elpaso Co., Texas on Saturday, 2/27/1904.

"The above Bible record now in possession of Mrs. Wallace Harris, Cochran, Ga. It formerly belonged to Mrs. Anna Harris Halsey, daughter of Eliza A. E. Bailey and William Gay Harris, Bibb Co., Ga."

BAILEY-MAY-COLLINS From Georgia DAR Collection

BIRTHS:

John Bailey 5/27/1792
Mary May, wife of John Bailey, 12/22/1796
Children of Mary May Bailey and John Bailey:
Caroline Bird Bailey 2/18/1816
Henry May Bailey 8/18/1818
John Jackson Bailey 8/24/1822
Mary Bailey 12/3/1824
Edmund Washington Bailey 3/11/1827
James Blackstone or M. C. Bailey 1/19/1830
Robert Neal Bailey 2/23/1832
Eliza Ann Ellen Bailey 11/17/1836

Bailey-May-Collins Bible contd....

MARRIAGES:

John Bailey and Mary May 1/19/1815
William B. Johnston and Caroline Bailey ---
Henry M. Bailey and Mary A. Gates 4/5/1853
Robert N. Bailey and Marian Louise Battle ---
William Gay Harris and Eliza Ann Bailey 1/5/1854
George Mozo and Carrie E. Bailey 4/7/1881
George Edna Mozo and J. E. Guilford 11/8/1905
Henry Bailey Mozo and Nell Florence Tyer 6/1/1907

DEATHS:

Caroline Bird Bailey died 8/13/1838
Henry May Bailey 12/16/1882
John Jackson Bailey 8/13/1845
Mary Bailey died 10/4/1834
Edmund Washington Bailey 10/20/1852
James Blackstone Bailey 4/16/1880
Robert Neal Bailey died at two o'clock in evening on Friday, 9/13/1861
Eliza Ann Ellen Bailey Harris, died 7:50 in evening on Friday, 2/20/1920
William Gay Harris 1885
Mary A. Gates Bailey, wife of Henry May Bailey, 5/9/1905
Carrie E. Bailey, wife of George D. Mozo, 5/22/1910
George D. Mozo 1/4/1885

"The above Family Bible is in the possession of Mr. Bailey Mozo who resides on Coleman Ave., Macon, Ga."

"Some Additional Notes Showing Collins Family Connection: (information from records kept by Mrs. Anna Harris Halsey)
John Bailey born near Wilmington, N. C. His parents moved to Georgia beginning 18th century, settled near Sandersville. He married May May near Sandersville. John Bailey's parents were John and Judah Bailey. After death of John Bailey, Sr., his widow, Judah Bailey married Thomas Collins. Judah Bailey Collins died Nov. 6, 1839. Thomas Collins died March 1842. Both are buried in Bailey Family Cemetery at Bailey's Mill on Columbus Road, Macon, Georgia.

Judah Bailey Collins and Thomas Collins had the following children:

Robert Collins who married Eliza C. Smith (1800-1861)
Charles Collins, b. 1797, d. 1865 married Sophia F. Rossetter on 1/1/1835 at Macon, Ga.
William Collins married Latisher McElmurray
and two daughters - Sidney and Annie Collins."

PEACOCK
GA DAR Collection

Robert Peacock, son of Simon and Zilpha, his wife, was born 9/13/1792 in Wayne Co., N. C.

Welthy Howell, daughter of Benjamin Howell, and his wife, America, was born 5/5/1794

Robert Peacock and Welthy Howell were married 7/29/1813, moved to Georgia 1/18/1817.

Children of Robert and Welthy Peacock:

BIRTHS:

Benjah 5/3/1814
Spicy Ann 3/6/1816
Howell 6/29/1817
Ginsy 12/15/1819
R. M. O. 2/18/1822
Dellemar Clayton 5/27/1824
Edna Zimmerman 5/6/1826
James Bryson 4/10/1828
Simon Morris 1/25/1830
Rebecca Melvina 7/30/1832
America Howell, daughter of David and Sarah Howell, was born 8/13/1814
Robert Peacock and his second wife, America Howell, were married 9/15/1833

Children of Robert and America Peacock:

BIRTHS:

Sara Ann 8/23/1834
Patience Pertee 12/15/1835
Marietta McQueen 2/25/1858
Polly Virginia 10/19/1839
John Tyler 9/5/1841
Letitia T. R. 10/25/1845
Laura Rebecca 11/5/1846
Margaret M. 11/11/11848
Jasper R. 2/4/1851
Ulala 4/27/1854
Robert Peacock died 12/9/1861
America Peacock Morrow died 9/8/1883

"This is a correct record, taken from family Bible owned by Robert Peacock, now in possession of Mrs. George Jackson of Baconton, Ga., his daughter."
/s/Mrs. J. N. Peacock and H. Albert Kelly, Jr.

AMANDA HOLLAND LITTLE BIBLE

MARRIAGES:

Mr. F. L. Little and Mrs. A. M. Little was married 10/18/1849 by Rev. Parker Rice at Villa Rica
Mr. W. L. Mayes and Mrs. Lou Mayes was married 7/13/1871 by Rev. Eaton, Atlanta, Ga.
Mr. Fred W. Petty was married to Miss A. T. Mayes 7/5/1896 by Rev. John J. Jenkins, Tallapoosa, Ga.
Mr. Solomon V. Patterson was married to Miss L. Mayes 1/8/1905 by Rev. Mixton at Tallapoosa

BIRTHS:

Mr. F. L. Little 1/29/1827
Mrs. A. M. Little 4/13/1833
(died 7/5/1919)
Miss Marry L. Little 7/5/1851

Mr. J. E. Little 10/4/1858
Mr. J. W. Little 4/29/1862
Master F. M. Little 9/29/1865

HYROM
Owner: Mrs. Winnie Mae Smith Reynolds
1008 Bru, N. W., Cullman, AL 35055

H. J. Smith bought this book from Mancel Garrett 3/23/1912.

BIRTHS:

Hyrom Jackson Smith 4/16/1841
Elisha Smith 7/18/1815
Elenor Smith 8/22/18--
Hyrom J. Smith 4/16/1841
M. E. Smith 12/17/1851
Joseph Henderson Smith 8/9/1876
Savannah Roseann Smith 8/13/1878
Elsie Magnolia Smith 8/9/1881
Sylvester Smith 8/25/1883
Sandford Anderson Smith 5/26/1886
Lovell Clay Smith 8/9/1890

DEATHS:

Littleton Hooten 1873
William Hooten 1873
Marthan Hooten 1896
Elenor Smith 4/25/1897
Elishie Smith 3/22/1899
M. E. Smith 3/16/1903
H. J. Smith 4/2/1933

CHAPEAU BIBLE of Charleston, S. C. and Savannah, Ga.
Owner: Mrs. John S. Moss
700 Myrtle St., N. E., Atlanta, GA (1931)

Thomas T. Chapeau and Ellen Chazal, both of Charleston, S. C., were married at St. Mary's Church, Charleston, S. C., 11/20/1866.
Thomas Chapeau died at Savannah, GA 5/25/1903
Ellen, his wife, died at Savannah, GA 11/12/1911

The following were the children of this union:
Austin Chazal Chapeau, born Charleston, S. C. 9/11/1868, died Savannah, GA 6/1/1884
Eleanor Chapeau, born Charleston, S. C. 8/4/1870, married Alexis Nicholas of Mulhouse, France, at Savannah, GA 4/19/1898
Armand L. Chapeau, born Charleston, S. C. 7/25/1874 married Elizabeth Woltz of Jacksonville, FL 6/6/1906
Elise Chapeau, born at Savannah, GA 7/30/1876, married John S. Moss of Atlanta, GA, at Savannah, GA 12/20/1921
Pauline Chapeau, born Savannah, GA 12/30/1878, married at Savannah, GA to Walter Jamieson of Brooklyn, N. Y. On 11/29/1911
Ellen Duncan Chapeau b.7/13/1883 Savannah, died Atlanta 2/25/1922.

OLIVER FAMILY BIBLE.
Owner: Mrs. George Clay Murray, Dadeville, AL

BIRTHS:
Florence McCarty Oliver, daughter of McCarty Oliver and Susanna Oliver, 3/10/1809
Hannah Kimbrough Banks, daughter of James Banks and Catherine Banks, 1/22/1813
James McCarty Oliver, son of F. M. & H. K. Oliver, 5/12/1831, Elbert Co.
Matilda Louisa Allen 6/1/1833, daughter of W. P. and Nancy A. Allen
Catherine Virginia Cater, daughter of Thomas J. Cater and Amelia E. Cater nee Wimberly, 1/27/1844 (2nd wife)
Children born to James McCarty Oliver & Matilda Louisa Allen Oliver:
Amelia Kimbrough Oliver 11/1/1850.Baptised 1853 Rev. McCarty Oliver
Woodson Allen Oliver 8/7/1853. Baptized by Rev. McCarty Oliver, 1853
Florence Ann Oliver 9/10/1855. Baptized by Rev. McCarty Oliver
Olivia Susanna Oliver 3/11/1859. Baptized by Rev. McCarty Oliver
James McCarty Oliver 6/21/1861. Baptized by Rev. McCarty Oliver
Samuel John Oliver 3/24/1866. Baptized by Rev. Samuel Harwell

MARRIAGES:
James McCarty Oliver and Matilda Louisa Allen 1/10/1850
James McCarty Oliver and Catherine Virginia Cater 2/5/1884
James McCarty Oliver, Jr. and Ada E. Shepard 9/1/1889
James McCarty Oliver III and Ruth Athlove Griffin 10/12/1928

DEATHS:

Matilda Louisa Allen Oliver 10/1/1882
Woodson Allen Oliver 5/13/1887
James McCarty Oliver 8/23/1896
James McCarty Oliver, Jr. 11/16/1902
    Presented to Mrs. J. M. Oliver by her father 1889. Philadelphia National Publishing Co., 724-6-8 Cherry Street. Entered according to Act of Congress in the year 1884 in the office of the Librarian of Congress at Washington, D. C.

MARRIAGES:

Lucile E. Oliver and George Clay Murray 9/19/1911
Kathleen A. Oliver and Robert Lee Smith 11/28/1912
Louise E. Oliver and Alva Pierce Wright 6/27/1913
Mary Stone Oliver and Maurice Linden Robertson 8/7/1919
Edith Allen Oliver and William Thomas Morton 7/1/1920

BIRTHS:

James McCarty Oliver, son of James M. and Matilda Allen Oliver 6/21/1862
Ada Estelle Shepard Oliver, daughter of O. T. and M. M. Stone Shepard 3/9/1866
Lucille Estelle, daughter of James M. and Ada E. Oliver 5/11/1890
Louisa Esten, daughter of James M. and Ada E. Oliver, 5/11/1890
Kathleen Ada, daughter of James M. and Ada E. Oliver, 5/22/1892
Mary Stone, daughter of James M. and Ada E. Oliver, 7/23/1893
James McCarty, son of James M. and Ada E. Oliver, 11/14/1897
Edith Allen, daughter of James M. and Ada E. Oliver, 7/1/1901
James McCarty Oliver died 11/16/1902
Ada E. Oliver and Frank P. Wallace married 6/6/1906
Born to Louise Oliver Wright and Alva Pearce Wright:
Oliver Kemper 4/10/1914
Henry Clay Kemper 7/17/1915
Shepard 6/7/1919
Born to Lucile Oliver Murray and George Clay Murray:
Eloise 12/4/1914
Florence 8/12/1918

William D. Stone, son of Michael D. and Sarah Elizabeth Stone born 12/24/1842
Mary Ann Maria Stone, daughter of Michael D. and Sarah Elizabeth Stone, born 7/21/1845
Michael D. Stone and Sarah E. Smith married 2/13/1842
Michael D. Stone died 12/3/1862
Sarah Elizabeth Stone died 6/8/1872
Newspaper clipping - "Mrs. Sarah E. Stone was born in Camden, S. C. 8/8/1822, last 20 years a member of Baptist Church, died residence,Tallapoosa Co., AL."

A. J. WEST BIBLE
Owner: Mrs. L. O. Hooper, 356 Shotwell St., Bainbridge, GA

Andrew Jackson West, 6th child of Nancy Marinda Griggs & John B. West
Andrew Jackson West born Ashville, N. C.
Nancy Marinda Griggs born Ashville, N. C., died 1878, daughter of Henry Griggs and Anne Towe, died 1832.
Nancy Marinda Griggs and John B. West married Ashville, N. C. 1820
Andrew Jackson West born Buncombe Co., N. C. 6/15/1832, came early in life to Blairsville, Ga. Later to Ellijay, Ga., Gilmer Co.
Andrew Jackson West married,Gilmer Co. 6/14/1855 Leah King Osborn.

Children:
Harriet Morgan West b. 4/4/1856 m. George Thomas Stribling 7/9/1851
Henry Sammones West born Spring Place, GA 11/14/1857 married Marion Lampkin 11/30/1887
Lou Kansas West born Ellijay, GA 1/22/1860 died Martin, GA 7/19/1918 married John Newton Telford (born 5/6/1854) 10/17/1878.
Annie Grady West born Ellijay, GA 3/12/1863, died 5/23/1931 married Westminster, S. C., James Clarence Rudisill 10/12/1884
John Calhoun West born Homer, GA 11/5/1865 married 6/16/1892 Dahlonega, GA, Sarah Wandsleigh Price, born 9/30/1869, daughter of the late William Price of Dahlonega, GA
Garnett Lee West born Homer, GA 5/17/1868 married 6/23/1891 Lallah Rook Remington, born 8/5/1874, daughter of Aborn Remington.

Grandchildren of Leah King Osborn and Andrew Jackson West:
Harriett Morgan West married George Thomas Stribling, born 7/9/1851.

Children:
Dr. Garnett Bob Bee Stribling born 11/29/1882
Henry Eugene Stribling born 4/1886
Lilliam Grady Stribling born 8/27/1888
Myrtle Annie Stribling born 6/7/1890
Henry Sammons West born Spring Place 11/14/1857 m. 11/30/1887 Marion Lampkin born 9/29/1862, daughter of Lewis Lampkin, Athens.
Children:
Lucy Leah West born 5/4/1889
Andrew Lewis West born 8/12/1891 (a doctor)
Mary Haines West born 9/10/1893
Marion Francis West born 8/1/1895
Lou Kansas West 1/22/1860-7/19/1918 m. 10/17/1878 John Newton Alfred born 5/6/1854, son of Harvy Telford of Commerce. GA
Child - Iris Telford born Homer, GA 7/4/1881
Anie Grady West (my mother) born Ellijay, GA 3/12/1863 died 5/23/1931 married 10/12/1884 James Clarence Rudisill, b. 3/22/1862, d. 11/16/1920, son of James Rudisill of Cornelia, d. 2/4/1883.
Children:
Dorothy Annie Clare West Rudisill born 7/26/1886 in Habersham Hall, Homerville, GA m. Oscar Lee Hooper 11/12/1907
Louise Grady Rudisill born 7/26/1897 in Atlanta, GA, died same day, buried Westview Cemetery.
James Clarence Rudisill b. 1/4/1900, died in service of World War 1/14/1918. Buried Jesup, GA. Age 18 years.
John Calhoun West born Homer, GA 11/5/1865 married 6/16/1892 Sarah Wandsleigh Price, born 8/30/1869, daughter of William Price.
Children:
Wandsleigh West born 6/11/1897 married 8/18/1917 Dr. Leland F. Way, born 11/27/1893
Norma Bell West born 7/9/1901 Atlanta, GA married Robert Ried Plowden
Garnett Lee West, born Homer, GA 5/17/1868 married 6/23/1891 Lalla Rook Remington born 8/5/1874, daughter of William Aborn Remington.
Children:
Maud King West born 8/5/1892 married Owen McConnell
Thelma Remington West born 6/10/1894 married Lewis Holloway
Edith Woodfin West born 5/1/1897

Great Grandchildren of Andrew J. West:
Lilliam Iris Telford born Homer, GA 7/4/1881
Daughter of Lou Kansas West and John Newton Telford.
Garnett Bee Bee Stribling born 11/29/1882 married Talitha Loretta Franklin born 10/29/1887.
Children:
Nian Marie born 2/18/1910
William Stokes born 4/1/1911
Mona Louise born 5/3/1914
George Young born 5/1917
Henry Eugene Stribling went west, never married.
Lillian Grady Stribling died in 1894
Myrtle Annie Stribling married Ellis Bryant (one child).
Stribling Children Parents:
Harriett Morgan West and George Thomas Stribling married 1/19/1882
Marion Lamkin and Henry Samones West married 11/30/1887
Children:
Lucy Leah West born 5/4/1889 married (1st) Walter Rylander Mathis 11/1907 (2) Robbie Redwine (one child).
Children by first marriage: Marion R. Mathis
Children by 2nd marriage: Henry Edward Mathis.
Andrew Lewis West born 8/12/1891
Henry Haines West born 9/10/1893
Marion Francis West born 8/1/1895 married Henry Ried
Annie Grady West b. 3/12/1862 m. James Clarence Rudisill (3/22/1862-10/12/1884). Children:
Dorothy Annie Clare West Rudisill born 7/26/1886 married Oscar Lee Hooper, born 8/29/1885 married 11/12/1907.
Children:
Wandsleigh Rudisill Hooper born 11/29/1915
Margaret West Hooper born 1916, buried in Ft. Lauderdale, FL
James Clarence Rudisill, Jr. b. 1/4/1900 in Atlanta, GA, died 10/14/1918
Louise Grady Rudisill born 7/26/1897, died same day, buried Westview Cemetery, Atlanta, GA
John C. West and wife, Sarah Wandsleigh Price married 6/16/1892.
Children:
Wandsleigh Price West married Dr. Leland Way
Norman Bell West married Robert Ried Plowden

Garnett Lee West and Lalla Rook Remington married 6/23/1891.
Children:
Maude King West married Owen McConnell
Thelma Remington West married Joseph William Holloway
Edith West married ---

NATHAN BARWICK BIBLE of Washington Co.
Jared Irwin Chapter, DAR, Sandersville, GA

BIRTHS:

Nathan Barwick 4/27/1822
Sarah A. E. Barwick 6/12/1827
Martha Ann Susan 12/16/1843
Elizabeth Ava 11/6/1846
William Eason 9/13/1848
Nathan Zackariah 9/27/1850
Sarah Ann 9/8/1852
Sophiah Malinda 6/21/1854
Mary Elefare 7/16/1856
Marja Ann 6/2/1858
John Davis 2/11/1860
Stancel Bartow 2/15/1862
Winford Frances 9/1-/1864
Amarintha and Joseph Johnson 10/16/1866

Nancy Cornelia 7/19/1869
Sarah Catherine 5/14/1864
Sara L. Moreland 6/19/1873

MARRIAGES:

Nathan Barwick and Sarah A. C. Shepperd 4/10/1842
William Thomas and Martha? H. S. Barwick ----
William H. Harp and Elizabeth Ava Barwick 12/12/1866
Littleton Moreland and Martha A. S. McCollane? 8/8/1872
T. K. Murphy and Martha A. S. Morland 10/18/1877
W. T. Adams and Marg E. Barwick 12/2/1877
W. Culpepper and Margann Barwick 1/8/1878
Ann V. Magu-- and ----------
John A. Myrick and Nannie C. Barwick 11/25/1899
T. W. Godson and Lora L. Morland 12/2/1894

DEATHS:

Sarah Ann 8/11/1854
William Eason 10/17/1860
Ann Davis --/29/1864
Sarah Catherine 9/28/1866
Nathan Zackariah 11/24/1867
Sophiah? Malinda Barwick Flowers 11/17/1937
Amarintha Barwick Morgan 3/17/1945
Ayres? Barwick 2/1747
Nathan Barwick 5/4/1874
T. Moreland 2/7/1875
Martha A. S. Murphy 5/12/1881
Marjann Culpepper 11/27/1882
Joseph Johnson 5/25/1889
Marintha 3/17/1945
Nancy ---
Sarah A. E. Barwick 10/9/1908
Elizabeth ----
Winifred Frances Barwick Summerlo 9/30/1934

WILLIAM TANNER ADAMS of Washington Co.
Jared Irwin Chapter DAR, Sandersville, GA

BIRTHS:

William Tanner Adams 10/24/1850 (married in Washington Co.)
Mary E. Barwick 7/16/1856
1st wife's children:
Martha G. Adams 11/5/1871
Archelas B. Adams 12/12/1872
Lacora E. Adams 4/13/1874
William Luther Adams 7/7/1875
Amarintha E. Adams 7/27/1876
2nd wife's children:
Clara C. Adams 9/26/1878
Irvin H. Adams 5/22/1880
Nathan Joseph Adams 7/30/1882

Oscar James Adams 12/28/1884
Lillie Clyde Adams 1/2/1887
Sarah Ardelia Adams 7/22/1889
Calvin Emmett Adams 8/22/1891
Mary Winifred Adams 1/6/1894
Johnnie May Adams 5/6/1896

DEATHS:

Archelas B. Adams 9/19/1874
Lacora E. Adams 5/28/1875
Amarintha E. (Duggan) Adams 7/31/1876
(Their baby, three days old, died 7/31/1876)
Irvin H. Adams 8/22/1882
Clara C. Adams 9/30/1885
Oscar James Adams 6/11/1886
William Tanner Adams 8/10/1903
Mary Elefare (Ellephaire) Barwick Adams 2/3/1947

MARRIAGES:

William T. Adams and Amarintha Duggan 1/26/1871 (Washington Co., GA., she was age 16)
William T. Adams & Mary E. Barwick 12/2/1877 (Washington Co., GA)

BARRETT BIBLE
Original in possession of Mrs. Doy (Lillian) Latham
827 Sunset Blvd., N. W., Gainesville, GA 30501

MARRIAGES:

Sumter Dist., S. C., On Tuesday morning, 12/23/1828, married William Goodwin Barrett, b. 3/31/1801, being 27 years, 8 months and 23 days old, and Massey Birdrian, b. 8/29/1805, 23 years, 3 months, 25 days old.
W. G. B. Born Fayetteville, N. C.
M. P. Born Chaston, S. C.
In Charleston, S. C. On Tues. Morning 7th May 1850, married by Rev. James Cuthbert, William G. Barrett & Mrs. Esther Deleisseline Mouk.

DEATHS:

Died on Sunday evening the 25th day of November 1894, my dear sister Mary Leonora Barrett, 64 years old. James R. Routin?
Athens, Ga. 20 April 1851, Ellen Barrett, stillborn 6/15/1852
Cornelius Dupre Barrett was born --
Dec. 1, 1853, Sarah Boardman Barrett was born -
Thomas Henry Barrett was born 10/31/1855, son of W. G. And E. D. Barrett.
On Monday 9/227/1841 was scalded to death in a tub of hot water into which she had accidentally fallen or as we rather think pushed into it by the dog, Jupiter, whose name she repeated several times after the accident - Elizabeth Massey Graves Barrett, being 4 years and 8 days old.
On Monday evening 8 o'clock 11/14/1842 died Peter Birdrian Barrett of inflamation of the brain, aged 7 months, 4 days.
Died on Thursday morning 9/5/1844 our dear little daughter, Sarah Levenia Creasy Barrett, being 15 months and 17 days old of inflamation of the brain and bowels.
Died on Monday evening 10/8/1849 my dearest wife, Mrs. Massey Goodwin Barrett in the 45th year of her age....W. G. Barrett.
Died on 8/2/1876 my dear father, William Goodwin Barrett in the 76th years of his age....Jane A. Thornton.

BIRTHS:

Sumterville, S. C., Martha Alice Barrett, first daughter of William G. and Massey G. Barrett 10/4/1829
Sumterville, S. C. , Mary Lenora Barrett, second daughter of William G. and Massey G. Barrett 12/21/1830
Shaws Place, Upper Salem, William Samuel Ferdrian Barrett, first son of William G. and Massey G. Barrett, 7/13/1832
Vicinity of Bethel Church, Edward Benjamin Barrett, second son of William G. and Massey G. Barrett, 1/1/1834
Vicinity of Bethel Church, Jane Hasseltine Judson, third daughter of William G. and Massey G. Barrett, 6/6/1835.
Frog Branch, S. C., Elizabeth Massey Graves Barrett, fourth daughter of William G. and Massey G. Barrett, 9/18/1837.

Frog Branch, S. C., John Isaiah Barrett 5/3/1839, third son of William G. and Massey G. Barrett.
Bishopville, Upper Sams, James Legh Richmond Barrett, fourth son of William G. and Massey G. Barrett, 7/7/1840
Sandy Ridge, 2 miles south of Sumterville, S. C. Peter Perdrian Barrett, fifth son of William G. and Massey G. Barrett, 4/10/1842.
Sandy Ridge, 2 miles south of Sumterville, S. C., Sarah Lavenia Gready Barrett, fifth daughter of William G. and Massey G. Barrett, 5/18/1843
Sandy Ridge, 2 miles south of Sumterville, S. C., Margaret Anna Barrett, sixth daughter of William G. and Massey G. Barrett, 6/28/1848

DEATHS:
John ___ Barrett 7/31/1862, Athens, Ga.
Rockmart, Ga, my dear brother, 6/27/18-5, Rev. Edward Benjamin Barrett, in the 61st year of his age. J. W. Irvinton.
Francis Stanton Barrett b. 4/5/1842 married 2/2/1869 Mariah Josephine Magee, b. 7/19/1844. Children:
Lyman Elmer Barrett b. 7/13/1870
Rosa Waneta Barrett b. 11/7/1872
Minnie Megee Barrett b. 5/31/1875
Eudelle Agnew Barrett b. 10/20/1877
Paul Stanton Barrett b. 12/25/188-
John Roger Barrett born and died --------

HOMER V. BIRD BIBLE of Hall Co., GA

MARRIAGES:
Homer V. Bird and Ella Jackson at Bellevuet 2/6/1898. License issued and recorded in Wichita Co., Texas.

Family Record:
John Bird and Annie Faucette m. 10/1809. Son, Terral Bird, 6/14/1812
John S. Bird b. Hall Co. 1/28/1849, died 4/9/1889, married 10/16/1868 Lizzie Whelchel, b. 1/20/1849, died 6/5/1925
J. F. Jackson b. Illinois 10/16/1849 d. 4/22/1932 married 3/4/1874 M. S. Graves, b. Missouri 9/18/1850, d. 5/24/1938.
H. V. Bird b. 12/4/1870 Hall Co., Ga., d. 4/6/1951 m. 2/6/1898 Ella Jackson, b. Knobnaster, Missouri 12/5/1877, d. 1/1/1956
Gertrude Bird b. Bellevue, Texas 1/25/1900, child of H. V. and Ella Bird

John F. (Jack) Bird b. Bellevue, Texas 1/19/1902, child of H. V. and Ella Bird

Horace C. Bird b. Ryan, OK 6/16/1917
J. Philip Bird b. Ryan, OK 1/31/1917
Gertrude m. Leslie L. Swinn at Buthrie, OK 8/4/1939
1963 John F. Bird, Brig. General, U. S. Army, Retired.
Horace V. Bird, Rear Admiral, U. S. Navy

JAMES OLIVER BANKS BIBLE

James Oliver Banks, His Bible, 1845
To my son, Willis Banks, b. & d. 1902. /s/J. O. Banks
To my son, Wylie Coleman, 1929. /s/Willis Banks

MARRIAGES:

Willis Banks and Mary Winfrey Oliver 8/3/1819
Willis Banks and Mary Gracy 9/3/1822
Jeptha V. Harris and Mary Oliver Banks 6/30/1860
Thomas Gray Banks and Mary M. D. Waldron 10/23/1851
James Oliver Banks and Martha J. Coleman 1/28/1852
James O. Banks and Lucy Watkins Young 5/10/1870
Daughter, Mary Gray and F. W. Pope
Daughter, Mary Gray and Hampton Osborne
James Oliver Banks and Julia Coleman 6/6/1888
Willis Banks and Jeanie Dunlap 6/26/1895
George Young Banks and Katharine Joyce 12/27/1894
Wylie Coleman Banks and Marie Williams 1/2/1901

BIRTHS:

Willis Banks, b. Columbus, MS, 5/23/1853, m. 6/26/95, died 7/14/34
Jennie Banks, b. Eutaw, AL 1/16/67, married 6/26/95, died 9/25/50
Wylie Coleman Banks, b. Eutaw, AL 12/29/96, married 7/2/49
Mary Bacon Banks, b. Eutaw, AL 2/24/99, died 7/15/99
James Oliver Banks, b. Bent Oak, MS 7/27/1900
Janie Harrington Lyly?, b. Kenefee? Co., MS 9/6/1898, married 7/2/49

BIRTHS:
Martha J. Coleman 4/23/1833
Daughter, Mary Gray Banks 7/13/1853
Son, John Coleman Banks, 10/1/1855
Son, Willis Banks, 5/22/1857
Son, Coleman Banks, 9/1/1859

Son, George Young Banks, 2/7/1861?
Son, John Oliver Banks, 12/26/18--
Daughter, Lucy Young Banks, 11/4/18--
Son, Wiley Coleman Banks, 1/6/18--
Daughter, Anna Hamilton Banks 8/24/1879
Son, Reuben Raymer? Banks 3/3/1884
James Pope 12/15/1877

Willis Banks 4/23/1791
Mary Winfrey Oliver, my wife, 2/5/1803
Mary Oliver Banks 7/10/1820
Mary Gray, my wife, 8/13/1797
John James Banks 8/6/1823
Thomas Gray Banks 12/10/1824
Daughter, Francis Scott Banks 2/19/1826
Son, William Lemuel Banks 9/7/1827
James Oliver Banks 9/6/1829
Dunston Banks 8/15/1833
Daughter, Lucy Ann Banks 11/24/1834

DEATHS:
Mary Winfrey Banks, my wife, 8/1/1820
Son, John James Banks 10/15/1824
Daughter, Lucy Ann Banks, 9/25/1835
Son, William Lemuel Banks, 2/13/1836
Daughter, Francis Scott Banks, 8/16/1844
Willis Dunston Banks 9/25/1833
Willis Banks, D. 9/19/1852 brother's res. Dunston Banks, Columbus, MS
Son, John Coleman Banks d. 6/26/1856 Amos Travis res, Gainesville, AL
Mary Gray Banks, wife of Willis Banks, died at residence of Mrs. Susan Gray at Tuscaloosa Co., 10/11/1857

Son, Coleman Banks, 3/7/1860
James Oliver Banks 11/10/1904
Wife, T. F. W. Pope 5/23/1912
James Fernanandi Pope, son of F. W. And Mary Gray Pope, 4/30/1916
Wilson Banks 7/14/1934

AYCOCK-LACKEY FAMILY BIBLE

Joel Aycock and Neaty Lackey, his wife, was married 2/13/1842
Our father, Joel Aycock, d. 3/23/1895
Our mother, Neaty Aycock, d. 7/28/1888
Our brother, Joel Aycock d. 12/13/1864, hospital, Augusta, GA
Our brother, M. D. Aycock d. 8/29/1888
Our sister, Martha R. Guinn, d. 7/5/1891
Our sister, Margaret E. Shannon, d. 2/27/1910
Our sister, Mary Caroline Taylor, d. 6/20/1911
Our brother, W. H. Aycock, d. 11/6/191-
Our brother, W. H. Aycock, d. 11/6/1815
Our sister, Virginia Thomas, d. 1/23/1923
Eva Aycock Manly d. 3/31/1945
Our---, ---/28/---

BIRTHS:
Elizabeth Lackey 4/12/1792
William Lackey, her eldest son, 8/4/1810
Charles Lackey 12/4/1812
Mary Ann Lackey 11/18/1814
Caroline Lackey 5/10/1816
Noah Lackey 3/2/1818
Martha Lackey 6/1/1820
Nealy Lackey 7/28/1823
-------Lackey 12/----
William Lackey d. 12/23/1846. 10/1849. (Date written under first date)

MARRIAGES:
William Lackey and Elizabeth, his wife, 3/26/1808
Reuben Cook and Martha Lackey 1/26/1840
Joel Aycock and Neaty Lackey 2/17/1842?

DEATHS:
William Lackey 12/23/1846
Pheriby L. Mable 11/3/1857
William Lackey 5/4/1853
Martha Cook 9/14/1854
Mary Cook 10/11/1859
Joel Aycock 3/7/1832
Joel Aycock, Jr. 12/13/1864, in the hospital, Augusta, GA.
M. D. Aycock, Sr. 10/3/1847
Rebecca Aycock 10/1804

BIRTHS:
Joel Aycock 2/25/1819
Neaty Aycock 7/28/1823
Pheriaby E. Aycock 7/12/1843
Martha R. Aycock 2/16/1845
Joel Aycock 9/6/1846
Middleton D. Aycock 3/18/1849
Virginia Aycock 1/5/1851
Mary C. Aycock 2/8/1853
Margaret E. Aycock 4/9/1855
William Aycock 1/11/1860
Eva J. Aycock 1/6/1868
Joel Aycock, Sr. 2/18/1776
Rebecca Aycock 3/1778
M. D. Aycock 9/16/1823

DEATHS:
Elizabeth W. Avret 1/20/1854, aged 65 yrs,, 18 days
The Rev. Alexander Avret 8/27/1858
Alexander Avret 6/10/1887
Sarah Avret 2/1/1897
George E. Avrett, wife of John G. Avrett, 9/14/1919
John Glen Avret 11/29/1924
Jane B. Arrington 9/30/1852
James Arrington 6/27/1845?
John Luther Avrett 11/28/1896
Edmund T. Avrett 2/11/1811, son of John G. and Georgia

BIRTHS:
James and Jane Arrington's daughter, Francis Amanda, 1/23/1839
Joseph and Amanda Avret, daughter of Frances Ellen, 12/20/1839
Margaret A. Avret 11/4/1846
Barbry H. 7/8/1843
William A. 3/14/1846
Louie K. 12/14/1848
Acile? T. 5/14/1851
John 10/17/1854
Thompson A. Blackburn 3/4/1874
Edmon T. Avrett 6/29/1877
Magie Avrett 4/29/1879
Fannie B. Avrett 10/4/1892

DEATHS:
Mary L. Z. Avret 12/22/1834
Louisa Manerva, daughter of Joseph and Amanda Avret, 7/5/1845?
James Arrington 6/27/1848
Cornelia A. L. Avret 11/7/1841
John F. Lucky, son of Mary and J. M. Lucky, 11/18/1847
Mary Jane Avret, daughter of Lavenia and C. C. Avret, 3/8/1851
Hove ----- 2/17/1852
Robert C. Avrett b. 9/26/1881
Salie Avrett 10/22/1883
William L. Avrett 9/6/1885

BIRTHS:
Alexander Avret 2/1/1788
Elizabeth W. Pharoah 1/1/1788
Their children:
1st, Christopher Columbus 12/1/1808
2d, Mary 10/7/1810
3d, Jane Barnes 1/10/1813
4th, Alexander 5/2/1815
5th, Joseph Benson 7/14/1818
6th, Elizabeth 7/16/1820
7th, John Wesley 6/18/1822, 8th, Judith Benton 4/1/1822,
9th, Sarah Mariah 6/12/1826, 10th, Frances Tobiah 2/22/1828

C. C. Avret and M. ? Avret's son, Samuel Alexander, b. 12/1/1834
C. C. Avrets and Levings, daughter, E. Ann, b. 4/17/1838
Mary Jane 5/1839
1. John and Mary Lucky's son, William, b. 8/31/1837
2. Alex Samuel 8/17/1839

John Luther Avrett b. 11/20/1895
Clifford A. Avrett b. 11/26/1890
Lillie Mae Avritt 6/2/1898

MARRIAGES:

Alexander A ret and Elizabeth Wallis Pharoah 1/24/1808
Christopher C. Avret and Mary L. G. Allin 11/28/1833
John M. Lucky and Mary Avret 11/30/1836
James Arrington and Jane B. Avret 1/8/1837
Joseph B. Avret and Amanda McNair 1/17/1839
C. C. Avret and Levenia Murphey 12/22/1836
Alexander Avret and Sarah Lucky 12/5/1839
John W. Avret and Frances A. Arrington 2/31/1850
John G. Avrett and George E. Thompson 12/2/1875
John W. Blackburn and Margaret A. Avret 12/27/1867

ATKISSON BIBLE
Owner: Mrs. Ellis McDonald
4117 Ashford- Dunwoody Rd
Atlanta, GA (1970)

MARRIAGES:
Joab Atkisson and Matilda Ellis Rabun 5/8/1821
George Baber Atkisson and Caroline Buffington 6/7/1867
Grace Atkisson and ---isy Gurwell 9/1891
Jude Atkisson and Jesse Hansford 12/1894
George Ellis Atkisson and Mamie Wallace 2/1912
------Atkission and George Edward McDonald 1/9/1932
-----Atkission and Marion Domesly?
Horace W. Atkission and Katy Wenthan? 194-

BIRTHS:
Joab, son of Michael Atkisson and Cecelia Oglesby, b. 6/15/1798 Fluvanna Co., VA
Matilda Ellis, dau. of Thomas Baber and Sarah Oglesby, b. 8/23/1800
Frances Atkisson, daughter of George and Caroline Atkission, b. 8/1868
Horace Atkisson b. 1/1870, d. 1938
Maud Atkisson b. 1/1871
Eva Atkisson b. 1/10/1877 (d. 5/13/1964)
Annie Atkisson b. 12/3/1878
George Ellis Atkisson b. 9/12/-----
George Stanhope Atkisson b. 1/1894
Sons of Horace and Daisy Atkisson:
Horace Gunnel Atkission 6/1895
Daughter of Horace and Daisy Atkisson
Olivia Atkisson 3/1897
Mary Ella, daughter of Maude and Wise Hansford 12/11/1895
Son, George B. Hansford, b. 3/18/1901, Stephens, Oglethorpe Co., Ga.
BIRTHS:
Thomas Horace Rochester 10/23/1823
Frances Ann Harden 11/29/1827
Marcella 6/4/1828
Victoria 3/7/1835
Henry 5/29/1840
George Baber 9/14/1842
Daughter, G. E. and Vinnie Atkisson
Ellis Atkisson b. 12/7/1912
Daughter, Edith Atkission 8/18/1914
Son, Horace Atkisson 11/16/1916
Son, Ellis Atkisson and George McDonald 5/1932, twins
Daughter, Brazos - 1950
DEATHS:
Thomas Horace Rochester 12/12/1832, aged 9 yrs, 1 mo., 20 days
Marcella Rochester 4/15/1833, aged 4 yrs, 10 mos, 11 days
Victoria Rochester 3/8/1835, aged one day
Henry Rochester 11/1840, aged 6 mos, --- days
Mrs. M. E. Atkisson 2/18/1873, aged 72 yrs, 5 mos, 25 days
J. Atkisson 3/15/1878, aged 79 yrs, 9 mos, 3 days
Frances A. H. Atkisson 7/19/1880, aged 82 yrs., 7 mos, 20 days

George Stanhope Atkisson 7/1897
George Baber Atkisson 6/7/1923 (7/2/1923 struck through)
George Ellis Atkisson 2/17/1918
Caroline Atkisson 2/28/1938
Horace L. B. Atkisson 12/11/1938

DEATHS:
Maude Atkisson Hansford
Treve McDonald 8/22/1846
Brazos McDonald 7/20/1961?
Eva Atkisson 5/13/1964

BACCUS BIBLE

Owner: Mrs. Thurmond Baccus, Social Circle, GA 30279

Bible illustrated by John Franklin. Copyright 1863.

BIRTHS:

Thurmond Joseph Baccos 12/23/1894
Bertha Leona Studdard Baccus 11/26/1800
Hulda Ellen Baccus 7/16/1921
Sarah Francis 6/7/1922
Doris Elizabeth Baccus 11/21/1923

DEATHS:

Mary W. Baccus 12/29/1892
Mahulda Baccus, wife of Ellick Baccus, 11/28/1895
Our little babe depaarted this life the day it was born 9/2/1897?
Alexander Hamilton 9/23/1926

MARRIAGES:

E. H. S. Baccus, son of Joseph and Mary Baccus, married Mahulda Hawk, daughter of Thurmon and Mary Hawk 12/30/1878
Cleophus A. Baccus, son of Mr. and Mrs. A. H. Baccus, married Edna Sawyer 6/3/1922

BIRTHS:

Of the children born unto Elick and Huldy:
Mary A. E. Baccus b. 9/10/1881
Eler O. Baccus 10/28/1884
Estellar J. Baccus 2/24/1888
Francis C. M. Baccus 9/19/1892
Joseph T. Baccus 12/23/1894
Our little babe was b. 9/1897
On 7/18/1899 was born unto us our little babe, W. B. F. Baccus
On 9/24/1903 was born unto us our little babe, Cleophus A. Baccus

MARRIAGES:

Thurmond J. Baccus and Leona Bertha Studdard at G. Studdard's home 12/25/1919, in presence of family and friends. /s/Ed Caudwell, Monroe, GA.

RALPH BANKS' BOOK/Rachel Banks

DEATHS:

Son, Elbert 10/8/1817, aged 7 years, ----mos.
Ralph Banks 10/25/18--, aged 71 years
Rachel Banks 7/11/1851, aged 82 yrs, 2 mos, 5 days
Willis Banks 9/19/1852, aged 61 years, 3 mos, 26 days
Sarah Sims 10/19/1874, aged 81 yrs, 5 mos., 14 days
Henry Banks 9/15/1876, aged 41 years, 10 mos, 13 days
John Banks 9/187--, aged 72 yrs, 10 mos., 22 days
Lemuel Banks 9/10/1854, aged 48 years, 8 mos, 16 days
Priscilla Britt 2/2/1853, aged 50 years, 4 mos, 30 dayss
Mary A. Napier 9/17/1858, aged 59 years, 1 mo., 7 days
Dunslan Banks 9/2/1881, aged 80 years, 9 mos.
James F. Banks 12/16/1867, aged 75 years, 8 mos., 11 days
Richard Banks 5/6/1856, aged 6 years, 6 mos., 13 days
Ralph Banks 6/2/1871, aged 75 years, 1 mo., 26 days
Thomas A. Banks 7/21/1835, aged 46 years, 7 mos., 2 days
Marion Banks 1/16/188-

BIRTHS:
John Troup Banks 11/22/1828, lived 34 yrs, 3 days
Willis Dunstan Banks 2/15/1830, lived 34 years, 6 mos, 16 days
George Young Banks 9/16/1831
Watkins Banks 2/24/1833, lived 31 years, 5 mos., 18 days
Edward Sims Banks 4/15/1834
Susan Martha Banks 10/29/1835 (daughter), died 6/29/1893
Rockingham Gilmer Banks 3/8/1837, died 11/1899
Eugene Banks 4/23/1838, lived 26 years, 23 days
Elbert Augustin Banks 1/15/1840, died 9/9/1902
William Kelly Banks 4/3/1841, lived 33 years, 8 mos., 7 days
Sarah Lucy Banks 11/1842, died 2/6/1928
Anna Josephine Virginia 9/28/1844, died 7/1906
MARRIAGES:
Gideon James Peacock and Josephine A. J. Banks 1/28/1873
John Banks and Sarah Watkins 2/14/1828, Elbert Co., Ga.
Marriages of their children:
George G. Banks and Susan Cook Mitchell 4/18/1854, Columbus, Ga.
Edward Sims Banks & Pauline D'Lanuacy? 1/5/1859, St. Lukes Church
Gilmer R. Banks and Catherine Burney 7/16/1861, Tallahassee, FL
Edward Ellis Yonge and Sarah Lucy Banks 3/27/1872
DEATHS:
John Troup Banks 11/25/1862 at family home in Wejanton?
Eugene Banks at Resaca 5/15/1864
Willis Dunstan Banks at Atlanta 8/14/1864
Watkins Banks, Georgia State Troops, was killed at Atlanta 8/15/1864
John Banks (father) 9/18/1870
Son, Mitchell Banks, wife of George G. Banks, 6/29/1871 near Columbus
William Kelly Banks 12/1-/1874 at family home on Wyanlas?
Sarah Watkins died Wyemton? 1/31/1881 (Mother)
George G. Banks at Hillside home in Stewart Co., GA 12/25/1887
Mattie Banks died near Cottage Mills, Chattahoochee Co., GA 5/26/1888
James Watkins (2nd son)
One of his daughters married Dr. Asa Thompson, Huntsville.
Sarah married Willis Harris
Jane m. Minor Tate
Martha m. Ben Talliaferro
Susan m. Dr. Richardson, Glenville, AL

Sophia m. Judge Eli Shorter (Columbus, Ga., sons in New York)
Eliza m. McGehee
Son, Robt. H.
John Watkins, son of James, m. Susanna Daniel of Chesley 10/27/1798
BIRTHS:
Lucy Woodson, daughter of John Watkins and Susanna, his wife, b. 2/27/1800
Daniel, son of John Watkins and Susan, his wife, 4/27/1801
Sarah, daughter of John Watkins and Susannah, his wife, 5/14/1803
Mary, daughter of John Watkins and Susanna, his wife, 1/16/1805
Martha, daughter of John Watkins and Susannah, his wife, 9/15/1807
Susanna, daughter of John Watkins and Susannah, his wife, 6/29/1810
DEATHS:
Mary Watkins 5/13/1818
Susan, wife of John Watkins 1/6/1827
Lucy Woodson, wife of George H. Young of Waverley 7/7/1852
Sarah Watkins, wife of Col. John Banks 1/31/1881
Daniel Watkins died on ---

JOHN HERGAN ASH BIBLE

John Hergan Ash b. 1/13/1799 d. 9/4/1822, aged 30 years, 4 moS, 9 days
Susannah Burnsides, mother of John Hergan Ash and George Adair Ash, d. 3/12/1826, aged 56 years
Georgia Anna Gorham Ash, daughter of George and Eliza Ash, d. 3/22/1827, aged 1 years, 2 months, 10 days
Eugenia R-----Ash, daughter of George & Eliza Ash, d. 5/29/1831, 9 mos.
Eliza Ash, wife of George A. Ash (6/1/1794-9/28/1839), 45 yrs, 5 mo, 23 days.
Charles K. Ash d. 9/25/1891
George Adam Ash b. 12/23/1793 in Savannah
Mary Eliza Ash, dau. of George and Eliza Ash, b. 12/13/1818, Savannah.
Charles Burnsides Ash, son of George and Eliza Ash, b. 8/16/1821, in New Haven, CT.
Susannah Burnsides Ash, daughter of George and Eliza Ash, b. 1/4/1824, Savannah.
Georgia Anna Gorham Ash, daughter of George and Eliza Ash, 1/12/1826, Savannah.
Geo. Henry Wyer Ash, son of Geo. & Eliza Ash, b. 5/25/1828, Savannah

Eugenia Rosemond Ash, daughter of George and Eliza Ash, b. 8/28/1830, Savannah.
William Rahn Ash, son of George and Eliza Ash, b. 6/20/1832, Savannah.

MARRIAGES:

George A. Ash of Savannnah to Miss Eliza Gorham of Newhaven, CT by Rev. Dr. Kollock, 2/17/1814
Charles B. Patterson and wife, Susannah B. Ash, 7/18/1838
Benjamin Grovenstein and wife, Mary E. Ash, 3/17/1841
My son, Charles R. Patterson and Donna M. Lester 10/20/1869
My daughter, Ida F. Patterson and Henry J. Wade 12/23/1869
Brother, John H. Ash and Miss Lula Foy 6/4/1874

WILLIAM BARNETT BIBLE
Owner: Mrs. William C. Warren, Jr.
3669 Paces Valley Rd, N. W., Atlanta, GA 30327 (1966)

"This bible was the property and contains records of William Barnett, Sr. (1756-1831) whose son, William Barnett, Jr. (1793-1886) married his cousin, Lucy Barnett (1794-1886). She was the daughter of his brother, John Barnett (1752-1833).
William Barnett, Sr. was the great-grandfather of my mother, Florella Harper Glenn. (1845-1927).
Bible was published 1816. /s/Thos. Glenn Cauker?."

BIRTHS:
Polly Barnett 1/1/1800
-----Barnett born before Polly Barnett 1/1/1798
Francis Elizabeth Ogburn 12/21/1824
William Barnett 4/14/1756
Fanney Jones 3/2/1760
Rebkah Barnett 3/8/1779
James Barnett 9/3/1780
Nancy Barnett 10/17/1782
Richard Davis Barnett 1/15/1785
John Barnett 8/31/1787

Fanney Barnett 12/2/1789
William Barnett, Jr. 1/25/1793

BIRTHS:
Zalsay? Davis Barnett 11/6/1795

DEATHS:

James Barnett 4/1782
Nancy Barnett 4/4/1790
John Barnett 4/5/1790
_____Barnett in three weeks after he was born
Polly Ogburn 3/1/1825
Frances Elizabeth Ogburn 5/25/1825
William Barnett, Sr. 2/3/1831
Fanny Barnett, wife of William Barnett, 9/21/1846, in the 87th year of her age

MARRIAGES:

William Barnett and his wife, Fanny Jones, 2/10/1778

JOHN COLLINS BIBLE
Donated to Georgia State Archives
by William W. Greer, Jr., M. D.,
3013 Bowling Green Drive
Walnut Creek, CA 94598

BIRTHS:

John Collins 5/31/1805
Phebe Collins 11/7/1809
Benjamin J. B. Collins 10/24/1834
Sarah B. Collins 12/21/1835
Ann Maria Collins 7/13/1838
Virginia Collins 10/20/1840
Creed Collins 12/14/1847

DEATHS:
Benjamin J. B. Collins 3/14/1835
Virginia Collins 5/16/1842
Sarah B. Collins 3/22/1861
Ann Maria McKinley 12/2/1864
Jennie L. Crumrine 2/21/1876
Creed Collins 4/23/1909

BIRTHS:
Angeline Collins 12/5/1844
William Collins 5/5/1847
Jerry Lind Collins 8/8/1850

DEATHS:
Angeline Collins Michael 3/30/1920

MARRIAGES:
John Collins and Phebe Brice 8/22/18333

DEATHS:
Phebe Collins, wife of John Collins, 8/17/1865
John Collins 6/4/1873 in the 69th year of his age.

HETTY JANE HOLLAND BIBLE of Columbus, Ga. and Russell Co., Alabama, Georgia State Archives

On front cover:

"Grandmother Curran
Hetty Jane Holland"

BIRTHS:
James C. Holland 12/27/1804 Hancock Co., Ga.
Orlando Stinson Holland in Thomaston, Upson Co., Ga. 10/6/1826
James Thomas Holland 6/3/1834 in Columbus, Ga.
Jesse Day Holland 5/3/1839 in Russell Co., Alabama
Hetty Holland in Jefferson Co., Tennessee 12/6/1801

Orlena Holland 6/26/1829 in Muscogee Co., Ga.
Emily Ann Holland 7/13/1830 in Columbus, Ga.
Sarah Elizabeth Holland 12/1/1832 in Columbus, Ga.
Mary Hannah Brewington Holland 4/11/1837 in Russell Co., Alabama
Hetty Jane Holland 3/26/1841 in Russell Co., Alabama
Mary H. Daniel in Columbus 10/21/1859
Charles Marion Curran in Henderson, Alabama 3/21/1865
Holland Kinon Curran in Washington City, D. C. 5/25/1827
Harry Hall Holland 7/20/1854 in Russell Co., Alabama
James Edward Daniel 5/31/1858 in City of Columbus, Ga.
Ervine Walter Holland in Russell Co., Alabama 1/26/1859

DEATHS:
Jesse Day Holland 9/17/1847 in Walker Co., Ga.
James C. Holland 9/19/1853 at his residence in Russell Co., Alabama
O. J. Smith 6/29/1858
Hettie Holland 1/14/1884 at residence of J. T. Holland, Lee Co., AL
Sarah Elizabeth Holland 8/20/1833 in Columbus, Ga.
Orlena J. Smith 6/29/1858 in Russell Co., Alabama
Mary H. Daniel 5/7/1861 in Columbus, Ga.

MARRIAGES:
James C. Holland and Hetty Day in Rhea Co., Tennessee 1/1/1826

WALLER BIBLE of Hancock Co., Ga.
The Arkansas Historian, Oct-Dec issue 1967. Sent to me by a Waller descendant in 1971 (now deceased)

John Waller Senior was born 3/1749
Elizabeth Waller was born 9/1746

BIRTHS OF CHILDREN:
Handy Waller 12/1768
Daniel Waller 8/10/1772
John Waller 6/8/1775
William Waller 1/9/1777
Charles R. Waller 9/14/1780
Elizabeth Waller 2/26/1783
Nathaniel E. Waller 10/12/1787

Nathaniel Waller married his wife, Elizabeth, 2/29/1833
Charles R. Waller married his wife, Emily, 4/23/1803

DEATHS:
Charles R. Waller 5/24/1858
Emily Waller, wife of Charles R. Waller 2/19/1860
John Waller, son of Charles R. Waller and Emily Waller, 6/26/1890

John Waller married Sarah Brown
Mrs. Emily (Waller) Oliver, daughter of John and Sarah Brown Waller, was born 8/5/1846

BENJAMIN F. HILL BIBLE
Donated to Georgia State Archives by Mrs. Mae Hill Purce, Indian Springs Drive, Forsyth, GA

MARRIAGES:
Benj. F. Hill married Araminta Autorrietta Alexander 12/7/1865
Ben F. Hill, Jr. and Stella Viola Baker 12/19/1895
Joe Baker Hill and Kate ?Orten Simpson 10/26/1922
J. Nancy Hill and James Persons ---20/1927
Henry? Edgefield? And Mae Hill 8/3/1930

BIRTHS:
B. F. Hill, Sr. 10/29/1837
A. A. Hill 4/10/1843
Mary Lizzie Hill 10/4/1866
Benj. F. Hill, Jr. 1/20/1871
Georgia Ella Reeves Hill 10/4/1882
Stella Viola Hill 11/24/1875
Joe Baker Hill 8/1/1897
Julia Thorpe Hill 5/8/1900
Ella May Hill 12/4/1909
Miriam Antionette Hill 4/27/1906
Stella Ora Hill 10/7/1909
Joe Jorden? Hill, Jr. 10/23/1924
David Ralalend? Hill 3/22/1931
Miriam Audrey Hill 9/19/1932

DEATHS:
Georgia Ella Reeves Hill 5/22/1888
Nettie A. Hill 3/14/1916
Benjamin Franklin Hill, Jr. 1/28/1918
Benjamin Franklin Hill 6/25/1924
Elizabeth R. Alexander 2/28/1886
Leonidas B. Alexander 3/1/1865

DAVID CALDWELL BIBLE
of Pittsylvania Co., Virginia and Jasper Co., Georgia

Sent to me in 1969 by a Caldwell descendant (now deceased). Original owner was David and Elizabeth Caldwell.

Bible published in 1818 by M. Carey & Son, Chesnut Street, Philadelphia, Pa.

BIRTHS:
David Caldwell 6/24/1769
Betsey, his wife, 3/17/1774
Their children:
William Hurley Caldwell 3/3/1792
Lucey Haskins Caldwell 4/1/1793
Matthew Caldwell 6/3/1794
John Caldwell 12/25/1796
Creed Caldwell 6/23/1798
Sally Caldwell 12/23/1799
Polley Caldwell 5/16/1801
Nancey Caldwell 7/10/1804
Patsey Caldwell 3/3/1809
David Allen Caldwell 1/2/1811

BIRTHS:
Betseyann Caldwell 8/5/1813
John Floyd Caldwell 3/10/1819
Mary Adney Parker 12/10/1832
Martha Ann Caldwell 3/16/1832, daughter of W. P. Parker
Patterson A. Parker 11/3/1834
William R. Parker 10/10/1836
John Floyd Parker 1/18/1839

Nancy Ann E. Parker 11/26/1840
Cloe Amanda Parker 4/7/1845
David C. Parker 12/3/1842
Martha Frances Parker 7/5/1847
Louisa Virginia Parker 1/20/1849
Sarah L. Parker 9/16/1851
Martha Ann Elizabeth Caldwell 12/21/1843
Mary Melissa Caldwell 10/17/1845
Julia Marion Caldwell 8/28/1847
Amanda Permelia Caldwell 8/8/1849
Robert Floyd Caldwell 12/20/1851

MARRIAGES:
David Caldwell to Elizabeth Tanner 1/6/1791
Lucey H. Caldwell, dau. of aforesaid, 3/26/1812, Edmond Caddenhead
Matthew Caldwell, son of aforesaid, to Mourning Satterwhite 9/2/1813
Salley Caldwell, daughter, to Chaney Pitts 4/19/1818
Creed Caldwell, son of above, to Rachel Clayton 12/22/1819
Nancey Caldwell, daughter, to Edward W. King 2/1/1820
Nancy King, widow, 1/7/1824 to Harrison V. Revill
Martha Caldwell to Williams P. Parker 1/7/1832
David A. Caldwell to Ary An Owens 7/23/1833
John F. Caldwell to Martha Ann Thrash 12/4/1842
John H. Williams to Mary M. Caldwell 10/26/1869
James Parker to Julia M. Caldwell 11/8/1871
Robert F. Caldwell to Minnie Frances Jackson 10/26/1876
Amanda P. Caldwell to F. D. Brewer 3/10/1878
Martha A. E. Caldwell to John Lawrence 7/18/1878
James M. Caldwell to Wilmoth J. Harry 4/24/1883
DEATHS:
William H. Caldwell, son of David and Betsy, 2/8/1797
John Caldwell, son of above, 10/20/1809
Polley Caldwell, daughter, 10/30/1809
Lucey H. Caddenhead, daughter of above, 4/20/1814
Betseyan Caldwell 2/12/1825
Nancy Revill, daughter of above, 6/29/1839
Sarah Pitts, daughter of above, 12/16/1859
David A. Caldwell, son of above, 4/9/1861
Elizabeth Caldwell, wife of David Caldwell, 12/3/1861

Creed Caldwell, son of above, 2/16/1862
Matthew Caldwell, son of David and Elizabeth Caldwell, 7/13/1862
John Floyd Caldwell, son of David and Betsy Caldwell, 12/20/1884, aged 76 years and 9 months and is buried at Ebenezer Church, Wood Co., Texas
Patsey Parker 2/6/1895
Martha A. Caldwell 3/2/1902
In memory of Polley Caldwell, who departed this life 7/8/1841, aged 62 years, 6 months and 4 days, and is buried at 18 miles south of Columbus.

Allen Caldwell, husband of the above-named, departed this line 6/19/1849, aged 73 years, 9 months and 19 days and lies by his beloved wife at the above named place.

ANDREWS BIBLE

Donated to Georgia State Archives by Mrss. William C. Warren, Jr., 3669 Paces Valley Rd, N. W., Atlanta, GA 30327 (1966)

Mark Andrews moved out of Essex into Cumberland 11/17/1759

BIRTHS:
Mark Andrews 7/2/1724
Ave Andrews, the wife of Mark Andrews, 7/9/1731
Elizabeth Andrews, the daughter of Mark Andrews and Ave, his wife, 8/7/1748
John Andrews 1/27/1749/50
Jesse Andrews 3/18/1752
Mary Andrews 2/14/1754
Hannah Andrews 12/9/1755
William Andrews 2/23/1758
Susanna Andrews 4/24/1760
Thomas Andrews 12/12/1761
Barnett Andrews 6/11/1764
Wyatt Andrews 8/29/1766
Ann Andrews 8/23/1768
Ave Andrews, the wife of Mark Andrews departed this life 10/29/1768
Mark Andrews departed this life 1/20/175--
Claborn ?? Nett was born the 13 ,177--

Died the 24th off----John Griffin----
Georgia S. 6/27/1792 landed in Green County on Big Creek with my family. (The above is faded)
John G. Barnett was born 12th day of Dec. 1799
Christiana Eastin, the wife of J. B. Barnett, was born 2/4/1813
J. G. Barnett was married to Miss Christiana Easton 2/3/1831
Nathan Thomas Barnett, son of J. G. Barnett and Christiana, his wife, was born 5/12/1832
Thomas G. Barnett was married to Miss Sarah Adams 5/27/1834
Mary Elizabeth Barnett was born 8/18/1835
John Adams Griffin Barnett was born 12/10/1839

HARPER-BARNETT BIBLE

Owner: Mrs. Stanton Pickens, 652 Hempstead Place, Charlotte, N. C. 28207 (1968)

MARRIAGES:
George W. Harper and Ann E. Barnett 1/19/1842 by Rev. Samuel Armstrong
W. F. Glenn and Florella C. Harper 1/31/1866 by Rev. Mark S. Andrews, Auburn, Alabama
George B. Harper and Emma R. Longmire 12/15/1869 by Rev. W. F. Glenn. Second wife was Mattie Lou Barnett.
W. E. Gilbert and Lucy F. Harper 10/12/1876 by Rev. W. F. Glenn
John J. Harper and widow Dottie Davis (nee Blanks) at residence of Mrs. Fred A Blanks, 454 Magazine Street, New Orleaans, LA 12/15/1886 by Dr. W. F. Glenn of Atlanta, Ga.

BIRTHS:
William F. Harper 5/30/1843
Florella C. Harper 12/27/1846
George B. Harper 6/15/1849
John J. Harper 1/30/1851
Robert F. Harper 7/2/1853
James P. Harper 2/3/1856
Lucy F. Harper 3/20/1859
George William Harper, father of above children, was born Wilkes Co., Ga. 11/25/1819

DEATHS:
George W. Harper, father of the above named children, died 9/22/1899 in Hickory, MS and was buried there.
Ann Eliza Barnett, wife of George W. Harper, died in Atlanta, GA 11/19/1895, buried Hickory, MS.
William T. Harper 6/26/1847
James R. Harper 9/30/1872
John J. Harper 9/20/1898 Monroe, LA and was buried there.
George B. Harper 4/1905 in Hickory, MS and was buried there.
John Jackson Harper, father of George W. Harper, was born 12/13/1789 and died and was buried at Auburn, Alabama. 2/20/1847.
John J. Harper (above) married Fanny Ogletree
--------Harper, father of John Jackson Harper married daughter of Nathaniel Jackson.

BIRTHS:
Ann Barnett and his wife, Lucy 2/23/1772-----and she departed this life 5/19/1822.
William Barnett 3/26/1773 and d. 1812
Ann Barnett 4/4/1775
John Barnett 2/28/1778 and d. 4/1812
Mary Barnett 12/16/1780 and died-------
James Barnett 8/23/1783, d. 9/25/1835
Thomas Barnett 2/23/1786
Nathaniel Barnett 8/25/1788 and d. 2/20/1842
Betsy Barnett 1/23/1792
Lucy Barnett 10/15/1794
Robert Barnett 5/31/1812
John Barnett, Sr. married his wife, Mary, 3/1823 and she died 10/3/1825
Job Barnett born 11/9/1824 dnd died 9/22/1825
Robert Barnett departed this life 12/14/1825
John Barnett, father of the above named children, departed this life 11/24/1833 in the 81st year of his age.
Nancy Walker, daughter of John and Lewessy? Barnett married 1797
James Walker was born 9/24/1798
David Walker was born 12/15/1803
William B. Walker was born 1/24/1805
Thomas Walker born 4/30/1807

Lucy Medlock Walker born 10/20/1809
Martha Walker born 11/15/1811
Samuel Walker born 2/26/1814
Henry Davis Walker born 5/20/1819
Henry----

DEATHS:
Joseph Mathis Barnett 8/21/1830, aged 2 months, 13 days
Anna Barnett 8/31/1855, aged 1 year, 2 months, 9 days
William Barnett 11/20/1858, aged 2 years, 1 month, 7 days
Harriet Barnett 4/20/1887, aged 52 yrs., 1 month, 8 days

BIRTHS:
Joseph Barnett 8/27/1784
Mary Barnett 12/12/1787

DEATHS:
William Boyd, Senior 2/25/1812, aged 60 years
Nancy Boyd 10/8/1797, aged 41 years
Joseph Barnett, Senior 6/3/1812, aged 52 years
Edwin Barnett 9/26/1817, aged one year and 13 days
Joseph Barnett 6/27/1832?, aged 49 years
Mary Barnett 5/16/1856, aged 69 years, 5 months

BIRTHS:
William Boyd Barnett 2/5/1810
Hamilton Barnett 6/13/1811
Clarissa Barnett 4/27/1814
Edwin Barnett 9/13/1816
Joseph Barnett, Jr. 5/--/1823
Joseph Martin Barnett 6/8/1850
John Hirart? Barnett 8/12/1850
Anna Barnett 6/22/1854
William Barnett 10/13/1856

MARRIAGES:
Joseph Barnett and Mary Boyd 4/27/1809
Hamilton Barnett-Ann M. Closeymore 9/6/1836
James H. Francis-Clarissa Barnett ---

BIRTHS:
John Griffin 9/3/1740
Mary Griffin 2/--/1754
John Griffin and Mary, his wife, were married 11/19/1772
Susanah Griffin, daughter of John and Mary, her mother, b. 9/5/1773
Ave Garnet Griffin was born 6/20/1776
David C. Jesse Andrews Griffin was born 2/14/1778
John Griffin was born 12/5/1779
Mary Griffin was born 9/11/1781
William Griffin was born 8/15/1785
Thomas Griffin was born 9/24/1787
James Griffin was born 7/7/1792
Wiat Andrews Griffin was born 9/23/1793
George Washington Griffin born 2/11/17--, departed this life 12/3/1799

The following was written on a separate piece of paper -
"John Griffin born in Virginia 9/3/1740 married 11/19/1772 Mary Andrews, born 2/14/1754. They came from Powhatan Co., VA and Greene Co., GA in 1792.
Dec. 24, 1791, I, John Griffin started to Georgia on Jan. 27, 1792. Landed in Green Co. in Big Creek with my family. John Griffin, son William, came to this place 1823."

MORGAN BIBLE of Berkshire Co., Massachusetts and Macon Co., GA
Lewis DAR Chapter, Eufaula, AL Collection, Contributed by Mrs. John W. Curtis, Eufaula, AL, &copied from Macon County History of Georgia

BIRTHS:
Cate Richards 3/7/1697
Elisabeth Price, their eldest daughter, was born the beginning of 1719
Cate Price 10/17/1720
Richard Price 10/17/1720
Richard Price Shreve the end of Feb. 1722
Cate Price Middle 2/1723
Sarah Price 3/30/1726
Elisabeth Price 4/10/1727
David Price 1/25/1729
This Bible was given to my son, Richard Price, by me. R. Price Tannon.

BIRTHS:
Catherine Morgan 5/16/1746
Elisabeth Morgan 5/22/1748
William Morgan 5/20/1750
Ann Morgan 3/19/1752
George Cadogan Morgan 5/11/1754
John Morgan 6/4/1756
Richard Morgan 7/24/1759
Sarah Morgan 9/29/1761
Sarah Price Morgan 12/11/1783
George Cadogan Morgan 8/2/1785
Sarah Price Morgan, dau. of George C. Morgan & Ann, 12/11/1783
Yarmouth, 8/2/1785, George Cadogan Morgan, son of Geo. C. & Ann
Uppertor Clapton, 9/6/1788, William Ashburner Morgan, son of George C. Morgan and Ann, his wife, 9/6/1788
Lower Clapton 7/29/1792, Richard Price Morgan, son of Geo. C. & Ann
Luke Ashburner Morgan 2/17/1792, son of Geo. C.& Ann,Lower Clapton
Edward Cobb Morgan 11/19/1793, son of Geo.C. & Ann, Lower Clapton
John Morgan 9/30/1795, son of George C. Morgan & Ann, at South Gate.
Septium Morgan 5/16/1797, son of Geo. C. Morgan & Ann, South Gate
Stanford Hill 6/24/1799, Henry Morgan, son of George & Ann, his wife
Stockbridge, William Frederick Morgan, 1st son, 4/26/1809, Jones, M. D.
Stockbridge, Thomas Hurry Morgan, 2nd son, 12/8/1810, Jones, M. D.
Stockbridge, 9/15/1812, Sydney Morgan, their third son, Perry, M. D.
Stockbridge, Henry Morgan, their 4th son, 1/8/1814, Fowler, M. D.
Stockbridge, 5/3/1816, Emma Morgan, their first dau., Fowler, M. D.
BIRTHS:
Stockbridge 6/21/1818 Nancy Hurry Morgan, 2d dau., Fowler, M.D.
Hudson, Columbia Co., New York, 2/21/1820, William Sydney Morgan, their 5th son, Samuel White, M. D.
Stockbridge, 12/30/1821, Mary Elisabeth Morgan,3rd dau, Fowler, M. D.
Elisabeth Jane Smith 12/16/1824, wife of T. H. Morgan
Grace Elisabeth Morgan, their 1st dau., born at Hamburg, Ga. 3/20/1847.
William Henry Morgan, 1st son, b. Hamburg, Ga. 12/10/1848
Mary Jane Morgan, 2d dau., b. Hamburg, Ga. 8/10/1850, Oliver, M. D.
Eliza Ann Smith, 2d wife of T. H. Morgan, 7/10/1820, Lexington, S. C.
Sarah Catherine Weed, dau. of David and Eliza Ann Weed, 4/22/1843
Julia Ann Weed, daughter of David and Eliza Ann Weed 11/25/1844

Flora Morgan, daughter of T. H. And Eliza Ann Morgan, Hamburg, Macon Co., Ga., 3/17/1853, Mrs. Dixon, M. D.
Nancy H. Morgan, daughter of T. H. And Eliza Ann Morgan, Hamburg, Macon Co., Ga. 3/5/1855, Mrs. Dixon, M. D.

MARRIAGES:
George Cadogan Morgan-Eunice Tolman, daughter of Ebenezer Tolman 6/30/1808, Rev. Stephen West at Stockbridge, Berkshire Co., Mass.
Thomas H. Morgan-Elizabeth Jane Smith, daughter of Jesse and Jane Smith 12/21/1845 by Benjamin Harris, J. P., Macon Co., Ga.
David Weed-Eliza Ann Smith ---
Thomas H. Morgan to his second wife, Eliza Ann Weed, widow of David Weed, 4/28/1852 in Macon Co., Ga. By Martin Edge, J. P.
James E. Mathis-Sarah Catherine Weed 8/21/1859 Macon Co., Ga. By Allen H. Greer, J. P.
McAllen Griggers-Julia A. Weed 12/5/1865 at Hamburg, Macon Co., Ga. By S. W. Bedenbaugh, D. D.
T. H. Morgan, Jr.-Virginia Joiner at Mr. Elmore's House by Rev. J. S. Elmore 2/14/1894.
Andrew E. Shely-Grace E. Morgan, oldest daughter of T. H. and E. A. Morgan 2/28/1867 at Hamburg, Macon Co., Ga.,S. W. Bedenbaugh, D.D.
James Robert Smith-Nancy H. Morgan, second daughter of T. H. and E. A. Morgan 2/24/1876 at Hamburg, Macon Co., Ga. B. A. Hudson, J. P.
Benton Weaver-Flora Morgan, eldest daughter of T. H. and E. A. Morgan, 12/5/1876 at Hamburg, Macon Co., Ga. Mathew English, J. P.
A. Eli Thompson-Ann Eliza Morgan, 3d daughter of T. H. and E. A. Morgan, 2/22/----, English house of him H. English, J. P, Macon Co., Ga.
T. M. Williams-Mary Jane Morgan, youngest daughter of T. H. and Elizabeth Jane Morgan, 11/8/1885 Hamburg, Macon Co., Ga. by Rev. Jacob Elmore.
Alice Griggers-T. C. Webb at Hamburg by Rev. J. S. Elmore 12/21/1893
Aden Lovell Greer-Mary Ruth Morgan, 2nd daughter of T. H. and V. M. Morgan 12/26/1917 at Oglethorpe, Ga. By Rev. E. F. K. Roof.
Thomas Leslie Coogle-Laura Ethel Morgan, eldest daughter of T. H. and V. M. Morgan 6/8/1918 at Oglethorpe, Ga. By Rev. E. P. K. Roof.
Roy Allen Coogle-Willie Belle Morgan, 4th daughter of T. H. and V. M. Morgan, 12/29/1918 at Oglethorpe Co., Ga. By Rev. E. F. K. Roof.
Wiley Eugene Webb-Ruby Allen Morgan, 3rd daughter of T. H. and V. M. Morgan 9/24/1919 at Oglethorpe Co., Ga. By Rev. E. F. K. Roof.

DEATHS:
William Frederick Morgan, son of George C. and Eunice Morgan, Stockbridge, Mass. 10/30/1812, 15 days, aged 3 years, 6 months, 4 days.
Sydney Morgan, 3d son, died at Stockbridge, Mass. 9/27/1812, 12 days
Eunice, wife of George C. Morgan, died Stockbridge, 6/19/1832, 51 yrs.
Stockbridge, 12/15/1845, house of George C. Morgan took fire...consumed the family with his aged mother barely escaping with their lives....perished in the building, aged 60 years, 4 months, 14 days.
Hudson, Columbia Co., Nyk. 3/16/1846, Ann Morgan, mother of George C. Morgan, died age 83 years, 11 months, 3 days.
David Weed, 1st husband of Eliza Ann Smith, died in service of US at Jalappa, Mexico 4/30/1848
Hamburg, Ga. 9/8/1851, Elisabeth Jane Morgan, 1st wife of T. H. Morgan, died leaving 2 daus. & one son aged 26 yrs, 9 mos. Hudson NY.
11/4/1867 Nancy H. Morgan, 2d sister d. 49 yrs, 4 mos, 13 das.
Wright, Illinois, 3/2/1852, Richard Price Morgan d. 92 yrs, 5 mos, 22 das.
Geneva, Vlane Co, Illinois, 11/2/1892, Silas W. Curtis d. 11/2----, aged 76 years, 10 months, 9 days, born 1/23/1816
Albany, Dougherty Co., Ga., Henry Morgan d. 1/8/1894, aged 80 years. He was born 1/8/1814.
Hamburg, Macon Co.,Thos Hurry Morgan, Sr.d. 1/24/1896, 85 y., 1 m., 16 d.
Emma Curtis, wife of Silas Curtis, d. 11/9/1897 Geneva, Hane Co., IL, d. 81 yrs., 11 mos., 6 days.
Pinehurst, Dooly Co., Ga., 10/9/1903, Annie E. Thompson, 3rd of T. H. and E. A. Morgan, died age 43 years, 5 months and 5 days.
Hudson, NY, 12/11/1903 Mary E. Skinner, 3rd sis.of T. H. d. 81 y, 11 m, 11 d.
Annie Virginia, 5th dau. of T. H. & V. M. Morgan, 11/1/1905, 1 yr, 1 mo., 7 das.
Hamburg, Ga., Eliza Ann, wife of T. H. Morgan d. 1/16/1910, aged 89 years, 6 months, 6 days.
Grace Elizabeth, wife of Andrew Shealy, d. 8/21/1913, 67 y, 27 m, 15 d.
T.M.Williams, hus.of Mary Jane Morgan, d.8/21/1913, 67 y., 27 m., 15 d.
Flora, w.of Benton Weaver, d. 2/3/1929, Byromville, 72 y., 10 m., 16 d..
William Henry Morgan d. 10/27/1922 Bryan, Tx, 73 yrs, 11 mos, 17 das.
Sarah Catherine, w. Jas Mathis, d. 6/13/1920, Bryan, Tx, 77 y., 1 m., 21 d.
William Benton Weaver, husband of Flora Morgan, d. 1929 Pinehurst, Ga
Amos Eli Thompson, hus.of Ann Morgan, d.1929 Pinehurst 33 yrs, 15 da.

BIRTHS:
Laura Ethel, 1st daughter of T. H. Jr. and Virginia M. Morgan, b. Hamburg, Macon Co., Ga., 11/15/1896, Field, M. D.
Mary Ruth, 2nd daughter of T. H. Jr. and Virginia M. M. Morgan, b. Hamburg, Macon Co., Ga., 2/22/1898, M. F. Crumby, M. D.
Rubye Allene, 3rd daughter of T. H. Jr. and Virginia M. Morgan b. Hamburg, Macon Co., Ga. 5/5/1899, Mrs. Bethia English.
Willia Belle, 4th daughter of T. H. and V. M. Morgan was born at Hamburg, Ga. 10/13/1900, M. F. Crumby, M. D.
Annie Virginia, 5th daughter of T. H. Jr. and Virginia M. Morgan was born at Hamburg, Ga. 9/25/1904, Derrick, M. D.
Daisy Lucile, 6th daughter to T. H. and V. M. Morgan was born at Hamburg, Ga. 1/23/1906, Derrick, M. D.
Elvie Hurry, 7th daughter of T. H. and V. M. Morgan, b. Hamburg, Ga. 7/29/1908, Derrick, M. D.
Thomas Joseph, 1st son of T. L. and L. E. Coogle b. Macon Co., Ga. 5/20/1919, H. C. Derrick, M. D.
Roy Morgan, 1st son of R. A. and W. B. Coogle, b. at Oglethorpe, Macon Co., Ga., 11/24/1919, C. A. Greer, M. D.
Sarah Elizabeth, first daughter of T. L. and L. E. Coogle was b. in Macon Co., Ga., 6/7/1920, H. C. Derrick, M. D.
Lilian, 1st daughter of R. A. and W. B. Coogle, born Macon Co., Ga. 9/3/1921, H. C. Derrick, M. D.
Virginia, 1st daughter of Eugene and Ruby Webb, Jr. b. at Oglethorpe 9/27/1921, H. C. Derrick, M. D.
Elvie Ann, first daughter of Aden and Ruth Greer, b. Macon 55/29/1923
Billie, 2d son of Roy & Willie Coogle b. Macon Co. 11/4/1923
Edward Curtis, 2nd son of T. L. and Laura Coogle was b. Macon, Ga. 11/24/1925, H. C. Derrick, M. D.
Wiley Eugen, 1st son of Eugene and Ruby Webb, Jr., born Oglethorpe 12/9/1925, H. C. Derrick, M. D.
Aden Lovelle, Jr., 1st son of Aden and Ruth Greer, born Holopaw, FL 10/4/1926, Fuqua, M. D.
George Herbert, 3rd son of T. L. and Laura Coogle, b. Macon Co., Ga. 11/13/1828, H. C. Derrick, M. D.
Mary Ruth, 2nd daughter of Aden and Ruth Greer, b. Macon, Ga. 9/25/1929, Thompson, M. D.
Robert Leo, 4th son of T. L. and Laura Coogle, born Macon Co., Ga. 2/2/1831, Dr. Derrick.

BIRTHS: *(sons-in-law)*
Theodore Middleton Williams, hus. of M.J.Morgan, 6/6/1846 Macon Co.
Amos Eli Thompson, husband of Annie E. Morgan, born 3/5/1859 in Dooly Co., Ga.
William Benton Weaver, husband of Flora Morgan, born 10/10/1855, Sumpter Co., Ga.
Andrew E. Shealy, husb. of Grace E. Morgan, b. 1/8/1843, Macon Co.
James Robert Smith, husband of Nancy H. Morgan, born 10/1/1849, Macon Co., Ga.
James E. Mathis, husband of Sarah C. Weed, born 8/4/1858, Macon Co.
Virginia M. Joiner Thomas, wife, born 11/12/1871, in Macon Co., Ga.

BIRTHS:
Thomas H. Morgan, 1st son of T. H. and Eliza Morgan, born Hamburg, Macon Co., Ga., 2/15/1858. Self and Grandmother Smith.
Ann Eliza Morgan, daughter of T. H. and Eliza Morgan, born Hamburg, Macon Co., Ga. 4/4/1860. Self, Mrs. Mathis.
John Hampden Morgan, 2nd son of T. H. and Eliza A. Morgan, born Hamburg, Macon Co., 1/30/1864. Self, Mr. Cox.
William, 1st son of T. M. and Mary Jane Williams, was born at their home on Duck Creek, Macon Co., Ga. 6/5/1894, Hicks, M. D.
Thomas Leslie Coogle, husb. of Laura Morgan, b. 5/19/1897 Oglethorpe, Ga.
Roy Allen Coogle, husb. of Willie Morgan, b. 4/25/1899 Oglethorpe, Ga
Aden Lovell Greer, hus.of Ruth Morgan, b. McMinnville, TN 4/20/1893

ABERCROMBIE-HILL-WARNER BIBLE of Meriwether Co.
Georgia State Archives, Atlanta, Ga.

"Presented to Martha Catharine Hill by her grandmother, Mrs. Martha Hill as a memento of her departed and christian uncle Abraham Thomas Hill. January 1846. Search the scriptures for in them yetink ye have eternal life and they an they which testify of me. W. D. M."

MARRIAGES:
At house & by Rev. M. D. Martin, A. J. Cheney m.M. C. Hill 2/2/1858
Alexander Franklin Hill m. Mary Jane Warner Thomas 7/4/1855 Meriwether Co., Ga.
Edmund Wellborn Martin married Sarah Hill 4/16/1877 Meriwether Co.
Burwell O. Hill married Ellen Pinson 2/22/1882 in Newnan, Ga.

Hiram Warner Hill married Lena Harris 9/24/1884 in LaGrange.

James Ogletre Tagner married Martha Hil 4/27/1886 in Meriwether Co.

Charles Gates Eckford married Mary Hill 4/23/1890 in Meriwether Co.

Dr. E. B. Terrell married Catherine Hill 12/27/1892 in Meriwether Co.

BIRTHS:
Alexander Franklin Hill 2/20/1831 Wilkes Co., Ga.
Mary Jane Hill 3/4/1832 Knoxville, Crawford Co.
Burwell Obadiah Hill 8/17/1856 Meriwether Co.
Hiram Warner Hill 7/18/1858 Meriwether Co.
Sarah Hill 5/1/1860 Meriwether Co., near Greenville, Ga., at her grandfather's home, Hiram Warren.
Martha Hill 4/1/1865 in Meriwether Co.
Mary Hill 5/20/1867 in Meriwether Co.
Alexander Franklin Hill 10/21/1869 Meriwether Co.
Catherine Hill 8/27/1871 Meriwether Co.
Albert Meriwether Hill 7/12/1874 in Meriwether Co.
Robert Johnson Hill 8/15/1876 in Meriwether Co.

Maternal Line:

BIRTHS:
Edmund Abercrombie 1/12/1778
Mary Pollard, wife of E. Abercrombie, 12/25/1778

Children of the above couple:

Sarah Watts Abercrombie 7/15/1802 in Hancock Co., Ga.
Malinda Booth Abercrombie 1/5/1805 and died 12/1/1805
Robert Abercrombie 6/15/1808, died 5/8/1809
Mary Abercrombie 12/16/1809 and died 12/1815

Paternal Line:

BIRTHS:
Hiram Warner 10/29/1802 and died 6/301881, born in Williamsburg, Mass.
Theron Warner 7/26/1806 in Williamsburg, Mass.
Rodolphus Warner 9/28/1808 in Williamsburg, Mass.
Obadiah Warner 1/8/1811 in Williamsburg, Mass.
Eliza Ann Warner 12/23/1813 in Williamsburg, Mass.
Miranda Warner 5/3/1815 in Williamsburg, Mass.
William Henry Warner 3/16/1817 in Williamsburg, Mass.
Jane Marion Warner 4/18/1820 in Williamsburg, Mass.
Charles Howard Warner 5/25/1822 in Williamsburg, Mass.

DEATHS:
Hiram Warner 6/30/1881 in Atlanta
Sarah Watts Warner 4/4/1860
Alexander Franklin Hill 1/15/1888
Catherine Hill Terrell 7/28/1898 in Greenville, Ga.
Edmund Wellborn Martin, son of E. W. Martin and Sarah Hill Martin, died 1/8/1906 in
Atlanta.

BLUE-MITCHELL-McDUFFIE-WILLIFORD BIBLE
Owner: Harry Blue, 1035 Rosedale Rd, Atlanta, GA 30306 (1881)

On inside cover:

Miss Caroline L. Mitchell was born 3/16/1825 and died 9/3/1878

MARRIAGES:
F. A. Blue-M. E. Mitchell 7/9/866
J. H. Wiliford-Annie Blue 8/22/1889
John Blue-Edna Donald 3/28/1892
Mann McDuffie-Carrie Blue 5/3/1896
D. P. Blue----(illegible)

BIRTHS:
Francis Archibald Blue son of Mary and John Blue, 1/25/1842
Mary Eliza Mitchell, daughter of Stephen and Caroline Lovedy Mitchell, 11/16/182--
John Blue, son of F. H. and M. E. Blue, 2/15/1867
Annie Blue, daughter of F. A. and M. E. Blue 12/24/1865
Daniel A. Blue, son of F. A. and M. E. Blue, 1/12/187--
Baby boy was born 9/26/187-
Charles Edwin Blue, son of F. A. and M. E. Blue, 4/16/1874
Caroline L. Blue, daughter of F. A. and M. E. Blue, 3/10/1876
Katie Adell Blue, daughter of F. A. and M. E. Blue, 2/24/1878
Stephen Agustus Blue, son of F. A. and M. E. Blue, 7/31/1880
Mary Virginia Blue, daughter of F. A. and M. E. Blue, 11/6/1881
Norman Mitchell 10/10/1885
Annie Clifford McDuffie, daughter of M. L. and R. L.? McDuffie, 4/1/1897?

DEATHS:
F. A. Blue 6/3/1883
James ---- Wiliford 10/5/1896
----------------------- ----/10/1896
James H. Williford 3/15/1897
Archie Elide Blue 8/7/1801
Carrie May Williford 6/11/102
M. E. Blue 9/30/1902
John Blue 5/28/1904
Mary Blue ---- 1903
John Edwin Blue, son of ------ and Edna Blue, 8/10/18---, died 8/20/1893
James Archabald Wiliford, son of L. H. and Annie Wiliford, 6/29/1890
Joseph F. Wiliford, son of L. H. and Annie Wiliford, 11/29/1891
Annie Bell Wiliford, daughter of L. H.and Annie Wiliford, 1/10/1893
Carrie May Wiliford, daughter of L. H. and Annie Wiliford, 2/14/1894
Edna Blue was born 2/28/1894?
--------, so of Dan and ------- Blue was born 8/9/1888?
Wilie? Ed?, son of Dan and -alia Blue, was born 4/10/1872?
----------------------------daughter born 6/1900
John Thomas?, son of ---- and Edna Blue, was born 2/18/1903

HILL BIBLE
Owner: Lawrence Hill
2092 Heritage Drive, Atlanta, Ga 30345

DEATHS:
Ann Hill, wife of William Hill, Sr., departed this life on 11/23/1835, who was the mother of Robert Hill, William Hill, Jr., Molly Hill, Adam Hill, James Hill, Nancy Hill, Margaret Hill and John Hill, aged about 73 years.

Charles Henry, son of John and Sarah Hill, 12/31/1853
Samuel, son of John and Sarah Hill 4/24/1854
Sarah Hill, wife of John Hill born 2/------ 8/2/----
Adam Hill ----/7/1865
Robert Hill 4/21/1867, aged 76 years, 5 months, 22 days
Margaret White, daughter of William Hill, Sr. and Annie Hill, 1/15/1870, aged 65 years, 9 months and 10 days
Hamlin F. Lewis, son of L. D. H. and Sarah A. Lewis, 12/21/1870, aged 9 years, 3 months, 3 days
John Hill 6/5/1869, aged 72 years, 5 months and 5 days.
Joseph A. Hill 8/12/1889

BIRTHS:
William Trayler Hill 8/16/1837, the son of John Hill and Sarah Hill
Champion Travis Hill, son of John Hill and Sarah Hill, 3/6/1839
Sarah Annie, daughter of John and Sarah Hill, 9/19/1840
John Calvin, son of John and Sarah Hill, 11/2/1842
James Adam Hill, son of John and Sarah Hill, 7/24/1844
Robert Lewis, son of John and Sarah Hill , 3/26/1846

DEATHS:
Molly Hill 9/29/1802, aged 8 years, 4 days
William Hill 9/5/1821, aged 65 years
William Hill, Jr. , son of William Hill, Sr., 11/14/1828, aged 36 years, one month, 26 days
James Hill, son of William Hill, Sr. 8/12/1833, aged 34 years
Nancy Marlot, daughter of William Hill, Sr., 8/27/1833, aged 31 years.

Laurence Hill 5/9/1894
Edwin Hill 10/6/1867
Capt Hill 8/16/1837
John Hill 1807
William Hill 1792
William Hill (1756) 1746

BIRTHS:
Charles Henry, son of John and Sarah Hill, 9/17/1852
Samuel, son of John and Sarah Hill, 4/9/1854
Frank Pickins, son of John and Sarah Hill, 5/27/1855
Hamlin F., son of Dixon H. and Sarah A. Lewis 10/19/1861
John Hill Lewis, son of Dixon H. and Sarah A. Lewis 3/24/1864
Sarah Elmore, daughter of D. H. and Sarah A. Lewis, 11/6/1866
Mary H. Lewis, daughter of D. H. and Sarah A. Lewis, 7/24/1869
Dixon H. Lewis, son of D. H. and Sarah A. Lewis, 1/8/1878
George Was. White 2/21/1824
George Washington White
John Hill 1/1/1807
Molly Hill 9/25/1794
Robert Hill 12./9/1790
William Hill 9/12/1792
Adam Hill 11/11/1796
James Hill 2/5/1799
George W. White 2/21/1824
Pinkney White 5/24/1801
Ann Drewsils White 3/7/1827
Margaret Hill 3/5/1804
Nancy Hill 1/15/1802
Joseph Reed, son of John and Sarah Hill, 1/3/1848
Mary Louisa, daughter of John and Sarah Hill, 9/8/1849

MARRIAGES:
Robert Hill-Nancy Patton 11/26/1812
Peggy Hill-Pinkney White 5/1/1823
Nancy Hill- Annabel Marlor 9/25/1828
John Hill-Sarah Coleman, formerly Sarah Traylor 10/5/1836
D. H. Lewis-Sarah A. Hill 10/3/1860
T. Hill-Ruth A. Scott 1/8/1867

W. T. Hill-M. L. Edmundson 12/12/1866
James A. Hill-Mary Elmore Lewis 5/22/1866 in Kaufman Co., Texas

SAMUEL BELL BIBLE

Owner: Mrs. Donald V. Richardson, Conway, S. C. (1960)

BIRTHS:
Sarah Adline Hartsfield 10/5/1828
Samuel Bell 10/7/1823
George Virginia Bell , dau. Samuel Bell & Sarah Adline, wife, 9/27/1846
Daughter, Ella Bell, of Samuel Hill, 11/3/1850
Henry Thomas Hill, son Jas A. Bell & Sarah Adline, wife, b. 1/15/1855
Iola Bell, dau of Samuel Bell & Sarah Adline, 11/14/1855, d. 8/12/1930
James Samuel Bell, son of Samuel Bell and Sarah Adline, 12/1851 or 1857, died 12/15/1932

MARRIAGES:
Samuel and Sarah Adline, 2/22/1844
George Virginia Bell -Capt. L. Buck 3/1/1866 by Rev. W. A. Gregg
Elliss ------ Bell -Ives R. Malone??, 11/28/1849
John Morrison-Iola Bell in Brooklyn, N. Y. 2/22/1897, Rev. R.J.Van Dyke.

DEATHS:
George Bell 4/23/1842
Henry Thomas Bell, son of Samuel and Sarah Adline Bell 9/24/1854
Virginia Bell Busch? 11/27/192--
Ella Bell Tolar 7/15/1928?
Lorrsell? Bell ----
Sarah A. Bell ?1872

BIRTHS:
William Ruburthus Bell 1/2/1881
Carry Eva Bell 6/5/1884
Mattie Ruth Bell 9/10/1854
George Pearce Bell 2/28/1889
William G. Thomas 12/30/1808
Caroline J. A. Thomas 7/13/1818
James J. Bell 5/30/1853

Sarah Kathryn Cochran 10/1/1911
Sarah Ellen Bell 6/28/1917
Dorothy Jeane Bell 8/26/1923

DEATHS:
William C. Thomas 2/37/1887
Caroline J. A. Thomas 12/12/1888
Jams J. Bell 2/28/1900
Frank Thomas 9/2/1917
Tipp Anders 3/15/1921

MARRIAGES:
Calvin W. Cochran-Eva Bell 3/30/1909
Pierce Bell-Helen Waller 2/7/1916
James J. Bell of Decatur Co., Ga.-Sarah S. Thomas of Decatur Co., Ga. 3/17/1880, the brides home by the Rev. Abraham Belcher. Wits: W. S. Ballow, Mary Mathew, J. G. Fain

THOMAS BIBLE

BIRTHS:
William C. Thomas 12/30/1808
Carolina J. A. Thomas, the espoused of W. C. Thomas, 7/15/1818
Joseph H. Thomas, son of William C. and C. A. A. Thomas, 8/10/1835
Mary Ann Thomas 10/16/1837
James Wilson Thomas 2/10/1840
Annacaona Hantippe Thomas 9/1/1842
William Moses Thomas 6/4/1843
Nancy Catharine Thomas 3/21/1845
Franklin Alexander Thomas 2/15/1847
Milton Guyton Thomas 3/13/1849
Sarah Thomas 12/24/1851
Alie Asenath Thomas 8/12/1855
Franklin Andrew? Thomas 2/18/1862
DEATHS:
James Wilson Thomas 5/5/1862, aged 22 years, 2 months, 25 days, died in the service of his country
Caroline J. A. Thomas 12/12/1888

W. C. Thomas 2/27/1889
Frank A. Thomas 9/2/1917
Annacaona Hantippe Anders 3/15/1921
Allie Thomas Hodges 4/15/1936

MARRIAGES:
William C. Thomas and Caroline J. A. Thomas 7/3/1834

BATES -WALLACE BIBLE
Owner: Mrs. D. A. Greer
RFD#1, Bainbridge, Ga.

MARRIAGES:
-------------------------- to Mary Jane Bates 1/13/1857

Their children:
Emma L. Bates-S. L. Wallace 12/10/1889

MARRIAGES:
Octaso Lucinda Bates-W. A. Davis 6/24/1890
W. A. Bates and Mollie Marlin married 6/25/1890
M. H. Bates-Ida Martin 3/2/1895
Marvin Terece Bates - L. P. Walker 6/9/1904

Children of W. A. Bates and Mollie Martin:

Mollie Martin
Mona Bates married R.L. Edens of Tennessee
Anthony Whitfield Bates married Elizabeth Bremmer
Anne E. Dalbo
Wilhemina Bates married William Hugh Riddell
Ruth Alston Bates married Owen Reynolds
Emil Peter Dalbo

BIRTHS:
Mary J. Bates 2/28/1849?
A. J. L. J. Bates 11/25/1839
T. Q. Bates 10/1/1800
W. A. Bates 12/23/1861
Grissell G. Bates 11/24/1864
M. H. Bates 5/12/1870
O. S. Bates 7/4/1872
M. F. Bates 9/21/1881

BIRTHS:
Arthur Bates Wallace, son of Emma and S. L. Wallace, 7/22/1890
May Wallace, daughter of Emma and S. L. Wallace, 5/1/1892
Leola Wallace, daughter of Emma and J. L. Wallace, 6/8/1895
Kendred Wallace 9/24/1897, buried 27th
Howard W. Bates, son of M. W. Bates and Ida Martin Bates 7/10/1894

Children of W. C. and Molly Martin Bates:
Diedmonda Bates 8/17/1893
Anthony Whitfield Bates 6/18/1895
Wilhelminia Bates 3/15/1897
Ruth Alston Bates 7/15/1899
Susie Elizabeth Bates 10/----

Priscilla Goods Reynolds born 1/29/1903
Emil Jens Dalbo born 8/15/1926
Mona Samaria Dalbo 9/1/1928
Johanna Lorensen Dalbo 9/1931
Anthony Bates Dalbo born 4/5/1938

DEATHS:
Marion H. Bates died 3/18/1888
Hariet Bates 8/20/18--
Arthur Bates Wallace, son of Emma Bates and S. L. Wallace, 12/14/1891
A. J. L. Bates was stricken with paralysis on 4/29; lingered until 4/12/94
Anthony W. Bates 6/1876?
N. B. Bates 6/19/1899, aged 52 years, and 1 day
W. A. Bates 9/1930
Mollie Martin Bates 10/1933

HORNSBY BIBLE
Owner: Mrs. D. A. Greer, RDF #1, Bainbridge, Ga.

Thomas Jefferson Hornsby 3/27/01850
Sarah ---------, widow, was born 12/10/1849
Frances Lee Hornsby, 6/6/1873
Ezzard Arthur Hornsby 2/4/1875
Dora Mary Hornsby 5/15/1878
Jessie Maude Hornsby 3/17/1880
Thomas Jefferson Hornsby 4/6/1888

MARRIAGES:
Thomas Jefferson Hornsby and Sarah Antoinett Morton 5/1/1872

BIRTHS:
Effie Clyde Hornsby 11/26/1884
Cora Arva Hornsby 5/6/1886
Our baby was born 10/19/1888

BIRDSEY BIBLE
DAR, Lewis Chapter, Eufaula, AL

Family Bible belonging to: Samuel Robinson Birdsey and Katherine Landford Birdsey 8/16/1866. Given to Ralph Talmadge Birdsey 1908
Herbert Ford Birdsey 1936 -
Ralph Talmadge Birdsey II

MARRIAGES:
Samuel Robinson Birdsey of Fayetteville, N. C. and Katherine Sanford of Fayetteville, N. C. by Rev. J. C. Huske, 8/16/1866
John Allen Rowell-Margarett Sandford Birdsey at Ocala, FL by Rev. C. M. Gray 2/6/182--
Hiram Birdsey-Mary Anna Martin, Ocala, FL, Rev. C. M. Gray, 10/7/1892
John Sandford Birdsey-Grace Caroline Green at Ocala, FL by Rev. C. M.Gray 11/23/1898
Samuel Robinson Birdsey-Loretta Elizabeth Bullock by Grace Episcopal Church, Ocala, FL by Rob. B. M. Gray 1/7/1900

Ralph Talmadge Birdsey to Emily Harcell Fora 1/21/1908, Grace Episcopal Church, Ocala, FL by G. H. Harrison

BIRTHS:

Samuel R. Birdsey, Clinton, N. C. , 1/25/1836
Kate Lunsford Birdsey, Fayetteville, N. C., 12/12/1848
Albert Hiram Birdsey, Wilmington, N. C., 6/10/1868
Margaret Sanford Birdsey, Wilmington, N. C., 6/27/1869
Samuel Robinson Birdsey, Wilmington, N. C., 1/13/1871
John Sandford Birdsey, Wilmington, N. C., 11/12/1872
Ralph Talmadge Birdsey, Wilmington, N. C., 5/5/1875
George Thomas Birdsey, Wilmington, N. C., 4/12/1878
Marrion Jones Birdsey, Wilmington, N. C., 8/13/1880
Angus Bell Birdsey, Ocala, FL, 1/20/1886
Myra Hubbard Birdsey, Ocala, FL, 2/20/1888

DEATHS:

George Thomas Birdsey in Wilmington, N. C. 3/5/1879, age 10 months, 24 days
Marion Jones Birdsey died in Ocala, FL 5/19/1884, age 3 years, 9 months
John Allan Rowell died Memphis, TN, buried Ocala FL.
Samuel Robinson Birdsey 1915, Macon
Rosaland Davis Birdsey 1915, Macon
Katherine Sandford Birdsey, 1934, Maon
Ralph Talmadge Birdsey 2/17/1936, Macon, buried in Ocala, FL
Green Birdsey 1900 Montezuma
Albert Hiram Birdsey 12/1940
Samuel Robinson Birdsey, Jr. 6/12/1945 Macon, Ga.
Emily Ford Birdsey 10/21/1947 Macon, Ga.
Jack Wade 5/31/1949 Macon, Ga.
Angus Bell Birdsey 6/10/1951, Macon, Ga.
John Sandford Birdsey 10/15/1953. Macon, Ga.
Margaret Sandford Birdsey 4/29/1959, Macon, Ga.

DAVY EVANS BIBLE (London, SC, GA)
Owner: Mrs. C. P. Roberts, 343 Adams St., Decatur, Ga.

The following children were born to Davy Evans and Mary, his wife, who were married 4/15/1766 at Saint Warbins Church in -------, London:
Elizabeth Martha Sophia born 3/28/1767 at Wm Reads Charles---?
David Read Evans 2/20/1769, at Cowley Sheet------?
Mary 3/1/1771 at Beehive Compton-------
Emely 4/20/1772 at Beehive Compton----
William 5/3/1773 at Beehive Compton---
Joseph 6/15/1778 at Beehive Compton---- and All Briston? by the Rev. Dr. Kipps Long Ditch Urson?
David Reid Evans died at Winnsborough in State of S. C. on 8th----1843
Mary (Evans) Winn died in Monroe Co., State of Georgia Sept. 15, 1856 aged 85 years, 6 months and 22 days.

WILLIAM D. WILLIAMS AND NANCY ELIZABETH COLLIER FAMILY BIBLE

"To: Mr. W. D. Williams from his friends and associate teachers, Miss Hannah Guillan and Miss Ann Elizabeth Zachy, Georgia Academy for the Blind, December 25, 1871"

BIRTHS:
William Brown, son of A.M. & L.L. Williams, b. Hawkinsville 3/27/1879
Leonora Cickett Wills dau. of A.M. & L. L.Williams, b. Albany 9/14/1881
Jackie Tochie, dau. of A.M. & L. L. Williams, b. Americus 12/14/1887
Albert McCoy, Jr., son of A.M. & L. L. Williams, b. Americus 12/22/189-
William Williams, son of Tochie and R. W. MacDonell, born at City of Mexico, Mex. 10/21/18--
George, son of Tochie and R. W. MacDonell, b. Macon, Ga. 2/2/1884
Robert Walker, Jr., s. of Tochie & A.W. MacDonell, b. Durango, Mx. 9/3/1886
Nancy Collier, dau. of Tochie & A.W. MacDonell, b. Durango, Mx. 11/29/1888
William Dismuke Williams, son of John & Sarah Dismukes, b. Putnam Co. 9/8/1823
Nancy Elizabeth Collier, dau. of James Collier & Frances b. Greene Co., 1/15/1831
Francina Collier, dau. of W. D. & N. E. Williams, b. Talbotton 1/20/1851
Albert M. Carr, son of W. D. & N. E. Williams, b. Madison 4/18/1852
William Dismuke, Jr., son of W.D. & N. E. Williams, b. Oxford 8/27/1855

Howard James, son of W. D. & N. E. Williams, b. Talbotton 10/6/1858
Sarah Frances Eliza (called "Tochie"), daughter of W. D. and N. E. Williams, born at Macon, Ga. 9/8/1867
Lucins Elijah, son of W. D. & N. E. Williams, b. Macon, Ga. 12/9/1869

MARRIAGES:
William Dismuke Williams-Nancy Elizabeth Collier Talbotton 2/14/1850
Albert McCoy Williams-Lorens Sucky Brown at Americus Ga 12/1/1876
Sarah Frances Eliza (called "Tochie") - Robert Walker MacDonell at Macon, Ga. 12/28/1880
Howard James Williams-Mattie Kitty Jewett at Macon 1/29/1885
William Dismuke Williams, Jr.-Sarah Weeks Goodall, Macon 9/15/1887
Arthur Dudley Williams-Ethel Turner (Hancock Ga.) 2/27/1894

DEATHS:
Francina Collier, dau. of W. D. & N.E. Williams, d. Talbotton 5/18/1882
Lucins Elijah, s. of W.D. & N.E. Williams, d. Baltimore, MD 10/27/1891
George, son of Tochie and R. W. MacDonell, d. El Paso, Texas 8/17/1884
Albert McCoy, Jr., son of A.M. & L. L. Williams, d. Americus 12/16/1892
William Dismukes, son/John & Sarah D. Williams, d. Macon 12/10/1898
Nancy Callie, wife of W.D. Williams, died at Macon, Ga. 10/11/1899
Mariha Jewitt (Howard struck through), daughter of H. J. and Kitty Williams, b. Macon, Ga 11/9/1885
Henry J. Jewitt, son of H. J. and Kitty Williams, b. Macon, Ga. 12/1/1887
Hannah Guillan, dau. of H. J. & Kitty Williams, b. Macon 10/28/1895
Howard M. Hatton, dau. of H. J. & Kitty Williams, b. Macon 12/31/1896
Julia Goodall, dau. of W. D. and S. W. Williams, b. Macon 10/29/1890
Lucius Elijah, son of W. D. and S. W. Williams, born at Macon 9/13/1892
Howard James, son of W. D. and S. W. Williams, b. Macon 5/14/1894
Carrie, daughter of A. D. and E. T. Williams, b. Macon 11/16/1897

This is to certify that William D. Williams of Macon, Ga. and Miss Sallie W. Goodall of Macon, Ga. were by me united together in Holy Matrimony on the 15th day of Sept. 1887. In presence of: A. M. Williams M. G., Joe Singleton, Ida Singleton, E. W. Burke, Jennie Boone.

MARRIAGES:
William D. Williams-Sarah Goodall at Macon 9/15/1887
John W. Williams-Robert Hendrick Brinson at Macon 1/20/1912
Howard J. Williams-Inez Butler at Macon
Lucius E. Williams-Inez Taylor at Macon 8/1918
Sarah E. Brinson-Pete Mills, Millen, Ga. 8/19/1937

Robert Hendrick Brinson-Patricia Murry at Mass. 9/1942
Pete Mills, Jr.-Elva R. Clifton, Screven Co.,3/29/1964
Julia G. Mills-William A. McWhorter Jr., Millen Ga. 8/25/1968
Bonnie Brinson-Larry Greer, Atlanta
Sherrel Brinson-Roger S. Shepard
Lucius E. Williams-Lunnell 8/1948

BIRTHS:
Julia Goodall Williams, daughter of W. D. and Sallie G. Williams 10/22/1890 in Macon
Lucius Elijah Williams, s. of W.D. & Sallie G. Williams, 9/13/1892 Macon
Howard James Williams, s/W.D. & Sallie G.Williams, 5/14/1894 Macon
Sara Elizabeth Brinson, daughter of Julia W. Brinson and Robert H. Brinson at Macon 10/20/1912
Mary Louise Brinson, dau. of Julia & Hendrick Brinson, Macon 4/5/1916
Robert Hendrick Brinson, Jr., son of R.H. & Julia Brinson, Milton 4/10/1918
Bonnie Patricia, daughter of Robert Hendrick Brinson, Jr. and Patricia Murry, 6/27/1943, Ayr Mass.
Sharrell Ann, daughter of Robert Hendrick Brinson, Jr. and Patricia Brinson, 3/10/1947
Julia Dora Williams, dau. of Howard J. & Inez Williams, Macon 4/1918
Pete Mills, son/Sara Elizabeth Brinson & Pete Mills,b.Millen 11/10/1959
Sally Mills, daughter of Pete and Sara Brinson Hill, b. 11/22/1943
Julia Goodall Mills, daughter of Pete and Sara Mills, b. 5/22/1945

DEATHS:
William D. Williams, son of W. D. and N. C. Williams, 8/11/1917, Macon, Ga at Williams Sanitorium, 62 years of age
Sarah Goodall Williams wife of William D. Williams, 4/1934 Jacksonville, FL age 71 years
Julia Goodall Williams Brinson, w. of Robt H. Brinson, 1/11/1953 Millen
Robert Hendrick Brinson, son of Jasper and Elizabeth Gray Brinson, 6/15/1956 at Millen, Ga.
Mary Louise, daughter of R. H. & Julia G. Brinson, 4/25/1917, 1 year old
Sarah Mills, daughter of Pete and Sara Mills, 3/19/1944
Inez Taylor Williams, wife of Lucius E. Williams 9/10/1946
Sara Brinson Mills, daughter of R. H. and Julia Brinson, 2/18/1966
Pete Mills III, son of Pete Jr. and Elva Mills, 9/23/1968
Pete Mills, Sr., husband of Sara Brinson, 7/22/1970
Lucius E. Williams 6/21/1970, Orange Park, FL

Memoranda:

BIRTHS:
Isaac Peter Mills, III son of Pete and Eliza Mills Millen, Ga. 12/5/1966
Larry Taylor Mills, daughter of Pete and Eliza Mills, Millen, Ga. 10/27/1969
Sara Elizabeth McWhorter, daughter of Bell and Judy McWhorter, Shreveport, LA 3/16/1972
Julia Helen Mills 9/20/1972, daughter of Eliza and Pete Mills, Sr., Millen, Ga.

SOLOMON KIRKSY AUSTIN BIBLE of Henry Co., Ga.
Owner: Brenda A. Dickerson
3019 Union Church Road, Stockbridge, GA 30281

Family Record:
Brother John
Grandparents: (Newton Co., Ga.)
J. T. P. Austin b. 7/16/1845 Conyers, Newton Co., Ga., d. 9/17/1924, Madison Co., Ga.
W. H. M. Austin b. 8/1851 d. 5/25/1912

Children:
Robert Pennington b. 12/13/1877 Henry Co., d. 12/27/1877
Ivan Chester b. 5/5/1896 d. at Detroit, MI 2/23/1920
Verna Austin b. 3/2/1882 DeKalb Co., d. 9/4/1937, married 12/27/1904 C. W. Gardner

Miscellaneous:
J. T. P. Austin was b. 7/18/1845 in Newton Co., Ga., d. 9/17/1929 at Madison Ga., age 82 years, 2 months, 1 day.

Grandparents:
J. P. Austin b. 8/13/1808 S. C., d. 7/17/1873 Henry Co., Ga.
Mary G. Austin b. 1/12/1816 Newton Co., Ga., d. 6/23/1890 Henry Co., Ga.
Robert Hollingsworth b. Clayton Co., Ga.
Elminy M. Hollingsworth b. 9/14/1831 Henry Co., d. 6/13/1881 DeKalb Co. (Parker written over Hollingsworth)

Parents:
Solomon K. Austin b. 1/31/1855 Henry Co., Ga. d. 12/25/1940 Emory University Hospital, DeKalb Co.
Robert J. M. Austin b. 6/11/1864 DeKalb Co., Ga., d. 12/17/1926 W. M. M. Hospital, DeKalb Co.
They were married 1/25/1877 at home by Bro. Foot.
Children::
Gwernia Inez b. 3/5/1882 DeKalb Co., 9/14/1937 m. 12/27/1908 C. W. Gardner
Walter Manning b. 5/21/1884 DeKalb Co. m. 12/17/----Anna Mae Riley
Margerete Elminy b. 9/17/1886 DeKalb Co.
Jack Carlton b. 3/23/1889 DeKalb Co., d. 10/21/1929 m. 3/10/1910 Lois Margaret Buck
Robert Matha b. 7/18/1890 Henry Co. d. 12/6/1954 m. 12/16/1914 Otis Thurman
William Pierce b. 9/11/1892 Henry Co. m. 7/7/1923 Matha Knswuck?, d. 9/----
Byron Kirksy b. 9/3/1894 Henry Co. d. 4/3/1955 m. 1/3/1918 Mary Emily Turpin
?Luan Chister b. 5/16/1896 Henry Co. d. 2/231920 Henryford Hospital, Detroit, MI
J. Caesar b. 8/23/1897 Henry Co. m. 12/5/1917 Ruth Annie Turpin
Clifford Glenn b. 7/27/1899 Henry Co. m. 8/10/1929 Viola
Loy Parker b. 7/26/1901 Henry Co. m. 9/1/1926 Sarah Elizabeth Carroll

STEPHEN L. DICKSON BIBLE of Franklin Co., GA
Owner: Mrs. Harper Mahan, 3787 Norfolk #21, Houston, TX 77027

Lippincott Grambo & Co. (successors to Grigg, Elliot & Co.), No. 14, North Fourth Street. 1854
MARRIAGES:
Stephen L. Dickson-Elizabeth J. DeVane, his wife, 7/8/1843 in Pike Co., Ga. by W. W. Westmoreland, Esq.
Fred Eugene Lorenz and Ruth Dahl, Walla Walla, Wa. by Rev. Schmidt 11/13/1931
Camilla Agnes Lorenz, daughter of Henry and Mary Eugenia Lorenz to Dr. Carl A. Rietman 9/16/1925 at Coqulla, Ore. by Rev. W. R. Sanderson
L. Lee Mahan-Bee Harper, his wife, 5/27/1891, Grimes Co., Tx by Rev.-----

Henry Lorenz-Mary Eugenia, his wife, 6/1/1899, Bandon, Ore.
Joseph Alonzo Harper-Nannie Richardson, his wife, were married--------
Joseph A. Harper & Minnie Lee Meek, his wife, 2/1/1930, Clovis, N. M.
BIRTHS:
Stephen Light Dickson 9/13/1811 in Franklin Co., Ga.
Elizabeth Jane DeVane, wife of S. L. Dickson, 1/23/1828 in Pike Co., Ga.
Patrick Henry Dickson 1st son of S. L. & E. J. Dickson, 6/25/1844 Coweta Co., Ga.
---------, daughter of S. L. and E. J. Dickson, 4/16/1846 in Macon Co., Ala.
Camillus Coleman Dickson, second son of S. L. and E. J. Dickson, 6/8/1848 in Macon Co., Ala.
Wyley Peyton Dickson, 3d son of S. L. & E. J. Dickson, 11/8/1850 Macon Co., Ala.
Eugenia Elizabeth Dickson, second daughter of S. L. and E. J. Dickson 1/16/1854 in Lowndes Co., Ala.
Stephen Robert Dickson, fourth son of S. L. and E. J. Dickson, 8/18/1856 in Lowndes Co., Ala.
William Alonzo Dickson, fifth son of S. L. and E. J. Dickson, 1/20/1859 in Lowndes Co., Ala.
Rufus Devane Dickson, sixth son of S. L. and E. J. Dickson, 4/14/1861 in Lowndes Co., Ala.
Henry Bee Dickson, seventh son of S. L. and E. J. Dickson, 1/23/1864 in Lowndes Co., Ala.
Eugene Bee Dickson 11/16/1868 in Butler Co., Ala.
Births of Children of J. W. and E. E. Harper:
Bee Harper 10/5/1872 Grimes Co., Texas
Mary Eugenia Harper 9/27/1874 Grimes Co.,Texas
Joseph Alonzo Harper 3/9/1884 Waller Co., Texas
Births of Children of L. L. and Bee Mahan:
Bessie Eugenia Mahan 11/19/1892
Nancy Dickson Mahan 5/23/1895 Waller Co., Texas
Harper Norman Mahan 2/13/1902 Hempstead, Texas
Births of Children of Mary Eugenia and Henry Lorenz:
Fred Eugene Lorenz 5/25/1900 at Coquilla, Ore.
Camilla Agnes Lorenz 11/23/1902 Coquilla, Ore.
Births of Children of Joseph and Josephine Harper:
Moore Dickson Harper 2/20/1912 Travis Co., Texas
Joe Allen Harper 6/2/1912 Travis Co., Texas
Tommie Ray Harper 6/22/1921 Travis Co. Texas

Born to N. D. Mahan and Daniel Lamson Morrison, a son, Dan, Jr. 4/30/1920, Hempstead, Texas

DEATHS:
_____, daughter of S. L. and E. J. Dickson 9/3/1847 in Macon Co., Ala.

Patrick Henry Dickson, the first born of his parents, fell by a ball piercing his vitals on the 1st day of July 1862, in the battle of "Malvern Hill" near Richmond, of which he died the day following, July 2nd, having been for fourteen months a member of the Tuskegee Light Infantry in the 3rd Alabama Regiment. He was 18 years and 6 days of age.

Henry Bee Dickson 8/1868
Wylie Peyton Dickson 6/9/1870
Eugene Bee Dickson 10/9/1871
C. C. Dickson 8/26/1877
Elizabeth Jane Dickson 11/24/1878
Stephen L. Dickson 1/13/1880
Eugenia Elizabeth Dickson 7/29/1909
Joseph Harper 11/2/1886 Monaville, Texas

From paper found in Dickson Bible:

Thomas Green Dickson born 6/27/1804
William White Dickson born 2/19/1807
Wylie Pope Dickson born 5/20/1809
Stephen Light Dickson born 9/13/1811
Samuel Cants Dickson born 7/4/1817

DEATHS:
Stephen Dickson 1/7/1848
Thomas G. Dickson 6/14/1845
Wylie P. Dickson 6/18/1858

WILLIAM W. DICKSON BIBLE of Clayton Co., Ga.
Contributed to Miss Corrie Dickson, Jonesboro, Ga.
to Armchair Researcher, Vol. 2, No. 2

New York American Bible Society 1884

MARRIAGES:
1/12th Tuesday 68 by Rev. Daniel McLucas, W. W. Dickson to Annie E. Butler

BIRTHS:
William W. Dickson 6/25/1843
Annie E., wife of W. W. Dickson, 10/26/1851
Charles D. Dickson 11/26/1869
John S. Dickson 2/4/1872
Robert L. Dickson 2/14/1875
Walter J. Dickson 9/12/1878
Howard H. Dickson 11/8/1880
Benjamin H. Dickson 8/2/1883
Pearl Dickson 11/9/1887

DEATHS:
William W. Dickson 3/4/1925
Annie E., wife of W. W. Dickson, 5/2/1933
Howard H. Dickson 1/30/1936
Walter J. Dickson 12/21/1939
Benj. Hill Dickson 12/6/1942
Charles D. Dickson 4/28/1950
John S. Dickson 11/29/1951
Robert L. Dickson 4/7/1956
Pearl Dickson 7/4/1978

Bible, Philadelphia, printed and published by Mathew Carey, No. 122 Market Street. August 19, 1805

Family Records:

John O. Dickson and Mary Dickson married 6/23/1833
John Orr Dickson, son of David Dickson, grandson of William Dickson, great-grandson of Michael Dickson, was born 6/1/1808
James Ottereson Dickson born 8/10/1811
Elisabeth Caroline Dickson born 11/18/1813
David Monro Dickson born 9/16/1815
Loriann O. Dickson born 10/14/1818
Elisabeth Ann Riley Dickson born 10/14/1820
William Hugh Crawford Dickson born 11/26/1822
Chandler Aubrey born 7/2/1787
David Dickson, son of William Dickson and grandson of Michael Dickson, born 7/23/1850 Old Style
Sarah Dickson, 1st wife to David Dickson, born 2/14/1750 Old Style
Martha Dickson, 2nd wife to David Dickson, born 3/22/1764
Anne Allen Dickson, 3rd wife to David Dickson, born 3/21/1772
W. Hugh Dickson born 9/14/1785
Michael Dickson born 12/9/1788
William Dickson born 3/20/1790
Elizabeth Dickson born 2/16/1791
David Dickson, Jr. born 3/22/1792
James Dickson born 7/10/1794
Thornton Smith Dickson born 8/21/1801
Nancy Campbell Dickson born 3/2/1804
Patsey Ealse Dickson born 11/30/1805
John Orr Dickson born 6/1/1808
Robert David Dickson born 1/2/1810
Martha Dickson Smith born 12/8/1827
David Manson Dickson born 8/17/1835
Thomas Hyde Dickson, son of David Dickson Jr., born 2/1/1812
Nancy Eliza Dickson born 3/28/1813
Martha Letitia Dickson born 9/10/1814
David Harris Dickson born 10/1815
Julia Maria Dickson born 3/1818
Zebulon Montgomery Pike Dickson born 7/1819
David Dickson Smith, son of Jepthey Smith & Nancy Smith, b. 3/6/1825
William Hugh Smith born 4/9/1826
Elizabeth Posy Dickson born 3/10/1814

Sarah Dickson, wife to David Dickson, d. 9/7/1785, 35 yrs, 7 mos, 3 daS.
Martha Dickson, 2nd wife to David Dickson, d. 9/9/1796, 32 yrs, 5 mos., 18 das
Elizabeth Dickson, dau. of David Dickson, d. 11/16/1792, 1 yr, 9 mos.
Elizabeth Echols died 9/2-/1828, aged 58 years, --- mos, 6 days
Ealsey Orr died ----/23/1828, aged 7-- years, 2 months.
Christopher Columbus Dickson born 10/17/1825
John Landers Dickson born 5/13/1828
Martha Jane Dickson born 5/21/1830
Johathan H. Glass born 5/5/1779
Nancy Eliza Dickson, first daughter of David Dickson, died 9/14/1813
David Dickson died 5/23/1830
Anna Dickson died 1/30/1840, aged 28 years, 7 months, 26 days
Mary Dickson, wife of John O. Dickson died 5/8/1847
Thornton S. Dickson died 10/29/1867
Charles A. Dickson died 9/1873
John O. Dickson died ---/23/1883
Robert D. Dickson born 1/2/1810
Matheny Dickson born 8/14/1813
Manson Dickson born 8/15/1833
Mary Ann Dickson born 2/17/1835
Elisabeth C. Dickson born 9/27/1836
Annie Allen Dickson born 12/23/1838
David Sumpter Dickson born 4/15/1841
William Wyatt Dickson born 6/24/1843
Sherman Glass Dickson born 9/8/1845
Robert David Dickson died 8/30/1891
Manson Dickson died 9/26/1833
Mary Ann Dickson died 10/10/1835
Elisabeth C. Dickson died 12/3/1911
Annie Allen Dickson died 3/22/1847
David Sumpter Dickson died 5/14/1847
William Wyatt Dickson died 3/4/1925
Sherman Glass Dickson died 2/25/186-
John Marshal Dickson born 5/31/1848
Martha Louisa Dickson born 1/25/1851
Charles Robert Dickson born 6/4/1853

Amer Saphrona Dickson born 3/17/1856
John Marshal Dickson died 8/15/1891
Charles Robert Dickson died 5/7/1896
Emer Saphrona Dickson died 1/15/1943

GEORGE BROWN EVANS
Owner: Mrs. Joe M. Whitworth
971 Wessel Rd., N. W., Gainesville, GA 30501 (1970)

BIRTHS:
George Brown Evans 1/26/1847
Elizabeth Acadia Evans 6/26/1848
Louisa Francis Evans 7/12/1851
Evan Evans 7/3/1855
Sarah Augusta Evans 4/5/1857
Mary Cuella Evans 1858
------Evans -----

DEATHS:
Seaborn Ardin Evans 12/26/1845, aged 1 years, 9 months, 20 days
Elizabeth Acadia Evans 10/28/1854, aged 6 years, 4 months,---days
Cornelius Jefferson Evans 6/27/1862, age 17 years and 18 days
Mrs. Josephine Evans wife of Ardin Evans and daughter
of--------McMichael, 3/25/----
Cassy A. Evans, son of G. B. and Louvenia Evans, 1/26/1850?

MARRIAGES
Ardin Evans and Josephine McMichael 9/15/1842

BIRTHS:
Seaborn Ardin Evans 3/6/1844
Cornelius Jefferson Evans 6/9/1845
Ardin B. Evans 8/24/1822
Josephine McMichael 11/8/1827

ABRAHAM PERKINS BIBLE of Georgia

JONATHAN PERKINS, HIS BOOK 1827
AFTER MY DECEASE, IT IS MY SON, CHASE.
ABRAHAM PERKINS, HIS BIBLE PRESENTED HIM BY HIS BROTHER, CHASE PERKINS SEPT. 28. 1859

BIRTHS:
Abraham Perkins 4/10/1735
Mary Perkins 1/17/1733
Ann Perkins 11/8/1758
Jonathan Perkins 10/17/1760
Esther Perkins 8/5/1762
Ruth Perkins 2/21/1764
Meribah Perkins 6/26/1766
Lydia D. Perkins 4/17/1768
Frodate Perkins 4/3/1770
Matthew Perkins 10/15/1772
Mary B. Perkins 11/27/1774
Jonathan Perkins 10/17/1760
Hannah Perkins 11/30/1761
John B. Perkins 5/16/1784
Chase Perkins 3/11/1786
Matthew Perkins 6/17/1788
Phebe Perkins 12/3/1791
Salley M. Perkins 3/31/1804
Abraham Perkins 10/13/1807
John B. Perkins 5/16/1784
Comfort Perkins 5/2/1789
Juliann Perkins 1/15/1810
Frederick T. Perkins 8/16/1811
Matthew Perkins 2/19/1817
John Perkins 8/6/1827

DEATHS:
Jonathan Perkins 7/25/1852, aged 91 years, 9 months, 8 days
Sarah M. Perkins, daughter of Jonathan Perkins, 3/1863, age nearly 61
John P. Perkins 2/1881 and was nearly 96 years old
Mathew Perkins 9/1826 and was 38 years old

BIRTHS:
Chase Perkins 3/11/1786
Susannah Perkins 10/201787
Hannah H. Perkins 12/28/1810
Thomas N. Perkins 6/20/1818

Chase P. Sanborn born 12/20/1829, son of Benaiah and Hannah Sanborn.

DEATHS:
Abraham Perkins 8/16/1804, aged 69 years
Mary Perkins 5/25/1823, aged 90 years
Matthew Perkins, son of J. B. O., 4/11/1817, aged 7 weeks
Matthew Perkins, son of Jona. 8/17/1826, aged 68 years
Hannah H. Sanborn, daughter of Chase Perkins 1/2-/183-, aged 19 years
Chase Sanborn 3/9/1800
Hannah Perkins, wife of Jona. Perkins 9/15/1837, aged 75 years, 9 months, 15 days

MARY CROSBY POOLE SCAIPE BIBLE
Owner: Ines St. Clou Lyon Anderson
Baytown, Texas (1957), John Lewis Chapter, DAR Baytown, TX

William Scaipe 12/13/1799-5/11/1837, buried Decatur Cemetery, Georgia
Mary Crosby Poole 4/19/1802-3/11/1893, buried Arizoma, La.
Died in Claiborne Parish, La. They married 10/23/1821

Children:
Nancy M. Mc. 8/7/1822-11/2/1824
Perlina S. A. 2/25/1824-12/15/1850 m.-------Lovejoy
James M. (Dr.) 2/28/1826-5/4/1875 m. Sarah Blockburn
Jessie Terry 4/18/1830-7/12/1862 died of battle wound
Charner Poole 3/21/1830-4/2/1892 m. Sarah Hollinsworth on 10/6/1853
Mary M. 3/3/1832-3/21/1867 m.-------Blackman
Vealento M. J.. born 3/22/1834
Margaret R. 6/17/1836-7/13/1872 m. Jarvis

Charmer Poole Scalpe 3/21/1830(Ga)-4/2/1895. He died in Claiborne Parish, La. Buried near Arizoma, La. Married 1st - Sarah Hollingsworth 4/23/1836 (Ga)-10/9/1875. She died in Claiborne Parish, La. buried near Arizome, La. They married 10/6/1853 in Georgia
Children:
Edith Olivia 9/2/1854-9/14/1890 m. Victor Ernest St. Cloud. They married 4/24/1877
She is buried Westview Cemetery, Atlanta, Ga.
Had daughter, Martha Ines St. Cloud who married William Andrew Lyon.
Charner Augustus 3/18/1856-5/26/1900 m. Leona Bookman 1/2/1877
Martha Elizabeth 11/28/1857-12/31/1891 m. Preston Smith 5/1/1883 (1st cousin)
James Madison 1/19/1860-8/11/1918 m. Tinie Calvin 12/18/1881
William Isaiah (Dr.) 5/16/1862- m. Blonde Griffin.
Roland Lee (Dr.) 6/11/1864-7/11/1904 m. Nannie Moore
Robert Hollingsworth (Dr.) 1/5/1867-12/25/1904 m. Nevada Gibbo
Ruth 1/1/1869-11/1950 m. George Edward Ramsey. They m. 6/7/1899
Margaret Alice 2/25/1872-1909 m. John Philip Ziegler. They m. 10/19/1897
Adam 9/29/1875-12/2/1895
Charner Poole Scaipe m. (2) Mollie Hester (widow with one son)
Children:
Fletcher Terry Scaipe

STOW-FERRELL BIBLE of GEORGIA/ALABAMA
Owner: Mrs. G. A. Ferrell, Eufaula, Alabama

Holman's Edition, THE HOLY BIBLE
A. J. Holman & Co., No. 930 Arch Street, Philadelphia, 1876

MARRIAGES:
Edward Stow-Rabun Susan Brantly, 11/28/1864 at Cotton Hill, Clay Co., Georgia
Lilia Stow-Benjamin Amzi Beach 11/9/1886, Eufaula, Alabama
Rabun Brantly Roberts-George Archer Ferrell 2/8/1918, Atlanta, Georgia
Leila Roberts-Francis Collier Rawls 4/15/ Prattville, Alabama

BIRTHS:
Edward Stow 1/30/1840
Rabun Susan Stow 9/23/1843
Rabun Stow 9/2/1865
Edward Stow, Jr. 12/17/1866
Lelia Stow 1/26/1868
James Anthony Stow 9/7/1869
Fredoria Stow 5/21/1871
Mary Lizzie Stow 10/9/1872
Addie Stow 9/6/1874
Brantly Stow 3/24/1876
Anthony Stow 6/29/1877
Kate Stow 1/6/1879
Lillie Stow 3/6/1882
Ruth Stow 8/21/1883
Walter Stow 2/3/1885
Naomi Stow 6/23/1888

George Arch Ferrell Sr. 9/20/1892
Oliver Toon Roberts 3/1/1869
Rabun Brantly Roberts 5/5/1897
Mary Roberts
Oliver Roberts
George Edward Roberts 10/22/1903
Ralph Roberts 8/28/
Leila Roberts 11/1/

Adeline Elizabeth Ferrell 7/31/1920
George Archer Ferrell, Jr. 4/6/1922
Toon Roberts Ferrell 11/4/1924
Francis Collier Rawls Jr. 3/22/1936
Charlotte Raiford Rawls 4/14/1938
Corella Rawls 10/8/1941

DEATHS:
Rabun Stow 5/7/1866
Fredonia Stow 3/18/1875
Lillie Stow 9/10/1882

CARTER BIBLE RECORDS
Owner: Glenda Callier Perkerson
Georgia State Archives

MARRIAGES:
Francis P. Bartow, son of E. R. and Lucinda Carter was born 8/5/1861
Warren Britt, son of E. R. and Lucinda Carter, was born 3/27/1864

GILBERT BIBLE RECORDS
Owner: Virgil Gilbert, Raleigh, Georgia
Georgia State Archives

MARRIAGES:
J. D. Gilbert-Mary F. Smith 1/11/1877

BIRTHS:
J. D. Gilbert 7/11/1855
Mary F. Smith 10/20/1861
Robert E. Gilbert 7/16/1878
C. F. Gilbert 10/14/1879
O. C. Gilbert 7/30/1881
O. A. Gilbert 11/5/1885
Laura Bell Gilbert 10/24/1887
Estelle Gilbert 8/22/1889
M. V. Gilbert 7/7/1891
Mante L. Gilbert 4/1/1894
W. S. Gilbert 5/26/1898
Lena M. Gilbert 8/3/1900
Lilla G. Gilbert 8/3/1900
V. B. Gilbert 9/29/1903

DEATHS:
Laura Bell Gilbert 3/4/1896
W. O. Gilbert 9/3/1908
Mrs. Mary F. Gilbert 11/21/1925
W. S. Gilbert 3/31/1929
J. D. Gilbert 11/19/1932

JOHN SEE BIBLE

John See was born 7/1/1812
Lavina S. See born 9/3/1814
Mary Ann See born 12/11/1831
"   " Ferdinand
Joshua L. See born 11/15/1834
Washington
John W. See born 11/27/1836
Lavina Bell, her Book 6/3/1829
Hartmell Harris See b. 6/6/1838
George Winfield See b. 10/24/1839
Sarah Barthella See b. 1/1/1842
Ernestine Elizabeth See b. 2/23/1842
Levi Pharoah See b. 12/8/1845
Barbary Virginia See b. 7/29/1847
David Tillman See b. 2/12/1849

WILLIAM MORGAN BIBLE

Owner: Virginia Speer Harris, Cochran, Ga.
Georgia State Archives

"This book was purchased December 3, Anno Domini 1804 by Wm Morgan. Price $8.50"

William Morgan, son of Luke John Morgan and Mary, his wife, was born 1/6/1766. Married Sally Ware, daughter of Peter Ware and Susannah, his wife, 1/6/1792. Sally Ware born 2/25/1765, died 3/13/1819. William Morgan died 10/30/1850

Henry C. Morgan, first son of William and Sally, born 10/28/1792
Roland Morgan, 2nd son of William Morgan and Sally, his wife, born 12/25/1794. Died 8/22/1795
Susannah Morgan, dau. of William Morgan & Sally, wife, b. 3/29/1796
Incy Morgan, daughter of William and Sally Morgan, born 12/16/1798. Died 3/23/1814. 16 years old.
William Morgan, Jr., son of William and Sally Morgan, b. 4/8/1803
Hiram Morgan, son of William and Sally Morgan, b. 4/8/1806
Elihu Morgan, son of William and Sally Morgan, b. 3/28/1809. Died 10/5/1813, 4 years old
Asa Morgan, son of William and Sally Morgan, b. 10/8/1811. Died 10/25/1812. 3 years old.

MARRIAGES:
Henry C. Morgan, son of William and Sally Morgan, - Susannah B. Harris, 9/15/1818. Susannah b. 3/29/1796.
Susannah Morgan, daughter of William and Sally Morgan-John H. Walthall 10/5/1820
Hiram Morgan, son of William and Sally Morgan, married Elizabeth Haistons 1/22/1826. Elizabeth Haistons b. 6/4/1810, d. 6/27/1852. They were parents of 12 children.
William Morgan, Jr., son of William and Sally Morgan married Henrietta Bridges 11/22/1827
"This book I give and bequeath to my beloved son, William Morgan, after my death. February 22, 1826. Hiram Morgan."

HIRAM MORGAN BIBLE

Owner: Mrs. Zach Arnold, 1374 Emory Road, Atlanta, Georgia
Henry Powell born 6/8/1765, died 2/9/1850
Asha Powell, wife of Henry Powell, born 2/28/1776, died 6/5/-----.
Their daughter was Polly Powell.
William Haisten married Polly Powell. Their daughter, Elizabeth Haisten, was born 6/4/1810 and died ----/26/1853 age 42 years, 23 days.
Hiram Morgan, son of Wm Morgan & Sally Ware 4/8/1806- 3/14/1856
Hiram Morgan m. Elizabeth Haisten 1/22/1826; they had 12 children.
William Henry Morgan 11/7/1826-10/1/1898 m. Deborah Wright on 2/26/1845
Asa Ware Morgan b. 10/27/1827 at Greenville, Ga. He m. Elizabeth Ann Jane Brown on 1/7/1858. Elizabeth A. J. Brown was b. 11/3/1840
Thomas Jefferson Morgan b. 10/1828
Sarah Ann Elizabeth Morgan b. 1834. She m. Young Frederick Wright 11/10/1846. He was son of Abraham & Ann Wright; b. 3/1/1827
Mary Anny Morgan b. 1836. She married Lewis Joiner on 9/28/1852
Susan Asha Morgan 5/11/1837-2/13/1881 m. Seaborn McLendon 3/13/1881.
Hiram Augusta Morgan b. 7/15/1839 m. Nancy M. Turner 1/26/1854.
John Terrantine Morgan 6/31/1841-3/19/1856
James Abner (Jemmie) Morgan b.3/28/1843
Martha Katharine Frances Jane Morgan b. 10/9/1845 m. Joel S. Strickland 7/9/1869
Incy Lavonia Morgan b.1/20/1847 m. Geo.A. Brown (d.10/1940 Atlanta.
Mariah Sophronia Morgan b. 1/20/1850 m. George Absalom Wright.

ASA WARE MORGAN BIBLE
Owner: Melvina Morgan, Woodbury, Ga.
Georgia State Archives

Asa Ware Morgan 10/27/1827-8/18/1900
Elizabeth Ann Jane Brown 11/3/1840-1/4/1936
Their Children:
Mary Ann Deborah Morgan 5/26/1859-10/29/1859
William Augustus Morgan 9/19/861
James Asa Morgan 9/22/1863-1/12/1919
Sarah Elizabeth Morgan 6/22/1869-3/17/1960
Thomas Jefferson Morgan 8/22/1869-10/8/1937
Martha Ann Elisa Jane Morgan 10/8/1872-3/7/1916
Young Frederick Allen Morgan 2/21/1875-6/3/1935
Annah Lee Morgan 5/14/1877-2/12/1900
Caludia Sophronia Morgan 6/19/1880-6/24/1952

JOHN NEWTON TURK BIBLE of Georgia
Georgia State Archives

DEATHS:
Mary Elisabeth Turk 5/24/1858 age 1 year, 5 months, 10 days
Mary E. Turk 4/22/1868 age 27 years 11 mos., 20 days
Lula Jane Turk 8/29/1870, 2 years, 10 mos, 18 days
Robert Lee Turk 9/23/1876, age one year, 23 days
Era Turk 9/16/1878, one year, 9 months, 5 days
John N. Turk 7/8/1882, age 56 years, 6 mos., 5 days
Jane Turk 4/15/1862, 69 years, 6 mos., 3 days, 51 years a member of the Presbyterian Church
Isabel Elizabeth Turk 7/19/1852, 20 years, 2 mos., 16 days
Cynthia Jane Ash 8/6/1852, age 24 years, 8 months, 8 days
Margaret Turk 11/3/1842, aged 82 years, 5 mos., 23 days, 66 years a member of the Presbyterian Church
John Mayes 24 Nov Octo 1827, aged 61 years, 7 mos., 24 days
Mary Hamilton 3/24/1852, age 65 years
William Turk 1/3/1877, aged 83 years, 6 mos., 14 days
Addison Turk 8/24/1879, aged 62 years, 5 mos., 29 days
John N. Turk 3/15/1883, age 11 mos.

BIRTHS:
William Turk 6/20/1794
Jane Turk 10/12/1792
Pliney Addison Turk 2/26/1817
William Harvy Turk 12/15/1818
Margaret Manerva Turk 1/5/1821
James Hall Turk 8/20/1823
John Newton Turk 1/3/1826
Cyntha Jane Turk 11/28/1827
Mary Malinda Turk 2/12/1829
Luesa Adaline Turk 1/6/1831
Isabel Elisabeth Turk 5/3/1832
Sarah Lititia Turk 11/10/1833

WILLIAM TURK BIBLE of Georgia
Owner: Grace Turk Seaver

BIRTHS:
Pliney Adison Turk 2/26/1817
William Harvy Turk 12/15/1818
Margaret Manerva Turk 1/5/1821
James Hall Turk 8/20/1823
John Newton Turk 1/3/1826
Cinthia Jane Turk 11/28/1827
Mary Malinda Turk 2/12/1829
Louesa Adeline Turk 1/6/1831
Isabella Elizabeth Turk 5/3/1832
Sarah Letitia Turk 11/10/1833

Births of Children of William and Margaret Turk:

John Turk 5/4/1785
Mary Hall Turk 11/8/1787
James Turk 2/9/1791
William Turk 6/20/1794

Margaret Hall Turk, mother of William Turk, was born 6/7/1760 in Iredell Co., N. C. and died in Ga. 11/30/1842, aged 82 years

DEATHS:

Isabella Elizabeth Turk 7/19/1852
Cinthia Jane Ash 8/6/1852
Jane Turk 4/15/1862
William Turk 1/3/1877
Pliney A. Turk 8/24/1879
John N. Turk 8/24/1879
William Harvy Turk 1/9/1885
Margaret M. Chambers 4/6/1895

KILGORE-TURK BIBLE of Georgia
Georgia State Archives
Donated by: Helen Turk Watson
1138 Ousley Place, Macon, GA 31210

BIRTHS:
Dr. James Kilgore 3/26/1828
Amanda S. Kilgore 1/25/1842
A. A. Turk 8/19/1847
J. T. Turk 3/11/1872
T. N. Turk 6/8/1874
Nora L. Turk 11/11/1879
Vincent A. Turk 3/22/----
W. F. Kilgore 4/2/1859
Nancy M. A. Kilgore 7/11/1861
T. B. Kilgore 8/24/1864
L. Y. Kilgore 4/25/1867
Charles Baxter Turk 9/24/1883

Struck through - Charles Baxter Turk died 6/20/1957
Struck through - Nora Lenna Turk died 1960

DEATHS:
Dr. James Kilgore 9/10/1867
A. S. Turk 9/12/1920
A. A. Turk 12/27/1938
Charles Baxter Turk 6/20/1959

DEATHS:
Nora Lenna Turk Archer 1960
W. B. Kilgore 11/19/1866
N. M. Kilgore 8/27/1867
L. J. Kilgore 8/19/1867
J. S. Turk 7/15/1873

MARRIAGES:
Dr. James Kilgore-Amanda S. Ballew 12/15/1856
A. A. Turk-A. S. Kilgore 4/2/1871

JOSEPH BOND BIBLE
Owner Charles Otwell Roberts
510 Coventry Road, Apt. 14A
Decatur, GA 30030 (1973)

His Book January 31st, 1819

Births:

Joseph Bond 5/17/1756
Jeney Bond, his wife, 10/15/1754
She died the 22 of May 1837

William Bond, son of Joseph Bond, 9/4/1779
Easom Bond 9/23/1780
Susanna Bond 2/19/1782
Nathan Bond 7/29/1783
Pollers Bond 1/17/1785
Gabriel Bond 9/1/1786
Jenney Bond 3/7/1788
Joseph Bond 2/2/1790
Charity Bond 3/6/1792
Milley Bond 8/16/1794
Lavinia Bond 9/1/1796

JAMES G. BOND BIBLE
Satterfield Collection
Georgia State Archives

MARRIAGES:
James G. Bond-E. J. Crittenden 11/3/1871
M. R. Bond-Alice Mize 12/27/1888
W. R. Sayer-Janie Bond 1/14/1891
F. M. Kay-Mary E. Bond 1/8/1905
W. A. Brown-Fanny E. Bond 12/26/1903
J. R. Bond-Sallie Hilliard 11/16/1905
L. R. Bagwell-Leo Nora Bond 12/25/1907
O. H. Bond-Sallie Duncan 11/16/1913
J. L. Bond-Ellie Andrew 12/15/1897

BIRTHS:
James G. Bond 1/6/1840
E. J. Bond 4/27/1846
Marcus R. Bond 9/8/1866
Joseph L. Bond 9/28/1868
Eleza J. Bond 10/4/1872
Francis E. Bond 9/24/1879
Elizabeth M. Bond 3/1877
Robert J. Bond 2/4/1879
William F. Bond 11/30/1880
Mavisra Ida 2/24/1883
Leonaril Bond 5/11/1885
Omer H. Bond 12/28/1887

DEATHS:
E. F. Bond 9/14/1870
Jane G. Crittenden 3/5/1898
W. F. Bond 11/1/1884

WILLIAM DUDLEY BOND BIBLE
Copied by: Mrs. S. C. Moon
431 Candler Street, Gainesville, GA (on 2/25/1954)
Owner: Miss Tandy Bonds, Eastman, Georgia

Dudley Bond, his book, 1853, Dec. 31st
Sacred to the memory of Thomas Essi, son of Martha M. and F. A. Bonds, born 2/22/1871, died 12/24/1874

MARRIAGES:
Dudley Bonds-Ann Mary Van Bibber 4/23/1815
Flavious Augusta Bond-Martha Maria Crawford 1/3/1859
Ann Mary Van Bibber (was our grandmother) was born and from Berkshire, England, moved to Virginia, later to Charleston, S. C., when she married William Dudley Bond, then they moved to Lawrenceville, Ga., Gwinnett Co.

Dudley Bond died 11/19/1857
Martha Jane Crawford, formerly Martha Jane Crawford Bonds, d. 2/23/1858
Mrs. Ann Mary Van Bibber Bond d. 1/25/1878
Henry Bond d. 4/25/1906
Flavius A. Bond d. 11/29/1912

Your grandmother Bond's name before she married was Frances Meredith, she was a native of Virginia, reared on the Yadkin River and your grandfather Bonds was reared at same place. He fought all through the Revolutionary War. Your own grandmother's name was Ann Evans. She was reared in or near Savannah, Ga.

Martha C. Bond left this world for Heaven 3/13/1914

Children of Mr. and Mrs. F. A. Bond:
Johnnie A. Bond died 11/1929
Jessie Lorina Bond d. 11/2/1917
Lula Bond Martin d. 1/2/1936
Precious, Mae Foster Bond d. 3/15/1937
Flavius Augusta Bond married Martha Maria Crawford 1/13/1859

BIRTHS OF CHILDREN:
Carry Delute Bond 5/9/1860
John Anderson Bond 12/10/1861
Jessie Lourine Bond 4/3/1866
Charlie Lafayette Bond 5/20/1868, died 1/20/1896
Essie Meridith Bond 2/22/1871, d. 12/24/1874
Mae Foster Bond 4/14/1873
William Wallace Bond 5/18/1875
Henry Clifford Bond 9/27/1877
Herman Bond 10/3/1879, d. 11/1887
Tandie Dudley Bond 5/26/1912
Martha Marie Crawford d. 3/13/1918
Jessie Lora Bond Ryals d. 11/3/1917
(Births) *Another handwriting:*
Carye Deluta Bonds 5/9/1860
John Anderson Bonds 12/10/1861
Jessie Loorine Bonds 4/3/1866
Charley Dafoot Bonds 5/20/1868
Essie Meredith Bonds 2/22/187
Mary Foster Bonds 4/14/1873
Flavious Augusta Bonds 9/22/1836
Martha Meridith Bonds 9/11/1841
William Wolis Bon 5/18/1875
Herman Bond 10/3/1879
Tandy Dudley Bond 5/26/1882
William Bond 10/18/1830
Hillary Bond 4/15/1832
Martha Jane Bond 12/5/1834
Flavious A. Bond 9/22/1836
Henry V. Bonds 7/23/1817
Caroline Bonds 12/16/1818
John J. Bonds 9/23/1820
Mary Elizabeth Bonds 2/15/1823
Zemily Bond 7/18/1826
Thomas M. Bond 3/23/1828
Ann Mary Van Bibber 2/3/1800
Dudley Bonds 11/27/1792, son of William Dudley Bond & Frances Merideth

Flavius Henry Crawford 6/27/1854, son of John F. and Martha Jane Bond Crawford
Hester Ann Crawford 2/12/1856
Alexander Lumpkin Bonds 3/28/1850
Laura Bonds 3/15/1855

DEATHS:
Elsey Bonds 12/24/1874
Herman Bonds 11/1881
Charlie Bonds 1/20/1896
Flora Bonds 11/3/1897, daughter of J. A. Bonds
Jessie Bonds 11/3/1917
Lula Bonds Martin 1/1/1936
John A. Bonds 11/1929
May Foster Bond 3/15/1937
Flora Lutch Bond, wife of John A. Bonds 3/17/1950

F. A. BLUE BIBLE
Owner: Harry Blue
1035 Rosedale Road, N. E., Atlanta, GA 30306 (1981)

Mrs. Caroline L. Mitchell was borned March 16, 1825 and died Sep 3 1873

MARRIAGES:
F. A. Blue-M. E. Mitchell 7/9/1866
J. H. Wiliford and Annie Blue 8/22/1889
John Blue-Edna Donald 3/28/1892
Manning McDuffie-Carrie Blue 5/3/1896

BIRTHS:
Francis Archibald Blue, son of Mary and John Blue, 1/25/1842
Mary Eliza Mitchell, daughter of Stephen and Caroline Lovedy Mitchell, 11/16/184--
John Blue, son of F. A. and M. E. Blue, 2/15/1867
Annie Blue daughter of F. A. and M. E. Blue, 12/24/1865
Daniel A. Blue, son of F. A. and M. E. Blue, 1/12/1873
Baby boy 9/26/187--
Charles Edwin Blue, son of F. A. and M. E. Blue, 9/16/1874
Caroline L. Blue, daughter of F. A. and M. E. Blue, 3/10/1876

Katie Adell Blue, daughter of F. A. and M. E. Blue, 2/24/1878
Stephen Augustus Blue, son of F. A. and M. E. Blue, 7/31/1880
Mary Virginia Blue, daughter of F. A. and M. E. Blue, 11/6/1881
Norman Mitchell 10/10/1885
Annie Clifford McDuffie--------------------

DEATHS:
F. A. Blue 6/3/1883
James A----Wiliford 10/5/1896
---------------- --/10/1896
James H. Wiliford 3/15/1897
Archie Elide Blue 6/24/1899
Willie Edgar Blue 8/7/1801
Carrie May Wiliford 6/11/1902
M. E. Blue 9/30/1902
John Blue 5/28/1904
Mary E. Blue --- 1903

BIRTHS:
John Edwin Blue, son of ----------Edna Blue, 8/10/-----, died 8/20/1893
James Archabald Wiliford, son of J. H. and Annie Wiliford, 6/29/1890
Joseph F. Wiliford, son of J. H. and Annie Wiliford, 11/29/1891
Annie Bell Wiliford, daughter of J. H. and Annie Wiliford, 1/10/1893
Carrie May Wiliford, daughter of J. H. and Annie Wiliford, 2/14/1894

-------------, son of Dan and ---- Blue, 8/9/-----8
Willie Edgar, son of Dan and --alia Blue, 4/10/19--
Charlotte, daughter of Edna Blue, 4/6/1900
John Thomas?, son of ---- and Edna Blue, 2/18/1903

THOMAS ATKINS BOOTH BIBLE
of Hartwell, Hart Co., Ga.

Rev. and Mrs. James Parker Vickery of Hartwell, Georgia announce the marriage of their elder daughter, Emma Vickery to Thomas A. Booth of Dewey Rose, Ga. 9/28/1890

BIRTHS:
Thomas Atkins Booth 5/12/1809, son of J. R. Booth and Elizabeth C. Booth of Dewey Rose, Ga.
Emma Vickery 8/28/1868, daughter of Rev. J. P. Vickery and Susie Shiflet Vickery of Hartwell, Ga.
Rossie Videau Booth 6/7/1893
Leona Booth 1/5/1895
Mildred Booth 11/25/1896
Albert Dewey Booth 4/4/1898
Jameson Van Buron Booth 2/2/1900
Ellen Bert Booth 7/28/1903
Thomas Carl Booth 2/24/1905
James Melvin Booth 10/27/1906
Susie Lee Booth 9/26/1908
Mr. and Mrs. T. A. Booth of Hartwell, Ga. announce the marriage of their daughter, Rossie Videau to Lonnie W. Walker of Hartwell, Ga. 7/9/1909

BIRTHS:
Julian Edgar Walker 7/31/1910
MacNorman Walker 5/21/1912
Thomas Inman Walker 10/17/1914
Susie Margaret Walker 9/17/191--
James Forest Walker 5/1/1919
Emma Geraldine Walker 11/27/1921
Forrest Walker died 1968
Mr. and Mrs. T. A. Booth of Hartwell, Ga. announce the marriage of their daughter, Leona Booth to James O. Chapman of Elberton, Ga. 1/26/1913.

BIRTHS:
Mary Louise Chapman 12/7/1913
William Thomas Chapman 6/7/1914
Emma Bert Chapman 5/13/1917
James Booth Chapman 4/30/1922
In loving memory of Mary Louise Chapman born 2/7/1913, died 6/17/1914. Funeral service conducted by Rev. S. C. West.
In loving memory of Emma Bert Chapman born 5/13/1917, died 5/28/1917. Funeral service conducted by Rev. J. D. Turner.

Sacred to the memory of Ellen Bert Booth born 7/28/1903, died, Funeral service conducted by Rev. J. C. West and Rev. T. A. Thornton.

Mr. and Mrs. T. A. Booth of Hartwell, Ga. announce the marriage of their daughter, Mildred Booth to James Bynum Cheek of Elberton, Ga. on 12/21/1919

Thomas Angus Cheek born 11/25/-----

Jamerson Vanburen Booth

Mr. and Mrs. James Turner of Fair Forest, S. C. announce the marriage of their daughter, Ethel Turner, to Thomas Carl Booth of Hartwell, Ga. 11/2/1924

Dewey Otis Booth born 9/23/192--

Homer O'Neil Booth born 4/1/192--

In loving memory of Dewey Otis Booth born 9/23/1925, died 9/25/192--

Mr. and Mrs. Moon of Royston, Ga. announce the marriage of their daughter Lillie Belle Moon to James Melvin Booth of Hartwell, Ga. 8/18/1928

Ray Edwin Booth died 10/5/1929

In loving memory of James Melvin Booth born 10/27/1906, died 7/3/1930

Mr. and Mrs. T. A. Booth of Hartwell, Ga. announce the marriage of their daughter, Susie Lee Booth to Paul Wilson Cole of Anderson, S. C. 6/24/1928.

Paul Wilson Cole Jr. born 9/24/1929

Mr. and Mrs. T. A. Booth of Hartwell, Ga. announce the marriage of their daughter, Leona Booth Chapman to George L. Richardson of Hartwell, Ga. 12/30/1930.

Sacred to the memory of John R. Booth who died 6/30/1864 in the time of the great cyclorama of the Civil War and his wife, Elizabeth Catherine Booth, who died 2/15/1892.

Elizabeth C. Booth was left a widow with seven children near the close of the civil war. She was left with no money and was in debt the only means of rearing and educating the children and paying the debts was farming. This noble Christian woman was loved by all who knew her. She lived twenty-seven years a widow, reared seven children to honorable manhood and womanhood.

John Wiley Booth and Nancy Adeline Pledger was married 12/10/1874

John Wiley Booth born 3/7/1852

Adeline P. Booth born 10/30/1856

Arrenia Ellen Booth b. 10/5/1875 m. 12/10/1899 to J. Luther Seymore, Dewey Rose, Ga.
Cathrinas Clifford Booth b. 3/17/1877 m. 3/19/1921 Susie Harper, Elberton, Ga.
Alexander S. Booth b. 10/22/1878 m. 12/10/1910 Hanna Renfroe, St. Louis, Mo.
John Lee Booth b. 2/24/1881 m. 1/12/1907 to Francis Ayers, St. Louis.
Essie Cathrine Booth b. 12/12/1882 m. 8/19/1900 to A. C. Johnson, Elberton, Ga.
George Conners Booth b. 6/28/1885 m. 10/11/1908 to Lillie Campbell
Katherine Aderline b. 8/8/1888 m. 6/5/1912 Fred Wood, Monroe, N. C.
Henry Grady Booth b. 9/2/1891 m. 11/19/1923 Toledo Hesse
Elmer Hoyt Booth b. 4/19/1894 m. 3/12/1917 to Rebecca Calloway
May Belle Booth b. 1/8/1897 m. 4/23/1919 Dr. W. L. Bond, Elberton, Ga.
John W. Booth d. 12/25/1924 buried Dewey Rose, Ga. 12/29/1924.
Funeral service conducted by W. A. Wray
Leona Booth b. Hart Co., Ga. 1/5/1895 m. first in Hart Co. 1/26/1913 to James Otis Chapman, b. 1880, d. 1975. divorced. She married 2nd 12/30/1930 to George Landrum Richardson who was b. Hartwell, Ga. 1/17/1876, d. Hartwell, Ga. 1/22/19--. There were no children by this second marriage. Mr. Richardson was first married in Hart Co. to Lena May McCurry on 12/31/1912. He had a son and daughter by his first wife who preceded him to the grave.

"Copied 1/28/1971 by L. L. S. while in possession of Leona Booth Chapman Richardson Abbacrombie, Main St., Anderson, S. C."

JOSHUA BOWDOIN BIBLE
Owner: Mrs. T. N. Ray, Norwood, Ga (1967)

Joshua Bowdoin b. 11/5/1803 d. 11/2/1880
Basheba? Bowdoin b. 7/1/1794 d. 7/8/1852
Josephus D. Bowdoin b. 4/18/1829
Elizabeth C. Patman b. 1/24/1831
Hypatia Catharine Bowdoin b. 10/5/1851, d. 4/10/1915
Josephus Patman Bowdoin b. 5/7/1866
Rosa Bowdoin b. 4/30/1862 d. 1/5/1911
Frank Dewitt Bowdoin b. 12/15/1865 d. 5/3/1918
Hypatia Virginia Bowdoin Anderson b. 8/12/1875
Bessie Lara Catherine Anderson b. 11/21/1877 d. 7/6/1960
Josephus Emina Anderson b. 7/26/1880 d. 11/22/1956

THORNBERRY BOWLING BIBLE of Oglethorpe Co., Ga.
Owner: Mrs. Charles W. Foppert
1803 Erlen Road, Melrose Park
Philadelphia, PA 19126 (1970)

BIRTHS:
Emily, daughter of Thornberry and Mary Ann, his second wife, 9/7/1830
Penelope Bowling 3/16/1832
Thornberry Jackson Bowling 3/30/1833
Mary E. Smith, wife of T. J. Bowling, 11/5/-----
Mary Anna, daughter of M. E. and T. J. Bowling, 2/1861
George Bowling 6/14/1863
Joseph Smith Bowling 3/1/1866
Harriet Newel Bowling 8/2/1867
Thomas Thornberry Bowling 11/27/1869
Walter Grogan Bowling 2/28/1892
William Franklin Bowling 8/8/1877
Harry Bowling 1/7/1881
different handwriting - (apparently "added")
Elizabeth O'Neill Bowling 4/13/1905
Walter Harrison 9/30/1909
same as 1st handwriting -
Thornberry Bowling 6/8/1777
Lucy Rainey, 1st wife of Thornberry Bowling, 2/12/1779
William and James Bowling, their sons, 2/19/1799
Lucy Ann Bowling, their daughter, 1/6/1801
Matthew Rainey Bowling, their son, 8/12/1802
Martha Watkins Bowling, their daughter, 12/26/180-
James Thornberry, their son, 2/4/1807
John Newton, their son, 9/27/1813
Winfred Jett Wright 10/6/1793
Mary Ann Aycock, his wife, 5/6/1793
Burl J. T. Wright, their son, 1/30/1815
Elisan William Wright 4/15/1816
Mary Adeline Elizabeth Wright 1/11/1818
John Lowen Wright 4/5/1819
Elicif Cordelia Wright 12/22/1820
Mertis Francina Wright 7/14/1822

Thornberry Bowling and Mary Ann Wright were married 6/19/1828

MARRIAGES:

Thomas E. R. Harris-Emily Bowling 5/18/1847
N. H. Wilson-Mertie F. Wright 9/1/1842
William Holmes-Elicif C. Wright 10/1/1845
C. J. Bowling-M. E. Smith 3/29/1860
J. F. Morton-Emily Harris 8/28/1861
Mary Anna Bowling-C. W. Berry 12/20/1894
Harriet Hewel Bowling-W. S. Branch 1/24/1895
T. T. Bowling-Bessie C. Bray 12/8/1897
Joseph S. Bowling-Florence Bell 5/16/1900
Harry Bowling-Ellen Cranford

DEATHS:

Thornberry Bowling 5/8/1839
William Bowling 4/2/1801
----Bowling 4/5/1801
Matthew Bowling 9/25/1822
------ 4/23/1825
Wright 7/24/1823
Mary Ann Wright 10/26/1826
I. J. G.? Wright 10/13/1826
E. W.? Wright 10/10/1826
Jane? Wright 7/29/1845
Mary Ann Bowling 11/27/1881
George Bowling 6/17/1889
M. Elizabeth Bowling d. 1/19/1905
Harriet Newel Bowling d. 2/3/1905
Penelope McMurray d. 8/22/1911
Thornberry Jackson Bowling d. 11/7/1919
Joseph Smith d. 8/25/1921
Will d. 12/1924
Thomas d. 10/1927

ROLLINS BIBLE
Included with the Bible of Thomas Young Brent
Owner: S. R. Chambliss, P. O. Box 137
Lithia Springs, GA (1965)

BIRTHS:
Harry Brent Rollins 8/23/1940 Atlanta, Ga. (son of James Richard and Ruth Brent Rollins)

Jacqueline Elaine Dennis 8/31/1949 Portsmouth, Virginia (daughter of William Madison and Jacquelyn Brent Dennis

Harry Brent Rollins, Jr. 12/23/195-- Atlanta, Ga. (son of Harry Brent and Gail Fitzgerald Rollins)
Michael Richard Rollins 9/4/1960 Portsmouth, Virginia (son of Harry Brent and Gail Fitzgerald Rollins)

Carol Howard Brent 11/4/1937 Atlanta, Ga. (daughter of Howard Crumly Brent and Louise Forrest Brent)

Catherine Louise Bedsole 11/20/1960 Texas (daughter of Terry and Carol Bedsole)

Peter Bedsole 5/29/1962 Texas (son of Terry and Carol Bedsole)

Wilmer Brent Haynes 10/29/---- Atlanta Ga. (son of Wilmer Carlisle and Kate Brent Haynes)
Danny Walker Haynes 10/6/1924 Atlanta, Ga (son of Wilmer Carlisle and Kate Brent Haynes)
Noel Baxter Haynes 6/21/1939 Atlanta, Ga. (son of Wilmer Carlisle and Kate Brent Haynes)
Scheryl Haynes 5/1962 Atlanta, Ga

DEATHS:
Wilmer Brent Haynes, son of Wilmer C. and Kate Brent Haynes and missing in action 6/24/1944
Danny Walker Haynes, son of Wilmer C. and Kate Brent Haynes 9/24/1944 in Casper, Wyoming

MRS. JAMES A. BUIE BIBLE
Owner: Mrs. Bert M. Janes
2082 Randolph Circle
Kennesaw, GA (1965)

BIRTHS:
Daniel Buie 5/8/1849
Sarah V. Buie 3/22/1863
Alzena Vaden Buie 8/19/1880
William D. Buie 7/20/1882
John C. Buie 5/7/1884
Sarah A. Buie 1/25/1887
Daniel B. Buie 2/12/1889
Mary Eunice Buie 9/19/1891

MARRIAGES:
Daniel Buie-Sarah V. Anderson 12/16/1879

JAMES A. BULL BIBLE
Georgia State Archives

Presented to Mrs. James A. Bull, 1885

James A. Bull-Elmira V. Chambers at Joseph S. Chambers 11/16/1858 in presence of Daniel McLucas and William Chambers. /s/Moses Harp.

Mitton S. Bull-Mattie T. Dixon 12/18/1881
John H.Conkle-Alice Bull 12/15/1886
Alonzo T. Bull-Susan Pearl Barron 7/19/1905
Jessie Annie Bull-Aline L. Richards 6/19/1906
Virginia Anne Bull-Corley Hall Dillon 12/29/1934

BIRTHS:

James A. Bull 12/11/1833
Elmira V. Bull 9/13/1840
Milton F. Bull 8/29/1859
Walter H. Bull 3/24/1861
Martha A. Bull 12/24/1865
Edgar A. Bull 2/16/1868
Ida S. Bull 10/24/1871
Willie A. Bull 3/20/1876
Alonzo T. Bull 4/22/1873
Jessie A. Bull 9/26/1882
Mary E. Bull 9/20/1884
Annie V. Bull 5/8/1907

DEATHS:

Walter H. Bull 12/21/1863
Edgar A. Bull 9/10/1875
Mattie T. Bull 11/22/1884
Mary Estella Bull 8/17/1885
Milton S. Bull 7/22/1889
James A. Bull 6/4/1891
Willie A. Bull 1/1/1893
Elmira V. Bull 7/9/1907
Ida S. Bull 5/5/1934
Alice Bull Conkle 12/17/1946
Alonzo T. Bull 9/16/1962
Jessie Bull Richards 12/19/1971

GREENBERRY STEPHENS BIBLE of Clayton Co., Ga.
From: Dkhz@aol.com (Debbie)

[DHZ note: Greenberry Stephens was the son of Simeon Sylvester & Elizabeth Stephens who are buried at Tanner's Baptist Church, Clayton Co GA. Evidence seems to indicate that Elizabeth was nee Estes, the daughter of Zephaniah & Mary "Polly" Clark Estes.]

MARRIAGES:
G B Stephens and E C Cook was married 12 April 1860
J A Leits and M F Stephens was married 21 Dec 1876
W T Stephens and M J Swiney was married 1 Feb 1880>
O H Turnipseed and M E T J Stephens was married 21 Dec 1882
G B Stephens and Emly Elizabeth Sanders was married 24 Feb 1884
T M New & J M Stephens was married 15 Jan 1888

Minnie A Stephens and S W Burks was married 13 June 1906

Alfred Columbus Stephens and Elizabeth Eberhart married 30 Dec 1906
Simon Silvester Stephens and Annie Rebecca Ross was married 6 Dec 1914
Julius Green Stephens and Beaulah Milam was married 18 Mar 1917

BIRTHS:
G. B. Stephens was born 9 May 1838
E. C. Cook was born 3o May 1834
E. E. Sanders was born 21 Mar 1854

Children of G B and E C Stephens:
M F Stephens was born 16 Dec 1860
W T Stephens was born 21 Jan 1862
M E T J Stephens was born 22 Oct 1864
J M Stephens was born 2 Dec 1866
R A Stephens was born 30 Sep 1868

Children of G B & E. .E Stephens:
A C Stephens was born 15 Jun 1885
M A Stephens was born 24 Nov 1886

[DHZ note: Minnie Alfaretta Stephens, above, was my great-grandmother.]
Simeon Sylvester Stephens was born 5 Sep 1890
Julius Green Stephens was born 20 Aug 1894

DEATHS:
M E T J Turnipseed departed this life 9 Sep 1883
T____ Octavio Turnipseed departed this life 11 Oct 1883
Celia Elizabeth Stephens wife of G B Stephens departed this life 18 Dec 1883
Monrow Leits departed this life 5 Jun 1893 2 o'clock PM
M T New departed this life 22 Mar 1892
W T Stephens departed this life 9 May 1910 in Ala 4:20 PM
G B Stephens departed this life 9 Apr 1920
Emily Elizabeth Stephens departed this life 1 Jun 1956 5:25 PM
Melvinnie Magdeline Stephens departed this life 5 Jan 1949 4:20 PM
Alfred Columbus Stephens departed this life 1 Jun 1956 5:25 PM
Minnie A Burks departed this life 7 Apr 1969

Grandchildren names:
A P Leits was born 23 Jan 1878
D V Stephens was born 25 Dec 1880
D R C Leits was born 26 Aug 1881
Simeon Monroe Stephens was born 1 Dec 1882
L O Turnipseed born 23 Aug 1883
L Octavia Stephens was born 5 May 1885
W C Stephens was born 16 Aug 1887
R E Leits born 6 Apr 1885
J H Stephens born 28 Sep 1889
D E Stephens born 22 Oct 1891
Monroe Leits born and died 2 Dec 1890
B____ Stephens born 2 Mar 1890
C____ Stephens born 17 Dec 1891
M S New born 30 Jun 1895
P M Stephens born 5 Jun 1896
R L Stephens born Aug 1899
T M New born 23 Sep 1899
M T New born 29 Mar 1892
L Myrtle New born 25 Oct 1897
T M New born 7 Aug 1902

R B New born 2 Oct 1904
William Henry Grady Stephens born 18 Apr 1908
Reuben Columbus Stephens born 25 Apr 1909
Robert Luther Stephens born 8 Oct 1910
[DHZ note: he had more grandchildren.]

Date of G B Stephens, Wife & Children joining the Church:
G B Stephens joined the Primitive Baptist Church by experience 10 Aug 1873
Elizabeth C Stephens joined the Missionary Baptist Church at Tanner's Church 7 Aug 1855 by experience; dismissed from same 4 Oct 1872 by letter
Elizabeth C Stephens joined Primitive Baptist Forest by letter 17 Nov 1873
M F Stephens joined church at Forest by experience 9 Oct 1878
M E T J Stephens joined the church at Forest by exp 4 Aug 1882
J M Stephens joined the church at Forest by experience 4 Aug 1882
G B Stephens was dismissed from the church at Forest May 1886
Emley E Stephens dismissed from the church at Forest by letter Aug 1886
Emley E Stephens joined Primitive Baptist Church at Forest Aug 1884
Minnie A Stephens joined the Primitive Baptist Church at Forest Aug 1903
Melvinnie M Stephens joined the Primitive Baptist Church at Forest Aug 1903
R A Stephens joined Missionary Baptist Church at The Rock in Spring of 1891
[DHZ note: The following newspaper clippings were found in this Bible.]
Death of I M Sanders. Mr Isiah M Sanders departed this life September 3 at the age of 58 years, 2 months and 23 days. He was born in Clayton County Georgia June 11, 1863. He came to Cass County, Texas in 1894, and to Hunt County in 1895, where he engaged in farming near Greenville with his cousin, Dr J W Lyle. After nineteen years of success there, they came to Harlingen in 1914, where he engaged in farming. He never married, but continued to live with Dr Lyle and their cousin Mrs Koger until death came. He was stricken with paralysis August 22 while in the field at work. He felt the approach of the stroke in time to call his little nephew who was near. Everything was done for him that could be done, but God's plan called for him to go at this time. He bore his suffering with much patience. No man in this section was more universally respected. He leaves a host of friends here besides many in the other places that he has lived in times past. He was not a member of any church, but we know where to find him as God, unlike man, looketh on the heart. No man was a better

friend to those in need than he. He leaves besides his relatives here, three brothers and two sisters. One sister and brother reside in Alabama, and two brothers and one sister in Georgia. His remains were laid to rest in the Harlingen cemetery after the funeral at the residence on Wilson tract at 4 PM Sunday, September 4. To the bereaved we would say; don't weep because of a new made grave, or feel sad for the vacant chair. Let's look from earth to heaven above, for he is living there. A friend.

[DHZ note: The "sister living in Georgia", is Emily Elizabeth Sanders Stephens. The family relationship with the Lyle is through the mother of Isaiah & Emily Elizabeth who was Amanda Lavina Lyle Sanders.]

In memory of Ida C Jones. Mrs Ida Catherine Jones, wife of William Jones and daughter of Isaiah and Vinie Sanders, departed this life January 14, 1896, aged 22 years, 11 months and 20 days...
[DHZ note: Ida was a sister to Emily Elizabeth Sanders Stephens.]

In Memorium. Martilla Ellen Adamson was born in Washington County, Ga on March 23rd, 1849, and died Jan 9th, 1874. She was the daughter of James S and Martha Cook, who moved to this county in 1854. In 1863, she lost her pious and devoted mother. In July 1862, she became a member of the Baptist Church at Tanners, baptized by Rev A K Tribble. She was married November 21, 1866 to A P Adamson with whom she lived until her death... [DHZ note: Martilla was the sister of Celia Elizabeth Cook Stephens.]

ROBERT E. WALL BIBLE
Owner: Dr. Frank Daniel, 726 Amsterdam Ave., N. E., Atlanta, GA 30306 (1972)

Parents:
Robert E. Wall 2/28/1777 Wilkes Co., NC-5/28/1850 Spartanburg, SC
Wilburn Wall 5/1/1812 Spartanburg, SC-11/4/1841 Cherokee Co., AL
CHILDREN:
Clarissa Wall 11/20/1821-10/5/1857 Walker Co., GA
E. G. Wall 8/5/1825 Ten-9/12/1858 Walker Co., GA
Mary A. Wall 8/19/1842 Walker Co., GA-12/2/1862 Walker Co., GA
T. A. Wall 5/19/1844 Walker Co., GA-7/16/1863 Walker Co., GA
John C. Wall 2/14/1848 Walker Co., GA-8/19/1875 Walker Co., GA
Eliza A. Wall 3/10/1852 Walker Co., GA-12/11/1873 Walker Co., GA

RICHARD W. CASSADAY BIBLE
Owner: Dr. Frank Daniel
726 Amsterdam Ave., N. E.
Atlanta, GA 30306 (1972)

BIRTHS:
Richard W. Cassaday 8/27/1804
Mary Walker 8/5/1799
Elizabeth Jane Cassaday 8/5/1825
Nancy Ann Cassaday 2/7/1827
Mary Lamanda Cassaday 2/9/1829
Elbert Sevier Cassaday 12/16/1830
Russell Marimore Cassaday 6/22/1833
Martha Emelia Cassaday 7/26/1835
Hannah Louca Cassaday 7/17/1838

Mary Walker m. Richard Cassaday 9/7/1824
The above taken from Knox Co., TN in "Teamell Cousins", pages 2, 3, 7 (copied 8/20/1964)

DEATHS:
Lewis Rowland Fletcher 8/20/1862 in camp, Confederate Soldier
Richard W. Cassaday in Chattooga Co., GA 7/9/1880 (This was taken from an old book that belonged to his daughter, Mrs. Lewis Rowland Fletcher (entered 3/9/1968).
Mary Cassaday 7/14/1849
Martha E. Cassaday 10/27/1857
R. M. Cassaday 12/19/1874
Elizabeth Jane Cassaday b. 8/5/1825 m. Wilburn Wall (2nd wife) 9/12/1858, d. 6/24/1901 in Walker Co., Ga., buried in Trinity Graveyard
Romney M. Cassaday was killed in a hail and wind storm in Dimmitt, Texas 7/1929

MARRIAGES:
Lewis R. Fletcher-Hannah L. Cassaday 7/23/1857
Thomason Amanda Wall-Russell Merriman Cassaday 7/21/1863
Nancy Ann Cassaday-William Rice 12/24/1846
Mary Lamanly Cassaday-David Biles 3/27/1852

BIRTHS:
Lewis Rowland Fletcher 5/10/1833
Hannah Loueva Fletcher 7/17/1838
Williamson Montgumry Fletcher 5/28/1858
Osker Alonzo Fletcher 9/20/1860
Talullah Alphonso Cassaday 6/9/1866
Romney Atticus Cassaday 2/14/1868

MARRIAGES:
Wilbern Wall-Clarisa Grogman 11/4/1841
William Wall-Elizabeth L. Cassaday 9/12/1858
John F. Thomas-Mary A. Wall 12/21/1862

BIRTHS:
Wilbern Wall 5/1/1812
Clarisa Grogan Wall 11/20/1821
Mary A. Wall 8/19/1842
Thomas A. Wall 5/19/1844
John C. Wall 2/14/1848
Sarah J. Willingham 7/25/1846
William Wall 6/28/1845
Sarah A. Wall 11/21/1847

BIRTHS:
Robert T. Wall 2/28/1777
Eliza A. Wall 3/10/1852
Elizabeth L. Wall 8/5/1825

Jonathan Wall, father of above Robert Wall, was born in Prince George Co., Maryland in 1744, died in Spartanburg Co., S. C. in 1836 (This place of death, probably in error, some data says he died Rutherford Co., N C)

DEATHS:

Robert T. Wall 5/28/1850
Clarissa B. Wall 10/5/1857
Wilbern Wall 9/12/1890
Eliza A. Wardlake 6/17/1890

BIRTHS:
Enoch Lewis Thurman 9/21/1858 Walker Co., GA-8/7/1906 m. on 8/3/1882 Lula Cassaday b. 6/9/1866, Walker Co., GA, d. 5/5/1957 Walker Co., GA
Children:
David Russell Thurman b. 7/7/1883 Walker Co., GA, d. 11/16/1936 in Chattanooga, TN
Ray Vaughn Thurman b. 5/24/1885 Walker Co., GA, d. 6/16/1947 in LaFayette, GA
Lillian Ruth Thurman b. 1/27/1888 Walker Co., GA
Amanda Lee Thurman b. 8/2/1890 Walker Co., GA
Sarah Lucile Thurman b. 1/31/1893 Walker Co., GA
Edna May Thurman b. 12/15/1897, d. 3/10/1898
Roy Atticus Thurman b. 10/21/1895 Walker Co., GA , d. 12/16/1967
Maude Irene Thurman b. 8/12/1900
Roy Atticus Thurman and Gertrude Smith were married on -----
Amanda Lee Thurman m. Dr. Eugene Weatherly 8/23/1823

JOHN A. JORDAN BIBLE
GA State Archives, Jordan Folder

BIRTHS:
John A. Jordan 11/30/1856
Mrs. M. C. Jordan 8/16/1858
Henry A. Jordan 9/24/1878
Mary E. Jordan 4/14/1881
Emmie M. Jordan 6/2/1883
Beulah E. Jordan 9/20/1885
James B. Jordan 9/22/1888
Lela Jordan 1/2/1897
Annie B. Jordan 12/1/1899
Maggie M. Jordan 7/22/1902

MARRIAGES:
John A. Jordan-Martha C. Johnson 12/23/1877
Henry A. Jordan-Kittie Mason 12/25/1902
James B. Jordan-Bessie Eubanks 9/8/1910
James W. A. Teasley-Emmie M. Jordan 9/18/1912

Beulah E. Jordan-Thomas J. Blackmon 8/31/1913
Maggie Malissa Jordan-Waco Agnew 12/22/1928
Annie Jordan-Elbert Estes 1/21/1918
Lowery M. Jordan-Clara Herndon 10/14/1919

DEATHS:

Lola Jordan 6/15/1893
Mary Ella Jordan 2/17/1905
Martha C. Jordan 6/5/1931
John A. Jordan 3/31/1935

THOMAS BURCH BIBLE
National Archives, Washington, D. C. (1960)

Elizabeth Burch, daughter of Thomas Burch and Sarah, his wife, b. 8/1/1786
Eunice Burch, daughter of Thomas Burch and Sarah, his wife, b. 3/16/1788
Jane Burch, daughter of Thomas Burch and Sarah, his wife, b. 5/18/1790
Ruth Burch, daughter of Thomas Burch and Sarah, his wife, 7/11/1792
Keziah Burch, daughter of Thomas Burch and Sarah, his wife, 5/18/1795
Benjamin Burch, son of Thomas Burch and Sarah, his wife, 11/26/1801
James J. Burch, son of Thomas Burch and Sarah, his wife, b. 5/24/1802?
William Stapleton Burch b. 6/14/1809

Thomas Burch, son of Benjamin Burch and Jane, his wife, b. 1/20/1757
Sarah Burch, wife of Thomas Burch, and daughter of James Jones and Elizabeth, his wife, b. 1/5/1766
And was married by William Cook, Esq. 10/18/1785

WILLIAM DAPESNEY BURCH BIBLE
Owner: Carol Burch Tooke
3748 Briarcliff Road, N. E.
Atlanta, GA 30345

BIRTHS:
William Dapesney Burch 10/9/1861
Aeolain L. Burch 2/14/1868 in Hart Co., GA
Margie Anna Burch 12/28/1887 Towns Co., GA
Willie Stokes Burch 2/10/1889 in Habersham Co., GA
John Adrain Roy Burch 12/29/1891
Roland Brown Burch 6/1/1894
Clyde Lanier Burch 11/28/1896

MARRIAGES:
Marjorie Burch-Eugene B. Jackson 11/17/1906?
W. D. Burch of Hiawassie, GA-Aeolain L. Burch of Mayesville, GA
At Hiawasse, GA 5/17/1885 in presence of W. H. McCline, M. D., T. W. Gilson

JACOB CHAMLEE BIBLE
Owner: Drusilla Chamblee
3626 Georgia Avenue
Hapeville, GA

"J. W. Chamlee, son of James Chamlee of Canton, Cherokee Co., GA"
Jacob Chamlee born 1/26/1752

Remainder of record illegible

JOHN UPSHAW BIBLE
From the Upshaw Collection,
Manuscript No. 18
University of Georgia Library
Athens, Georgia

Ages of John Upshaw's Children and Deaths:

John Upshaw b. 2/22/1755
Amey Upshaw b. 1/12/1757
John Upshaw and Amey Upshaw m. 3/7/1776
John Upshaw b. 12/24/1776
Sarah Upshaw b. 1/31/1779
Ann Upshaw b. 3/2/1781
Catherine Upshaw b. 1/12/1783
Leroy Upshaw b. 5/26/1785
James Upshaw b. 9/24/1789
Thomas Upshaw b. 10/19/1793
George Upshaw b. 1/5/1797
Middleton Upshaw b. 6/17/1799

DEATHS:
Amy Upshaw 12/28/1826
John Upshaw 10/8/1834

JOHN B. BURCH BIBLE
Owner: Raul W. Burch

John P. (Pinson)Burch 3/28/1806-2/22/1888
Jincy Burch 1/18/1808-5/16/1888
A. (Andrew) J. Burch 7/6/1830-
John Burch 7/10/1832-8/1/1908
Nancy E. Burch 3/27/1834-9/2/1876
Duquesne Burch 1/25/1837-
Mortimer Burch 8/23/1839-
Albert Burch 12/23/1841-3/5/1865
Elizabeth Burch 3/23/1844
Marshall Burch 7/15/1846-
Lafayette Burch 5/5/1849-

Note by Raul W. Burch: "Jincy Burch is Janette (Jane) Carolyn Burch Dillingham, daughter of Hiram Dillingham of Rabun Co., GA and Buncombe Co., N. C. Absalom Dillingham is Hiram's brother."

WOODY BURGE BIBLE
Owner: Lucy Cunyus Mulcohy
960 Hardmon Ct., N. E., Atlanta, GA (1969)

Births of Children of Woody and Judy Burge:
Allen Burge 2/5/1769?
Nancy Burge 3/24/1774
David Burge 1/8/1776
William Burge 10/29/1773
Priscilla Burge 3/22/1778
Elizabeth Burge 2/20/1780
Sarah Burge 3/4/1782
John Burge 1/28/1785
Judith Burge 8/9/1797
Nathaniel Burge 1/8/1790
Mary Burge 6/17/1792
Nancy Burge, wife of Nathaniel Burge, daughter of Joseph and Belerina Green, b. 12/23/1797
Joseph Green Burge, son of Nathaniel and Nancy Burge, b. 12/1/1816
William Twilly Burge, son of Nathaniel and Nancy Burge, b. 1/20/1820
Adolphus Green Burge, son of Nathaniel and Nancy Burge, b. 10/5/1823
Mary Elizabeth, daughter of Nathaniel and Nancy Gurge, b. 6/3/1826
Elizabeth Ann Burge, dau. of Nathaniel and Nancy Burge, b. 5/13/1828
Jane Adeline, daughter of Nathaniel and Nancy Burge, b. 2/2/1830
John Pinckney Burge, son of Nathaniel and Nancy Burge, b. 12/29/1834
James Robert McGee Burge, son of Nathaniel & Nancy Burge, b. 4/18/1839
Nancy Elizabeth Burge, dau. of William and Malissa Burge, b. 10/9/1846
Milly Texaner Burge, daughter of William and Malissa Burge, b. 5/9/1848
Sarah Susan Burge, daughter of William and Malissa Burge, b. 4/1/1850
Dora Jane Burge, daughter of William and Malissa Burge, b. 7/23/1852
MARRIAGES:
Nathaniel Burge-Nancy Green 11/18/1815
William T. Burge-Malissa Smith 2/3/1845
Daniel B. Conyers-Mary E. Burge 10/9/1844
Russel Hunter Cannon-Eliza Ann Burge 9/29/1847
John T. Spruill-Jane Adeline Burge 10/23/1851
Adolphus Green Burge-Hulda Ann Dykes 1849

HEIDT BIBLE
Owner: Janice McKinnon
P. O. Box 285, Cuthbert, GA 31740 (1980)

MARRIAGES:
Mr. Wilhelm Bort to Miss Sarah T. Bethena Heidt 4/26/1848

BIRTHS:
Elizabeth Heidt 5/12/1815
James Hamilton Heidt 1/17/1817
John William Heidt 5/10/1819
Gideon Jackson Heidt 3/23/1821
Ann Margaret Heidt 12/10/1823
Almirey Clementiney Berkins Heidt 9/20/1825
Sarah Ann Bethena Heidt 5/25/1827
D. S. B. Crocket Heidt 7/13/1829
Wily Hampton Heidt 6/6/1831
Eli Augustus Baldwin Heidt 6/11/1833
M. M. and A. M. Banister?
Eliza Carline Banister? 6/11/1853
Albert Maranda Barrington 8/28/1854
Sarah Seliel? Barrington 12/9/1855
William Agustus Barrington 9/17/1858
Marion Hen? Barrington 6/28/1860
John Matterson Barrington 6/28/1860
Anne Zember? Barrington 1862
Willis Garber? Barrington 12/-----

DEATHS:
John Heidt 9/17/1833
James Hamilton Heidt
John William Heidt
Gideon Jackson Heidt

JAMES M. BURKS BIBLE

Owner: Mary Livington Akin, Notasulga, Macon Co., Alabama (1945)

"Bought of E. H. Beall, Talbotton, Ga., 1846"

Written in margin - Narcissa Jane Burks departed this life on Sunday May 13, 1860, aged 45 years, 3 months and 13 days

BIRTHS:
James Madison Burks 11/28/1819 in Jasper Co., GA
Narcissa Jane Holmes 2/4/1815 in Washington Co., GA
James M. Burks & Narcissa J. Burks m. 3/31/1844 in Houston Co., GA
Mary Catherine Burks, daughter of James M. Burks and his wife, Narcissa J. Burks, 11/23/184-- in Talbot Co., GA
Robert Emmet Burks, son of James M. and Narcissa J., his wife, 8/1/1847 in Tallapoosa Co., AL
Martha Jane Eunice, second daughter of James M. and Narcissa J. Burks, his wife, 12/29/1852 in Tallapoosa Co., AL
Narcissa James M. Burks, our third daughter, 9/1/1854
James Madison Tharp 8/15/---- in Bibb Co., GA
John Holmes Talton 11/9/1839 in Houston Co., GA
James M. Burks departed this life 8/27/1854, 34 years, 3 months, 13 days
Robert Emmett Burks departed this life 6/5/1901, Dallas, Texas, 54 years
Charles H. Burks & Mary C. Burks m. 7/17/1866 Tallapoosa Co., AL
Samuel A. Burns and Narcissa J. M. Burks were married 5/7/1879
James Cooper Livingston & Stella Elizabeth Goulding Burks m. 12/1/1886
Stella Elizabeth Goulding Burks, daughter of Charles H. Burks and Mary Catherine Burks, b. 8/31/1868
Doric Edwin Emmet Burks b. 1/20/187--
Fannie Lou Burks b. 10/1/1873, d. 7/7/1874, aged 9 months, 7 days
Owen Akin, our first great grandchild was b. 11/5/1908 (written by his great-grandmother). Little Owen passed away 2/10/1912
Kenneth Judson Akin b. 7/1/1911 at Notasulga, AL
Willard Wise Livingston b. 11/23/1915 at Notasulga, AL
Robert Holmes Burns b. 2/5/1812 at Notasulga, AL
Charles Henry Burks d. 7/22/1912
Mary Catherine (Burks), wife of Charles Henry Burks, died 1/1926 at Notasulga, AL

Salmon Holmes Burns, only child of Samuel A. Burns and Narcissa J. Burks, d. 3/14/1936 in Birmingham, AL, buried at Notasulga, AL
Stella Burks Livingston died 6/10/1937 in Notasulga, AL
Narcissa J. M. (Burks) Burns died 5/1939 in Notasulga, AL

JOHN CALDWELL BIBLE, formerly of Ireland
Owner: Mrs. Hagood Clarke
4034 Beechwood Drive, N. W., Atlanta, GA (1966)

DEATHS:
John Caldwell, the elder, 10/29/1804

Deaths in the family of Andrew James and Harriet Caldwell:

Samuel Brewster Caldwell, the elder of that name, 10/7/1822, aged 20 months, 9 days
Harriet B. Caldwell 6/26/1846, aged 57 years
Elizabeth F. Caldwell 1/2/1848, aged 28 years
Helen Dmanery Caldwell 3/11/1848, aged 22 years
Andrew T. Caldwell 1/8/1862, 80th year
Catherine P. Caldwell 3/10/1881, aged 63 years

Obituary, undated, unknown newspaper -

"*It has been our province, lately to record the death of several valued citizens of Charleston, and we now add to the catalogue the name of William Caldwell, who departed this life yesterday, and after a lingering illness, which has prevented him with mixing with the busy world for many months. Caldwell, for a long series of years, was active largely engaged in commercial affairs, and in all the vicissitudes of lie bore an enviable reputation for -----, sterling honesty, and purity of motive. His....and usefulness was acknowledged by all who knew him. In his sufferings, he had the sympathies of all who possessed them. His decease will be regretted, and memory cherished by all who revere truth and ben----, coupled with honor and justice.*"

MARRIAGES:
10/11/1849 Samuel Brewster Caldwell to Susan Elizabeth Roe
5/22/1862 Richard Caldwell to Sarah Beattie.

BIRTHS:
In the family of Andrew James and Harriet Caldwell who were married 8/30/1815

Mary Freelove Caldwell 7/16/1816, and instantly departed this life
Catharine Parks Caldwell 12/21/1817
Elizabeth Freelove Caldwell 5/9/1819
Samuel Brewster Caldwell 1/29/1821
Samuel Brewster Caldwell (named after the decease of his brother) 8/22/1822
Helen Demeray Caldwell 3/20/1826
Richard Caldwell 3/4/1831

SAMUEL COBB BIBLE

Samuel Cobb married 2/9/1843 Emily Payne

Parents:
Samuel Cobb b. 5/30/1811 Hall Co.
Emily E. Payne b. 1/25/1819

Children:
Sarah F. Cobb 12/14/1843 Franklin Co.
Nancy M. Cobb 9/1/1845 Cherokee Co.
---------E. Cobb 1/30/1847 Cherokee Co.
David H. Cobb 9/23/1848 Cherokee Co.
Mary K. Cobb 4/18/1850 Cherokee Co.
Emily Cobb -----------------
William S. Cobb 8/25/1854
Marila L. Cobb 11/15/1857
John N. Cobb 6/16/1855

MARRIAGES:
Samuel Cobb and Emily E. Payne 2/9/1847
H. R. Cross and S. T. Cobb 1/16/1853
K. C. Johnston and A. E. Cobb 9/26/1851?
William H. H. Cross and N. M. Cobb 9/29/1861
Joseph McConnell and S. S. Cobb 10/21/1861

BIRTHS:
Martha L. Cobb 11/15/1851
Emily Cobb 6/1/1853
William S. Cobb 8/25/1854
John H. Cobb 6/15/1856

DAVID H. COBB BIBLE of Milton Co., GA
Georgia State Archives (folders)

MARRIAGES:

David H. Cobb of Milton Co., GA and Aby B. Griffin of same place 12/23/1869 at the bride's fathers by William J. Christian. Witnesses: J. W. Edward, James Baley

BIRTHS:
D. H. Cobb 9/23/1848
Abby R. Cobb 11/29/1851
John W. Cobb 11/27/1870
Charles K. Cobb 7/28/1872
Samuel N. Cobb 12/26/1874
David H. Cobb 10/8/1877
Mary A. E. Cobb 2/9/1880
Rosa P. Cobb 8/21/1882
Martha A. Cobb 10/8/1884
Ida Ophelia Cobb 6/24/1888
Laurence N. Pruett 10/27/1910

DEATHS:
John W. Cobb 8/10/1872
Mary A. E. Cobb 10/22/1880
Rosy L. Cobb 5/30/1892
Aby B. Cobb 7/17/1900
Charles R. Cobb 11/10/1902
Laurence N. Pruett 11/25/1910

MARRIAGES:
D. H. Cobb and Mary J. Willson 12/22/1904

JAMES H. COBB BIBLE
Georgia State Archives (folder)

BIRTHS:
James C. Cobb 9/17/1810
R. C. Cobb 6/25/1815
Joh R. Cobb 8/14/1841
James E. Cobb 11/8/1842
Anzlet? Burges? Cobb 9/2/1844
Rebecca Sugar Cobb 10/9/1846
Thomas H. Cobb 6/12/1849
Green C. Cobb 6/10/1851
William J. Cobb 6/28/1854
James R. L. Cobb 3/4/1878
Thomas H. Cobb, Sr. 12/21/1880
Edwin Parker Cobb -----
Thomas H. Cobb 11/8/1916
J. C. Cobb and R. C. Barney was married 9/2/1840

No of watch 3040
Liverpool 12 Holes gueto?
A. B. Cobb E. M.
W. J. Cobb and R. E. Scott was married 8/9/1877

DEATHS:
John R. Cobb 9/11/1892, making him 12 months and 20 days old
Rebca Sugar Cobb 5/31/1851, making her 1 year, 20 days old
James Edmund Cobb 9/23/1863, making him 20 years, 10 months, 15 days
Thomas H. D. Cobb 3/26th, making him 14 years, 9 months, 14 days
Edwin Parker Cobb b. 5/8/1883, died 3/19/1920, at the age of 36 years, 10 months, 9 days
J. H. Cobb died 2/5/1879, making him 49 years old, 21 months, 5 days
R. C. Cobb b. 6/28/1803? and d. 9/26/1879, making her 65 years, 3 months, one day
Robert------Cobb died ----18/1880
William J. Cobb died 12/231896, 44 years (wife, Rebecca C.)
Rebecca C. Cobb, b. 7/8/1857, d. 6/13/1920

JOHN W. JORDAN BIBLE
Georgia State Archives (folder)

MARRIAGES:
John W. Jordan to Melvina Elizabeth 3/13/1842
Richard Jordan to Sallie Jordan 11/28/1872
John T. Jordan to Mrs. Mattie E. Jordan 12/3/1899

DEATHS:
Richard Jordan, consort of Drucilla Jordan 9/14/1851
Drucilla Jordan, consort of William Jordan, 6/12/1845
Marion Augusta Jordan 7/30/1878
James Willis Jordan 12/23/1880
Melvina Elizabeth Jordan 6/22/1857
John W. Jordan, consort of Elizabeth Jordan, 3/2/1869
James W. Jordan b. 12/25/1842, and was killed at Battle of Seven Pines 5/30/1862, his age 19 years, 4 months, 6 days

BIRTHS:
John W. Jordan 6/25/1807
S------ Jordan ?
Nancy Jordan 1840
Richard Jordan 5/22/1805
John Richard Jordan 11/23/1850
Sallie Cahill Jordan 12/9/1855
Mary A. Jordan 4/25/1847
Sallie C. Jordan 12/9/1855
Margrett Elizabeth Jordan 12/17/1873
Marion Jordan 1/16/1876
John Thomas Jordan 10/15/1878

NEWTON M. JORDAN BIBLE OF WASHINGTON CO.
Owner: Bubby Jordan, Sandersville, GA (1965)

MARRIAGES:
Newton M. Jordan of Washington Co. and Susan Boatright of Washington Co. 9/19/1871 /s/Thomas J. Cumming
Lizzie E. Jordan to Irwin J. Joyner 12/12/1893

Pearl A. Jordan to William J. Frost 3/6/1895
Laura R. Jordan to William Jackson 12/15/1897
Neva M. Jordan to Eugene Frost 1/8/1899
Ella May Jordan to Theo Smith 6/18/1902
Alma M. Jordan to Hyman James 12/4/1904
Susie Ernestine Jordan to George C. Smith 7/18/1909

BIRTHS:
Newton M. Jordan 4/14/1847
Susan M. Boatright 1/8/1852
Pearl A. Jordan 6/28/1872
Elizabeth E. Jordan 3/12/1874
Laura R. Jordan 3/26/1876
Alma M. Jordan 1/6/1878
Neva M. Jordan 5/9/1880
Susan E. Jordan 6/14/1882
Ella May Jordan 5/8/1884
Newton M. Jordan 2/12/1886
Sallie W. Jordan 7/5/1887
Jessie Will Jordan 11/1/1890
An infant son born and died 7/25/1894

DEATHS:
Susan M. Jordan 7/25/189--
Newton M. Jordan 2/16/19--

MITCHELL BIBLE
Owner: Mrs. Louise Mitchell
Route 1, Box 210
Kingsland, AR 71652

BIRTHS:
W. W. Mitchell 6/1/1853
Joseph Lafac Mitchell 12/31/1854
Thomas Olanan Mitchell 11/30/1856
Mary L. B. Mitchell 5/14/1858

MARRIAGES:
William and Mary A. Carson was married 2/2/1826
John J. Mitchell and Elizabeth J. Mitchell was married 8/17/1852

DEATHS:
Joseph Carson, son of William and Mary Carson, departed this life 12/9/1826

BIRTHS:
William Carson, son of Joseph and Elizabeth Carson, 10/23/1805
Mary A. Carson 8/17/181--
Joseph Carson 11/13/1826
Elizabeth Jane Carson 4/27/18--
W. H. G. Carson 12/31/1880
Joseph J. Carson 7/19/1833
Sarah F. Carson 10/5/1839
Mary M. Carson 3/21/1862

THOMAS CARLTON OF WILKES CO.
Owner: Mrs. Mary German
Boomer, N. C. (1959)

BIRTHS:
Thomas Carlton 1/24/1790
Jane Carlton, wife of Thomas Carlton, 2/28/1796
Ruth Carlton, wife of Thomas Carlton, 7/11/1792

Sally Leanerah? Carlton, daughter of Thomas C. Carlton and Susan M. Carlton, 5/24/1857
Rebecca Girtrude Carlton, daughter of Thomas C. Carlton and Susan M. Carlton, 8/23/1859

Sarah Burch departed this life 3/6/1854

BIRTHS:
Eveline Carlton, daughter of Thomas and Jane, his wife, 1815
Allen Burton Carlton, son of Thomas and Jane, his wife, 1818
John Carlton, son of Thomas and Ruth, his wife, 8/23/1822

Danniel Milton Carlton, son of Thomas Carlton and Ruth, his wife, 9/28/1823
Henry Carlton, son of Thomas Carlton and Ruth, his wife, ----/28/1825
Joelander, son of Thomas Carlton and Ruth, his wife, 10/16/1827
Marthy, --------------

MARRIAGES:
Thomas Carlton and Jane Carlton, his wife, 3/23/1813
Thomas Carlton and Ruth, his wife, 1821
Thomas Carlton and Alen?, his wife, 10/18/1862?
Two more entries, undeciperable

DEATHS:
Jane Carlton, wife of Thomas, 4/10/1821
John Carlton, son of Thomas Carlton and Ruth, his wife, 10/12/1822
Henry Carlton, son of Thomas Carlton and Ruth, his wife, 6/17/1832?
Eveline Carlton, daughter of Thomas Carlton and Jane, his wife, 6/1847
Thomas C. Carlton, son of Thomas Carlton and Ruth, his wife, 7/7/1860
Ruth Carlton, wife of Thomas Carlton, 10/29/1862
Joelander Carlton 1/21/1865

JAMES CARLTON, SR. BIBLE OF GREENE CO., GA.
Owner: W. D. Carlton, Jr., 1630 Kenmore Street, S. W., Atlanta, GA (1965)

BIRTHS:
James Carlton, Sr. 7/13/1782
Rebekah G. Carlton, his wife, 8/28/1796 was married 2/24/1813

Richard G. Carlton, son of James and R. G. Carlton 12/23/1813
James M. Carlton 10/23/1815
Lorenzo D. Carlton 10/26/1817
William L. Carlton 6/16/1821
Travis H. Carlton 7/16/1823
John T. Carlton 9/5/1825
Benjamin F. Carlton 11/13/1829
Mary Ann Elisabeth Carlton 10/12/1833

Wesley Arnold Carlton 10/3/1837
Margarett W. Carlton, daughter of David and Mary Daniel 11/12/18---
William T. Carlton, son of John and Margarett Carlton, 9/13/1860
John W. Carlton 9/3/1861
Mildred C. Carlton 2/8/1863
Mary A. R. Carlton 10/18/1864
Maggie Bell Newsom, dau. of David A. & Margaret Newsom 4/14/1870
David Danel Newsom, son of David A. & Margaret W. Newsom, 6/7/1872
Annie Ruth Newsom, dau. of David A. & Margaret W. Newsom, 6/3/1875
Elizabeth Lucy (Bessie Lou) Newsom, daughter of David A. and Margaret W. Newsom, 7/3/1876

DEATHS:
John Wesley Carlton, son of John and Margarett Carlton, 12/16/18--3
John F. Carlton 9/2/1864
Mildred Corine, first daughter of John T. and Margaret H. Carlton 11/25/1864
Maggie Belle Newsom 9/--/----
Meta Etna Newsom, daughter of David and Margaret Newsom, b. 9/9/1877

ARCHIBALD CAMPBELL BIBLE

"Archibald Campbell was the son of John Campbell who came to America when the war with Great Britain began and went into the Revolutionary War as Captain."
MARRIAGES:
Archibald Campbell and Rebecca, his wife, were married 1/1/1784
Isaac B. Rowland-Frances A. Campbell 2/7/1828
John Thurston, first son of B. and T. A. Rowland, b. 6/7/1829
Abram Fannin b. 7/21/1830
Isaac Bloomer? b. 6/3/1832
Edwin Campbell b. 8/18/1834
Alexander MacKenzie b. 3/12/183--
Susan Campbell b. 9/3/1839
William Rosencrntz? b. 10/1841

DEATHS:
Duncan Green Campbell 7/31/1828
Susan G. 9/4/1831
Frances Alexander 12/24/1842
Mrs. Rowlands
John M. Campbell 1/25/1850
Edwin Eliza Campbell 11/30/1856
never married
Sarah Q. 12/29/1857
Mrs. Fluker
Fina McQueen Campbell, daughter of Archibald and Rebecca Campbell, in Atlanta, GA, 1/7/1876, age 73 years, 5 months, 21 days
Mary Ann McKenzie, eldest daughter of Archibald and Rebecca Campbell, 1/7/1877. in Waynesboro, Ga.
Rebecca Caroline Tracy, second wife of Edward D. Tracy, and daughter of Archibald and Rebecca Campbell, Macon, Ga.

BIRTHS:
James Archibald Campbell, first son, 8/22/1785
Duncan G. Campbell, second son, 2/16/1787
Walter Lewis Campbell, third son, 11/10/1788
Mary Ann Campbell, first daughter, 10/5/1790
Sarah Quinten? Campbell, second daughter, 7/10/1792
John Wesley (Campbell), fourth son, 3/20/1794
Betsey Hays Campbell, third daughter, b. 5/17/1796. d. in Milledgeville aged 16 years
Nancy Mansfield Campbell, fourth daughter, 1/12/1778, d. 8/17/1811, aged 13
William Archibald Campbell, fifth son, 2/23/1800
Flora MacQueen Campbell, fifth daughter, 7/17/1802
Margaret Jane Campbell 2/7/1804
Afterwards Mrs. George Towns Edison, Elina Campbell, b. 2/8/1805.
Rebecca Caroline Campbell 4/4/1807
Jason Griffin Campbell 8/1/1808
Frances Alexander Campbell 9/15/1810, wife of Isaac B. Rowland
Archibald Campbell who married Rebecca Kirk, was born in North Carolina, died 11/20/1820, buried in cemetery at Montgomery, Alabama, married 1/1/1784 Rebecca Kirk of Guilford N. C.

DEATHS:
Betsey Hays Campbell 8/12/1802
Nancy Mansfield Campbell 8/17/1811
Rebecca Kirk Campbell, wife of Archibald Campbell, 7/1816
Archibald Campbell, husband of Rebecca Kirk
Margaret Jane Campbell Towns 11/1826 in Montgomery, Alabama. She was wife of George Towns, afterwards Gov. of Georgia.

JOSHUA S. CALLAWAY BIBLE
Owner: Mrs. Cecil T. Hays
1708 Peachtree Street, N. W.
Atlanta, GA (1964)

BIRTHS:
Joshua S. Callaway 5/30/1789
Polley Callaway 2/25/1795
were married 2/12/1811

P. M. Milnor Callaway 10/10/1812
James Madison Callaway 1/1/1815
John H. M. Callaway 1/25/1817
Beniter A. Callaway 2/11/1819
Apsilla Ann Callaway 3/21/1821
Joshua Sandford Callaway 11/18/1824

Joshua S. Callaway and Elizabeth Smith were married 11/15/1827

Polly Milner Callaway 9/1/1828
Willis Joshua Callaway 10/1/1830

Joshua S. Callaway and Mary McCoy were married 11/13/1832

Elizabeth Shivers Callaway 9/21/1835
Eliza E. Callaway 4/24/1835
Ardecoe? G. Callaway 3/30/1837
Jacob King Callaway 1/18/1841
DeLamaster Callaway 2/22/1842
Ellen Wilie Jourdan Callaway 4/30/1844

Thomas George Jordan 7/22/1788
Lovicy Chambless 10/15/1793
Were married 7/21/1814
Ellen H. Jordan 6/6/1816
Henry H. Jordan 6/27/1817
Ira T. Jordan 1/9/1819
Narcissa E. Jordan 2/2/1822
Albert E. Jordan 8/21/1824
Samuel V. Jordan 2/5/1826
Mary L. Jordan 12/25/1827
Melissa A. Jordan 7/27/1822
Warren Q. Jordan 2/16/1837
Hellen G. Jordan 9/3/1832
William C. Jordan 7/10/1834
Elizabeth Clark Callaway, daughter of James M. Callaway, 11/9/1842

JOSEPH CALLAWAY BIBLE
Owner: Mrs. Cecil T. Hays
1708 Peachtree St., N. W., Atlanta, GA (1964)

BIRTHS:
Joseph Callaway 9/21/1754
Sabrina Callaway 3/14/1754
William Callaway 4/13/1773
John Callaway 2/14/1780
Joseph M. Callaway 7/2/1782
Joshua Callaway 10/9/1784
Luke J. Callaway 4/8/1787
Samuel M. Callaway 11/5/1789
Lydia Callaway 10/3/1793
Jesse Callaway 6/3/1796
Woodson Callaway 10/12/1803
Elizabeth Callaway 11/20/1807
Mary Callaway 4/17/1811

MARRIAGES:
Joseph Callaway-Rebecca Morgan 6/12/1777
Joseph M. Callaway-Polly Lee 11/25/1804

Luke J. Callaway-Jane McDole? 11/22/1810
Joshua Callaway-Margaret Crawley 7/4/1811
John Boren-Lydia Callaway 8/27/1812

DEATHS:
Sabrina Callaway 9/7/1801
John Callaway, Sen. 2/5/1804
Samuel M. Callaway 9/19/1815
William Callaway 2/12/1819
Lydia Ann Callaway 7/15/1819
Joseph Callaway, Sen. 11/15/1821
Elizabeth Callaway 8/9/1822
Luke J. Callaway 1/19/1868, aged 80 years, 9 months, 11 days
Mary Catherine Callaway 7/27/1906

CHARLES HOWARD CANDLER BIBLE of Atlanta
Owner: Mrs. William C. Warren, Jr.
3669 Paces Valley Road, N. W., Atlanta, GA 30327 (1966)

MARRIAGES:
Charles Howard Candler of Atlanta, GA to Flora Glenn of Atlanta, GA at residence of Dr. W. F. Glenn 12/3/1903, in presence of W. F. Glenn. /s/Warren A. Candler
Charles Howard Candler, son of Asa Griggs Candler and Lucy Elizabeth Candler and Flora Harper, daughter of Wilbur Fiske and Florella Harper Glenn, married 12/3/1903 at 683 Edgewood Ave., Atlanta by Bishop W. A. Candler.
Catherine Candler, daughter of Charles Howard and Flora Glenn Candler and William Chester Warren, Jr. (M. D., son of William Chester and Annie Dodd Warren were married 11/22/1927 at 980 Briarcliff Rd., N. E., Atlanta by Bishop W. A. Candler.
Charles Howard Candler, Jr., son of Charles Howard and Flora Glenn Candler and Ruth Tolbert Ozburn, daughter of Samuel Alonza and Lilla Belle Tolbert Ozburn were married 12/3/1928 at St. Luke's Eiscopal Church, Atlanta, Ga. by Rev. High Moon.
Mary Louisa Candler, daughter of Charles Howard and Flora Glenn Candler and Alfred Turner Eldredge, son of Alfred Stewart and Janie Bell Turner Eldredge were married 6/7/1933 at 980 Briarcliff Road, N.E., Atlanta, Ga. by Bishop W. A. Candler.

Charles Howard Candler, Jr. and Lee Edwards were married 12/12/1961 at Chapel of Glenn Memorial Church by Dr. Eugene Drinkard.

BIRTHS:
Charles Howard, Jr., son of Charles Howard and Flora Glenn Candler, 9/15/1904, 683 Edgewood Ave., Atlanta, Ga.

Catherine, second child, first daughter of Charles Howard and Flora Glenn Candler, 7/5/1906, 683 Edgewood Ave., Atlanta, Ga.

Mary Louisa, third child, second daughter of Charles Howard and Flora Glenn Candler, 2/23/1912 at 114 Elizabeth St., Atlanta, Ga.
Grandchildren of Charles Howard and Flora Glenn Candler;
Catherine Candler Warren, daughter of William C. and Catherine Candler Warren, Jr., b. 5/14/1929, Emory University Hospital, Atlanta
Charles Howard Candler III, son of Charles Howard and Ruth Ozburn Candler, Jr., b. 9/13/1930 Emory University Hospital, Atlanta, Ga.
William Chester Warren III, son of William C. and Catherine C. Warren, Jr. b 9/3/1931
Samuel Ozburn Candler, son of Charles Howard and Ruth Ozburn Candler, Jr. b. 5/6/1932
Ruth Candler, daughter of Charles Howard and Ruth Ozburn Candler, b. 6/5/1935
Alfred Turner Eldredge, son of Alfred Turner and Louisa Candler Eldredge, b. 10/4/1936, Coral Gables, FL

DEATHS:
Charles Howard Candler b. 12/2/1878 d. 10/1/1957
Ruth Candler Lovett b. 6/5/1935 d. 9/25/1964

Births of Other Grandchildren of Charles Howard and Flora Glenn Candler:
Howard Candler Warren, third child, second son of William C. Jr. and Catherine Candler Warren b. 5/15/1938, Emory University Hospital.
Flora Glenn Candler, fourth child, second dau. of Ruth Ozburn and Charles Howard Candler, Jr., b. 5/14/1941 Emory University Hospital
Ann Glenn Eldredge, second child, first daughter of Louisa Candler and Alfred Turner Eldredge, b. 10/6/1941, Jackson Merri. Hospital at Miami, FL, during Huricane Blow.

MARRIAGES:
Grandchildren of Charles Howard and Flora Glenn Candler:
Catherine Candler Warren and Lamar Qintero Ball, Jr. 6/30/1951 at Glenn Memorial Church by Rev. Warren Candler Budd, minister.
Charles Howard Candler III and Katherine Claire Clement 9/18/1951 at St. Mark Methodist Church by Rev. John L. Horton, minister.
William Chester Warren II and Mary Irene Ripley 4/11/1953 at Morningside Presbyterian Church, by Rev. Arthur Vann Gibson, minister.
Samuel Ozburn Candler and Beth Graham Denny 6/12/1954 at the Chapel of the Cathedral of St. Phillip by Rev. Wilson W. Sneed, minister
Ruth Candler and Robert William Lovett 8/23/1955 at Chapel of Cathedral of St. Phillip by Rev. Wilson W. Sneed, minister.
Alfred Turner Eldredge and Claire Middlebrooks 2/1/195-- at First Methodist Church, Athens, by Dr. Charles Boleyn, minister.
Ann Glenn Eldredge and William Royal Middelthon, Jr. 9/20th at Newport News, VA
Flora Glenn Candler and Thomas Fuller III 9/6/1961 at St. Martin-in-the-Fields Church, Rev. Sam Cobb, minister.

Births of Great-Grandchildren of Charles Howard and Flora Glenn Candler:
Charles Howard Candler IV, son of Charles Howard Candler II and Claire Clement Candler 4/21/1953 at Piedmont Hospital, Atlanta , Ga. 1st grandchild of Charles Howard Candler, Jr.

Lamar Quintero Ball III, son of Lamar Q. Ball Jr. and Catherine Warren Ball, 7/8/1953, at Chapel of Cathedral of St. Phillips.

William Chester Warren IV, son of William Chester Warren III and Mary Ripley Warren, 5/19/1954 at St. Joseph Infirmary, Atlanta, Ga., second grandchild of Catherine Candler Warren, Glenn Memorial Little Chapel.

Walker Tolbert Candler, son of Charles Howard Candler III and Claire Clement Candler, 3/22/1955 at Piedmont Hospital, Atlanta, Ga., grandchild of Charles Howard Candler, Jr.

David Ashley Ball, son of Lamar Q. Ball, Jr & Catherine Warren Ball, 4/7/1955, Georgia Baptist Hospital, Atlanta , Ga., 3d grandchild of Catherine Candler Warren.

Thomas Ripley Warren, son of Wiliam Chester Warren III and Mary Ripley Warren, 5/19/1956 at St. Joseph's Hospital, Atlanta, Ga., fourth grandchild of Catherine Candler Warren

Samuel Glenn Candler son of Samuel Ozburn Candler & Beth Graham Denny 8/12/1956 Panama City FL 3d gch of Charles Howard Candler Jr.

David Meriwether Lovett, son of Robert William Lovett and Ruth Candler Lovett, 3/20/1957 at Piedmont Hospital, fourth grandchild of Charles Howard Candler, Jr.

Beth Meredith Candler, daughter of Samuel O. Candler and Beth Denny Candler, 11/11/1957, Piedmont Hospital, 5th gch of Howard Candler, Jr.

Elizabeth Howard Lovett, dau. of Ruth Candler Lovett and Robert Lovett, 6/24/1958 Piedmont Hospital, 6th grandchild of Howard Candler Jr.

William Warren Ball, son of Catherine Warren Ball and Lamar Ball, Jr. 4/7/1959, Ga Baptist Hospital, 5th grandchild of Catherine Candler Warren.

Glenn Dodd Warren, son of William C. Warren III & Mary Ripley Warren, 6/3/1959, St. Joseph's Hospital, 6th grandchild of Catherine C. Warren.

Catherine Claire Candler, dau. of Howard Candler III & Claire Clements Candler 9/21/1959, Piedmont Hospital, 7th gch of Charles Howard, Jr.

Catherine McGregor Candler, dau. of Samuel O. Candler and Beth Denny Candler, 10/7/1959 Piedmont Hospital, 8th grandchild of Charles Howard Candler, Jr.

Alfred Turner Eldredge III, son of Alfred Turner Eldredge, Jr. and Claire Middlebrooks Eldredge, 2/7/1960, Miami, FL, 1st grandchild of Louisa Candler Eldredge.

Mary Candler Eldredge 11/13/1961, Drs. Hospital, Miami, FL, dau. of Alfred T. Eldredge, Jr. & Claire M. Eldredge, 7th grandchild of Louisa Candler Eldredge.

Charles Candler Lovett, son of Ruth Candler Lovett and Robert William Lovett, 8/24/1962, ninth grandchild of Charles Howard Candler, Jr.

Douglas Harper Candler, son of Claire C. and Howard Candler III 3/22/1963, tenth grandchild of Howard Candler, Jr.

Richard Alden Candler, son of Beth D. and Samuel Candler 7/7/1963, 11th grandchild of Howard Candler, Jr.

William Royall Middelthon IV, son of Ann E . and William Middelthon III 10/22/1964, Gainesville, FL., third grandchild of L. C. Eldredge.

Thomas Fuller IV, son of Glenn C. and Thomas Fuller III 12/12/1964, 12th grandchild of C. H. Candler, Jr.

James Kimbrough Warren, son of Mary R. and W. C. Warren, III, 1/2/1965, 7th grandchild of C. C. Warren.

ASA GRIGGS CANDLER BIBLE of Atlanta
Owner: Mrs. William C. Warren, Jr.
3669 Paces Valley Road, N. W., Atlanta, GA 30327 (1966)

MARRIAGES:
Asa Griggs Candler to Lucy Elizabeth Howard at Atlanta, First Baptist Church, 1/15/1878. /s/D. W. Gwin, Pastor.
Asa G. Candler, Jr. to Helen Magill 7/15/1901
Lucy Beall Candler to William Davis Owens 6/11/1903
Wallis T. Candler to Eugenia Righam 12/10/1907
William Candler to Bennie Teabrant of Cuthbert 2/5/1913
Walter T. Candler to Marian Penland 8//1919
Mrs. Lucy Beall Owens to Henry C. Henis? 1/15/1917
Asa G. Candler, Jr. to Florence Stephenson
Asa G. Candler to Mrs. Mary Little

BIRTHS:
Asa Griggs Candler 12/30/1851
Lucy Elizabeth Howard 9/28/1859
Charles Howard, first child of Asa G. and Lucy E. Candler 12/2/1878
Asa Griggs, Jr., 2nd child of Asa G. and Lucy E. Candler 8/27/1880
Lucy Beall, third child and first dau. of Asa G. and Lucy E. Candler 4/11/1883
Walter Turner, fourth child of Asa G. and Lucy E. Candler 10/5/1885
William Candler, fifth child, fourth son, 1/24/1890
Luvy Magill, first child of Asa G. Candler, Jr. 3/21/1902
Elizabeth Candler, 1st child of William D. & Lucy Beall Owens 6/8/1904
Asa Griggs third, 2nd child of Asa G. Jr. and Helen Candler, 6/10/1904
Charles Howard, Jr., first child of Charles Howard and Flora Glenn Candler, 9/15/1904

John Howard Candler, 3rd child of Asa G. Jr. & Helen Candler, 12/16/1905
Catherine Candler, 2nd child of C. H. and Flora Candler 7/5/1906
Laura Candler, 4th child of Asa G. Jr. and Helen Candler, 12/23/1907
Walter T. Candler, Jr., first child of W. T. and Eugenia, 5/17/1908
Asa G. Candler 4th, 2nd child of W. T. and Eugenia Candler, 8/19/1909
Eugenia, third child of Walter T. and Eugene Candler, 10/29/1910
William Davis, Jr., son of W. D. and Lucy Beall Owens, 4/1/1911
Martha and Helen, twin daus. of Asa G., Jr. & Helen Candler, 8/14/1911
Mary Louisa, dau. of Charles H. and Flora Candler 2/23/1912
Mary, fourth child of W. T. and Eugenia Candler, 11/4/1912
Samuel, son of Asa G., Jr. and Helen Candler 11/1/1914
Rena Elizabeth, first child of William Berrie? Candler 1/25/1914
William Jr., son of William and Berrie? Candler 7/2/1918
Henry Charles, Jr., son of Henry C. and Lucy Beall Hens? 12/22/1918
DEATHS:
Asa Griggs, third son of Asa G., Jr. and Helen Candler, 2/8/1905
Lucy Elizabeth, dear wife of Asa G. Candler, Sr., 2/22/1919
Asa G. Candler 3/12/1929
William Candler 10/2/1936, a tragic highway accident...in his prime, 46 yrs, 8 mos
William D. Owens 12/20/1914
Eugenia Bigham Candler, wife of Walter T. Candler, 9/3/1918
Helen Magill Candler, wife of Asa G. Candler, Jr., died ----------------

RICHARD H. HUNT BIBLE
Owner: Miss Ruby Mathews, Gadsden, Alabama

MARRIAGES:
Joseph Wolf-Hannah Doster 12/8/1825
J. C. Wolf-M. L. Hunt 12/26/1867
BIRTHS:
Richard H. Hunt 9/7/1813
Rhoda Ann Hunt 1/22/1818
Martha Ann Malissa Hunt 3/27/1840
Robert Turman Hunt 7/19/1842
Eugeneous Beamon Hunt 6/3/1846
Mary Laurah Hunt 6/17/1850
Rhoda Luvenia Hunt 3/10/1853

Rachel C. Wolf 9/15/1826
Elizaer Catherine 5/22/1828
Jacob Hill 2/16/1830
Permelia Emeline 12/26/1831
William Goren Wolf 10/20/1833
Mary Jane 1/20/1836
Phillip Tally 11/20/1838
Joseph H. Wolf 2/8/1840
Hannah Elizabeth 4/17/1843
John C. Wolf 3/18/1845

M. L. Wolf 6/17/1850
Theodosia E. 8/3/1869
Adolphus C. Wolf 9/13/1874
Servitus Alvie Wolf 7/21/1878
Nonie Ora Wolf 2/15/1882

DEATHS:

William G. Wolf d. Evins Port, VA 12/19/1861
Jacob Hill d. 1831
Rachel C. Summerlin d. 12/6/1860
William D. Gordon was killed at the Battle of Chickamauga 9/20/1863
Joseph Wolf d. 7/24/1877
Hannah E. Wolf d. 11/29/1881
Hannah Wolf d. 3/19/1882
Mary Jane d. 2/20/1870 Columbus, GA
John C. Wolf d. 2/23/1906
Mary L. Wolf d. 7/25/1900
Theodosia E. Mathews d. 2/28/1913
Nonie Ora Wolf died -
Crocket Adolphus died -
Servitus Alvie Wolf died -

WILLIAM ROSE BIBLE of Chattooga Co., GA
Owner: Mrs. Estella Burns Stewart
Rt. 4, Box 321, Huntsville, TX

Philadelphia, stereotyped and published by C. Alexander, 1834.

BIRTHS:
William Rose 3/7/1779

Births of his children:
Samuel H. Rose 4/8/1816
William H. Rose 5/1/1818
James M. Rose 10/1819
Fleming C. Rose 12/23/1820
Nancy Mary Rose 8/5/1824
George W. W. Rose 9/16/1826
John A. Rose and Emily C. Rose 7/16/1828
Eliza E. Rose 5/8/1831
Permelia E. Rose, daughter of William, 12/8/1841
Marcus DeLaFayette Rose, son of William, 6/6/1842
Charlotte E. L. Owens, daughter of J. M. Owens 7/1/1850
James M. A. Rose, son of G. W. W. Rose, 3/14/1851
Eliza Ann Amanda Rose, daughter of G. W. W. Rose, 5/1851
John T. Rose, son of J. M. Rose, 10/11/1851
Loduski C. Johnson, daughter of L. E. J. and E. C. Johnson, 8/1/1853
John M. M. Rose, son of John A. and Mary A.M. Rose, 9/18/1853
George W. J. Rose, son of same, 3/11/1855
John A.N. Rose, son of G. W. R. Rose, 3/23/1855

MARRIAGES:
William Rose-Lucy Draper 7/16/1801
William Rose-Charlotte Crosland 78/1815
William A. Rose-Elizabeth Pool 1/11/1841
Samuel H. Rose-Cisaley Nance 8/16/1842
Nancy Mary Rose-John M. Owens 9/13/1844
George W. W. Rose-Mary Cook 7/26/1846
James M. Rose-Mary E. Moseley 12/12/1851

John A. Rose-Mary An M. Johnson 1128/1852
Emily C. Rose-Landrum E. J. Johnson 1128/1852
Eliza E. Rose-Reuben T. Allmon 1/1853
Tolliver Owens, son of Abner Owens and Jane Owens, the daughter of Gideon Owens, married 5/31/1851

DEATHS:
Charlotty Lucy Elizabeth Owens 10/27/1890
Lucy Rose 7/18/1802, William Rose 1st wife
Tamer Rose 10/3/1802
George Rose, Sr. 12/31/827
Marcus DeLaFayette Rose 9/16/1867
James M. A. Rose 5/8/1851
A son died in non-age buried 5/18/1847
William Rose, Sr. 10/16/1857
Charlotty Rose, wife of William Rose, 4/14/1858
William Rose, Sr. 10/16/1857
Charlotta Cross Rose 4/14/1858
Ruben T. Allmon 7/19/186--
Sarah S. A. Allmon, the daughter of R. T. and E. E. Allmon, b. 5/15/1854
Nancy E. G. Allmon b. 3/24/1856
Jane Owens, wife of Toll Owens 10/18/1873

Tolliver Owens and Lucinda Warren married 12/25/1874

Floman M. P. Owens, son of M. J. Owens b. 8/21/1853
John M. M. Rose b. 9/10/1853
M. J. Rose b. 3/1855
Martha S. A. Rose b. --/25/1857
W. M. Rose 3/30/1859, children of J. A. Rose and A. M. M. S. Rose
Nancy Mary Jane Rose, dau. of G. W. W. Rose and Mary Cook, b. 8/26/1850
Nancy M. W. Rose b. 7/19/1851
Francis Barto Rose b. 6/16/1862
Elizabeth Lee Rose b. 10/8/1865
Samuel H. Rose, son of William and Charlotte Rose, d. 1/3/1864
Charlotty Lucy Elizabeth Owens d. 10/28/1870
Sarah E. P. Rose b. 1/11/1860

OLIVER PORTER of Madison, GA
Owner: Bates Block, 25 Valley Rd N. W., Atlanta, GA 30305 (1990)

MARRIAGES:
Oliver Porter-Margaret Watson 10/10/1783
Polly Porter-James Fears 10/31/1805
Peggy Porter-Isham S. Fannin 9/1/1809
Douglas Watson Porter-Annebelle Dawson 9/9/1812
Ann Porter-Adam G. Saffold 12/17/1812
Caty Porter-Jepthah Fannin 4/10/1814
Peggy Fanin, relict of Isham S. Fannin-Lazearus Battle 4/6/1818
John W. Porter-Ann M. Fannin 5/6/1824
Anthony Porter-Louisa Alexander 12/16/1825
Thomas S. King-Margaret Battle, widow of Lazarus Battle, 3/12/1827
James M. Porter-Athaliah I. Hook 9/12/1833

BIRTHS:
Oliver Porter 10/14/1763
Margaret Porter 4/20/1764
Polly Porter 11/12/1784
D. W. Porter 9/17/1786
Anthony Porter 12/8/1788
Peggy Porter 1/7/1791
Ann Porter 1/8/1793
Caty Porter 6/2/1795
John Porter 4/2/1797
William Porter 7/16/1799
Oliver Porter 7/14/1801
Nancy Porter 2/20/1804
James Madison Porter 8/30/1804

DEATHS:
Oliver Porter Junior 12/25/1803
Nancy Porter 10/22/1805
Douglas W. Porter 12/21/1823
Lazarus Battle 7/26/1824
Isham S. Fannin 4/27/1817
Margaret King 12/24/1830
Margaret Porter, consort of Oliver Porter, 3/30/1837

Oliver Porter 8/29/1838
William Porter 9/29/1841
James Madison Porter 5/24/1849
John W. Porter 1/8/1868 in Madison, GA
Ann M. Porter 7/31/1875 Madison, GA
Sallie Porter Graves 5/31/1876 in Madison, GA

OBEDIAH STEVENS BIBLE

BIRTHS:
Joseph Stevens 3/9/1787
Martha Stevens 4/22/1787
Obediah Stevens 5/7/1809
Haley Stevens 3/30/1811
Allen Stevens 6/16/1812
Jasper Stevens 9/27/1813
Thomas Stevens 10/22/1818
Elizabeth Stevens 2/8/1822
Martha Stevens 2/22/1824
Newton Stevens 12/19/1825
Walton Stevens 3/11/1829
W. C. Stevens 2/21/1831
J. R. Stevens 4/20/1824
W. W. Stevens 3/24/1837
C. A. Stevens 6/26/1844
Rose Watkins senior 8/20/177---
Milly Watkins 9/26/1779
Ben Watkins 10/12/1801
Elizabeth Watkins 12/5/1803
Nancy Watkins 10/12/1807
Charly Watkins 9/1/1809
Olive Watkins 9/25/1811
Martha Watkins 9/5/1814
William Watkins 3/22/1818
Rose Watkins 7/22/1822
James Appling 3/16/1825

JOHN COLLEY BIBLE

"This Bible is the property of John Colley bought September 4th 1804"

MARRIAGES:
Gabriel Colley 6/17/1809
Elizabeth Colley 5/17/1808
Elizabeth Tindall married to John Putett 2/12/1811
Nancy Colley to Kirby Goolsbe 7/25/1813
Mary Colley married 9/26/1816 to James V. Brown
Francis Colley m. F. L. Owens 12/24/1818
Louisa Colley to Welcome Fanning 3/23/1820

BIRTHS:
John Colley 9/14/1752
Gabriel Colley 2/23/1782
Francis Colley 2/20/1785
Eliza Colley 5/12/1788
Mary Coley 5/26/1790
Nancy Colley 1/3/1792
Spain Colley 1/22/1794
Louisa Colley 9/23/1801
Lieusinday E. Tindall 4/26/1809
Darmaris Goolsbe 4/25/1814
Sarah Colley of Henry Fran Jr. 6/4/1763
John C. Fanning 1/19/1821
Sarah F. Fanning 9/11/1822
Mary Fanning 7/5/1824
Nancy Fanning 3/9/1827
Martha Fanning 2/1/1829

DEATHS:
Parks Fanning 8/4/1835
Francis Fanning 10/1/1846
Abina Victoria Fanning 12/24/1846
Charles Ann Fanning 12/28/1850
Mrs. Louisa Fanning 10/1/1853
Welcome Fanning b. 7/14/1799 d. 10/3/1873

William S. Brown 1/16/1855
Bro. A. J. Orr 7/12/1860
John C. Fanning 4/19/1870
Sarah F. Fanning 11/30/1869
Webster Fanning 4/24/1903
J. A. Brown 1/10/1903
Mary P. Johnson 3/29/1904
Sabrina Ellen Fanning 6/23/1905

BIRTHS:
Webster Fanning 3/25/1831
Parks Fanning 3/9/1833
Sabrina Ellen Fanning (July or August)/13/1835
Charles Ann Fanning 9/23/1838
Victoria A. Fanning 11/16/1840
Bryan Fanning 10/18/1842
Frances Fanning 1/6/1845
Samuel D. Fanning 7/4/1862
Alace Estelle Fanning 4/23/1864

Nimrod Colley
Lieusinday Colley
Lewis Colley
John Colley 6/9/1815
Sarah Colley 12/21/1833
Thomas B. Tindall 20th or 27th Nov. 1809

NATHAN FISH of Jasper Co.
Owner: H. J. Powell, Monticello, GA

BIRTHS:
Nathan Fish 10/3/1779
Naomi Phillipes 7/14/1784
Clarasha Fish 11/29/1803
Poley Fish 8/20/1805
Calvin Fish 12/22/1807
Susan Fish 4/6/1810
Theren Happwah Fish 6/1/1812

Rusel Fish 9/16/1814
Thomas Gastin Fish 1/28/1817
Leonora Fish 4/5/1819
Vines Fish 12/9/1821
Curth 10/31/1824, d. same 1824
Curth 8/17/1826, d. same 1826

MARRIAGES:
Nathan Fish and Naomi, his wife, 3/20/1802
William MacCauley an Susan, his wife, 1/31/1828
Calvin Fish and Sarrina, his wife, 2/1830
Russel Fish and Eliza, his wife, 10/10/1833
Pollard Brown McMichael and his wife 1/12/1841

DEATHS:
Theren Happuch Fish 6/1/1812-924/1815, aged 3 years, 3 monoths, 24 days
Clarisa Fish 11/29/1803-1/28/1823, aged 19 years, 1 month, 28 days and was married 10 months and 14 days
Nathan Fish 10/14/1840
Naomi Fish 4/8/1846

WILLIAM BULLOCK of Franklin Co.
Owner: Mrs. Bessie Bullock
Lubbock, Texas

MARRIAGES:
William Bullock-Elizabeth Oliphant 9/30/1784
William Bullock-Spicey Bowman 8/23/1796

DEATHS:
Elizabeth Oliphant Bullock 6/24/1796

BIRTHS:
William Bullock 3/1/1764
Elizabeth Oliphant 10/29/1764
Winifred Bullock 10/14/1785

Sally Bullock 7/1/1787
James Bullock 1/30/1789
Susanna Bullock 1/17/1792
Edward Bullock 8/27/1797
David Bullock 2/20/1799
Elizabeth Bullock 8/22/1803
William O. Bullock 9/22/1805
John Bullock 3/8/1807
Zachariah Bullock 5/3/1809

JOHN KEMP, SR. BIBLE of Wayne Co.
Owner: Mrs. Virginia Kemp Ayer, Birmingham, Alabama (1963)

BIRTHS:
Sherod Sheffield 3/13/1782
Elizabeth Sheffield, his wife, 4/1/1793
John Kemp, Sr. 9/22/1761
Rhoda Kemp 10/22/1771
Joseph Kemp 5/13/1790
John R. Kemp 12/30/1794
Jane Kemp 10/9/1796
David Edwards Kemp 9/22/1798
Mary E. Kemp 5/17/1801
Eliza Woods 7/23/1809
Elizabeth S. Kemp 10/21/1820
William John Kemp 11/14/1824
Ann Jane Kemp 2/20/1804
John K. Fitchett, son of above, 6/26/1823
Joseph Stephen Kemp 3/22/1814
Moses Harvey Kemp 7/2/1816
Sherod Sheffield Akins 6/24/1815

MARRIAGES:
Sherod Sheffield-Elizabeth Kemp 11/22/1810
John Kemp-Rhoda Edwards 4/9/1789
John Fitchett-Ann J. Kemp 12/27/1821
Cordel C. Loper-Elizabeth--------2/12/1835
Sherod Sheffield Akins-Elizabeth Sherrod Kemp 6/24/1835
Bollin Boon-Mary E. Kemp 1/10/1827

DENNIS SULLIVAN of Burke Co.

BIRTHS:
John Sullivan 5/22/1811
Ferriby Sullivan 8/20/1813
John William Sullivan 5/21/1816
Elizabeth (Betsy) Sullivan 11/11818
James Sullivan 5/4/1820
Simeon Sullivan 10/1821
Mary Ann Sullivan 5/22/1823
George W. Sullivan 6/7/1826
Daniel Sullivan 8/31/1828
Susan Sullivan 8/31/1828
Polly Sullivan 11/8/1830
Andrew Jackson Sullivan 7/15/1833

JOHN WALLER BIBLE of Maryland and Hancock Co., GA
Owner: Mrs. Emily Oliver
Lisbon, Arkansas (1959)

John Waller b. 3/13/1749 and his wife, Elizabeth R. Waller, b. 9/1746

Births of Their Children:

Handy Waller 12/1768
Daniel Waller 8/10/1772
John Waller 6/8/1775
William Waller 19/1777
Charles R. Waller 9/14/1780
Elizabeth Waller 2/26/1783
Nathaniel L. Waller 10/12/1787

Nathaniel and his wife, Elizabeth, married 2/29/1833
Charles R. Waller and his wife, Emily, married 4/23/1803

SAMUEL WALDEN BIBLE
Owner: Mrs. R. Shefer Heard, West Point, GA

"A Free Gift of Dismukes, in the year 1757, to Mary Walden for the love of her mother, Mary Ellis. God be close to all!"

Samuel Walden, His Book

BIRTHS:
Fannie Walding 2/8/1757
Richard Walding 10/10/1760
William Walden 11/24/1768
Anne Walden 10/20/1773
Anderson Fambrough 1/24/1782
Samuel Boyd 10/8/1782
Nancy Inroughtee 12/10/1780
Fanny Boyd 1/28/1787
---------------Boyd 1/30/1791
Sarah Walding 12/10/1758
Owen Walden 12/26/1762
Lewis Walden 1/13/1771
Elijah Walden 4/10/1775
Byrd Fambrough 5/4/1778
Clayburn Inroughtee 3/10/1777
Mary Boyd 2/24/1784
--------Boyd 2111789
------------oyd 2/12/1793

Robert Dismukes Thompson, son of Sarah Thompson, daughter of John Thompson, was born 8/22/1791

Richard Boyd, Jun., son of Richard Boyd, b. 9/4/1795
Henry Boyd, son of Richard Boyd and Fanny, his wife, b. 5/2/1797
John Coleman Boyd, son of Richard Boyd and Fanny, his wife, b. 3/16/1802
Averilla? Boyd 1/11/1805
James M. T......this 11th Oct. 1762
John Boyd b. 3/161802
Richard Boyd deceased 9/28/1823

JONATHAN HEARN
Owner: Mrs. Alice Hamilton Sammons, Godfrey, GA

Jonathan Hearn, son of Samuel and Elizabeth Hearn, born 3/11/1760 Sussex Co., Delaware

His wife, Rhoda Parker, daughter of Jacob and Mary Parker, born 12/17/1763 in Sussex Co., Delaware

Asa Hearn, son, born 12/17/1783 Sussex Co., Delaware
Zabed Hearn, son, born 11/22/1785 Sussex Co., Delaware
Seth Hearn, son, born 1/2/1788 Sussex Co., Delaware, died 2/17/1821 Putnam Co., Ga.

Lott Hearn, son, born 3/18/1790 Sussex Co., Delaware, died 11/30/1844 Putnam Co., Ga. Married 1/13/1813 Frances McClendon, born 8/23/1796

Mary P. Hearn, daughter, b. 4/20/1792 Hancock Co., Ga. Married John Hamilton 12/14/1807 Jackson Co., Ga.

Samuel Hearn, son, born 1/31/1795 Hancock Co., Ga.
Jacob Hearn, son, born 7/29/1797 Hancock Co., Ga.
Elizabeth Hearn, daughter, born 1/29/1799 Hancock Co., Ga.
Judah Hearn, daughter, born 7/2/1801 Jackson Co., Ga.

William Hearn, son, born 8/31/1803 Jackson Co., Ga. Died 11/10/1873 married 11/15/1821 Anna Pennington who died 8/24/1851
Dr. James Hamilton died 12/28/1871
Nancy Furlow born 12/7/1781.
Nancy D. Montgomery died 10/23/1842
Travis M. Hearn, son, born 11/2/1819
Rhoda Ann Letha Hearn born 8/15/1822, died 9/15/1851 married 3/1/1838 Samuel G. Akens
Lucinda Amanda Hearn born 2/20/1824 married 11/19/1844 Thomas J. Weaver
William Hearn married 1/17/1861 Cynthia Catherine Calloway
William D. Weaver.

DUNCAN COLQUHOUN BIBLE of Cheraw Dist., S. C. and Talbot Co., GA

From: Leonardo Andrew Collection (deceased).
Owner: Edwin C. Calhoun
229 Alexander Hamilton Drive
San Antonio, TX (1974)

Duncan Colquhoun 12/18/1796-11/17/1851. He was married to Sarah McNeal born 8/19/1800-5/9/1863

Children:

Archibald Colquhoun b. 8/19/1819 m. Sarah Jane McMurray
Mary Colquhoun b. 4/13/1821 m. (1) Mr. Whatley (2) Mr. Phillips (3) Mr. Moore
Margaret Ann Colquhoun b. 2/26/1823 m. Robert M. Patterson in 1844
Isabel Colquhoun 12/13/1824-11/16/1828
Malcolm Colquhoun b. 7/16/1826 m. Catherine McKee
Rachel Colquohoun b. 3/29/1828 m. James Turner Phillips
Calvin Calhoun b. 8/29/1830 m. (1) Mrs. Fatima Snelgrove nee Fatima Buckner (2) Ann Miller
John C. Calquhoun b. 9/2/1832 m. Ebiline Watts
Ann Elizabeth Calquhoun b. 11/9/1834 m. Nathan Baugh
James Gamble Colquhoun b. 8/19/1836 m. Sarah Phillips
Richard Marks Colquhoun b. 3/31/1841 m. Manah Wesley Snelgrove

MARRIAGES:
Archibald Colquhoun 10/10/1842 to Sarah Jane McMurray

DEATHS:
Archibald Colquhoun died in Bienville Parish, LA 9/9/1855
Margaret Ann Colquhoun Patterson died 12/22/1905
Archibald Colquhoun, Sr. died 9/15/1839

JOSEPH FEW BIBLE of Chester and Spartanburg Co., S. C. and Warren Co., GA

From: Leonardo Andrea Collection
Owner: Mrs. W. B. Daniel, Eastman, GA (1925)

Joseph Few born 8/1/1710 in Pennsylvania, died 11/15/1762 married 9/18/1733 according to the Rules of The Friends to

Mary Aston born 3/25/1711 in Pennsylvania died 3/15/1762, same day as her husband

Children: (entries illegible)

Mary Few, daughter 9/12/1741-11/22/1807 married in Chester Co., PA 8/1/1759 to Joseph Buffington

Hannah Few, daughter, born 9/10/1744
Joseph Few, son, 5/25/1749-5/27/1750
Joseph Few II, son, born 5/25/1753

"The Bible was brought to Spartanburg County, S. C. by Mary Few Buffington who gave it to her daughter, Frances Buffington Friend, who took it to Warren Co., Ga. and continued the Bible as her own Bible".

Children of Thomas Friend and his wife, Fanny Buffington Friend of Warren Co., GA:

Edward Friend, son, born 1/14/1793 in Spartanburg Co., S. C., died 5/29/179--
Matilda Friend, daughter, born 7/16/1794 Warren Co., Ga.
Joseph Friend, son, born 1/11/1796 in Warren Co., Ga.
Benjamin Few Friend, son, born 7/9/1797 in Warren Co., Ga.
John Ozburn Friend, son, born 7/26/1799 Warren Co., Ga., died 8/25/1801
Phoebe Ozburn Friend, daughter, born 6/2/1801 in Warren Co., Ga.
Mary Few Friend, daughter, born---/13/1803, died 7/4/1804 Warren Co., Ga.
Eliza Buffington Friend, daughter, born 7/9/1805 Warren Co., Ga.

LEONARD DOZIER III BIBLE of S. C. and Elbert Co., GA
From: Leonardo Andrea Collection
Columbia, S. C.

Mutiliated page, other family pages missing.

Leonard Dozier married 1/30/1773 to Anne Gayle.

Their children:
James Dozier, born 9/2/1737
Susannah Dozier, daughter, born 11/16/1739
John Dozier, son, born 12/2/1741, died in S. C.
William Dozier, son, born 3/16/1743
Jemima Dozier, daughter, born 5/22/1746
Keziah Dozier, daughter, born 5/26/1749
Leonard Dozier, son, born 5/7/1751
Thomas Dozier, son, born 6/29/1753
Ann Dozier, daughter, born 1755
Richard Dozier, son, born 8/15/1760

Notation by Mrs. James Nuckols of Columbus, Ga.

"The first Leonard Dozier came from France and died in 1693 in Westmoreland Co., Va. His wife was named Elizabeth...."

MAJORS BIBLE
Owner: Mrs. A. F. Majors
Sylvester, GA (1925)
From: Leonardo Andrea Collection

"Brought from S. C. To Georgia...Only this page of Births shown in the Bigle and no relationship is given for any."

BIRTHS:
Sarah Majors 10/12/1803
David Majors 1/1/1806
Thomas Majors 12/24/1807
Mary Majors 4/28/1809

John Majors 4/3/1811
Rachel Majors 3/7/1813
Martha Majors 11/12/1814
David Majors 6/10/1816
Elizabeth F. Majors 8/19/1825
Sarah A. Majors 4/9/1827
Winnefred Majors 7/5/1828
William Majors 1/6/1830
David Majors 8/15/1830
Susan Majors 8/1/1832
Jonathan T. Majors 12/14/1834
Anderson Majors born--------, -----------1835
Louisa Majors 9/1/1836
Daniel Majors 9/13/1836
Thomas Clements Majors 8/29/1839
Malissa Majors 1/6/1840

CHARLES MARTIN BIBLE of Union Co., S. C. and Jasper Co., GA
Owner: Mrs. C. Grubbs, Sylvester, GA (1925)
Leonardo Andrea Collection

Charles Martin, 6th son of James and Esther Hogan Martin born 3/9/1827 in Union Co., S. C., died 11/25/1910 in Jasper Co., Ga.

Married 9/5/1846 to Rachel Anna Laslie, born 3/2/1829, died 3/21/1895

Mary Jane Martin, daughter, born 1/10/1848, died 2/16/1876 (Tombstone in Colquitt Co., Ga. Reads "Wife of Col. Bouley Baughn".
Elizabeth Martin, daughter, born 1/27/1852, died 5/9/1852
Catherine Aquilla Martin, daughter, born 11/21/1854, married 2/10/1874 to John Brunson Watson of Jasper Co., Ga.
Alice T. Martin, daughter, born 12/1/1857, died 5/2/1901 (Tombstone in Colquitt Co., Ga. Reads "wife of Abner Roberts"
Rachel Anna Martin, daughter, born 3/3/1861 married 2/29/1880 in Arlington, Ga. To Welborn J. Roberts
Daniel Laslie Martin, son, born 5/5/1864 (sketch of his life states he married Elizabeth Adams of Colquitt Co., Ga.)

Ida Martin, daughter, born 8/7/1867 married Jackson S. Cowart of Arlington, Ga."
Twin
Ada Martin, daughter, born 8/7/1867 married William Lane of Arlington, Ga.

"The Rev. Charles Martin was one of five brothers who became Baptist ministers. He preached and held pastorates in South Carolina and Georgia...See the Bible of his brother, James Martin, which has birth, death and marriage dates for James Martin, Sr., as well as the Bible entries for the family of James Martin, Sr.

JAMES MARION MARTIN BIBLE of Jasper Co.
Owner: Mrs. C. Grubbs, Sylvester, GA (1925)
From: Leonardo Andrea Collection

James Marion Martin born 7/12/1839 Jasper Co., Ga. Died 8/19/1923 at Shellman, Ga. Married 16th March in Florida to
Corrine Elizabeth Eubanks 10/4/1848-11/1/1874

Married 2nd at Hawkinsville, Ga. 2/28/1882 to
Lucinda Coley 4/9/1850-7/3/1869

Children by first wife:
John Eubanks Martin, son, born 5/9/1872 *married in Kentucky to Frances Elliott
Mary Lydia Martin, daughter, born 8/2/1874 *married in Dade City, FL to C. W. Croft

Children by second wife:
James Arthur Martin, son, born 8/28/1884 *married in Worth Co., Ga. to Effie Gleaton
Coley Truitt Martin, son, born 12/1/1886, died 4/1/1910 Shellman, Ga.

*Added in pencil along the margin in the Bible...no dates

John Martin, my father, born in Union Co., S. C. 1/3/1821, died in Shellman, Ga. 4/22/1917, married 11/18/1838 to Martha Truitt, my mother, born 5/27/1821, died 7/15/1905

James Martin, my grandfather, born in Charleston, S. C. 11/15/1788, died 11/18/1869 in Jasper Co., Ga. (Randolph Co. then) married in Union Co., S. C. 6/2/1810 to

Esther Borgan, my grandmother, born 4/18/1789 in Union Co., S. C., died 7/15/1867 in Randolph Co., Ga.

ABNER TATOM BIBLE (1755-1819) Norfolk, Va., Granville Co., N. C., 96th District, S. C., Lincoln Co., Ga., Madison Co., Ga.
From: Leonardo Andrew Collection

Abner Tatom b. 10/15/1755 married 5/3/1780 to
Mary Currin was born ----------------------

Children:
Elizabeth Ann Tatom, daughter, born 3/20/1781
James Tatom, son, born 2/23/1783
Absalom Tatom, son, born 8/7/1785
Cynthia Tatom, daughter, born 3/7/1788
Barnett Tatom, son, born 2/14/1791
John Tatom, son, born 11/17/1793
Nancy Tatom, daughter, born 6/10/1798
William Tatom, son, born 11/29/1801, died 11/1802
Also
"Abner Tatom is the fifth child of John Tatom, Sr. and his wife, Ann Wright of Norfolk, Va."
"Abner Tatom was the first clerk of the Superior Court of Lincoln County, Georgia and the above family data is found inscribed by him on one of the pages of the Clerk of Court Records."

CALEB EARP BIBLE of 96th District, S. C. and Franklin Co., Ga.
Owner: Mrs. J. T. Beasley, Lavonia, Ga (1925)
From: Leonardo Andrea Collection

BIRTHS:

Caleb Earp 2/7/1768
Margaret Earp 2/7/1771

Our Children:

David D. Earp 7/9/1795
Matthew Earp 7/12/1797
Daniel Earp 5/2/1799
Llewellen Earp 10/25/1801
Caty Earp 8/19/1803.....Catherine
James M. Earp 12/2/1805
Caswell Earp 1/6/1808
Statiba Earp 1/31/1810
Matty Earp 4/22/1812
Lavonia Earp 6/18/1814
Caleb Asbury Earp 5/1/11816

James McLevi Ellis born 9/2/1803 (or 1823)
John Cox born 5/25/1821

JOHN McMILLAN DELANY BIBLE
Owner: E. D. Reed
2749 Lanier Drive, Snellville, GA 30278

John McMillan, son of Daniel and Esther Delany, born 9/12/1791
Delilah Bruton, daughter of George and Susannah Durham, born 4/18/1801
John McMillan Delany m. Delilah Bruton Durham 2/17/1820

BIRTHS:
Rosannah M. Delany 3/10/1821
Alexander Delany 3/30/1822
James Delany 10/26/1823
Maryann Delany 2/22/1825
Matilda Moroney Delany 12/11/1827
George Durham Delany 10/15/1829
Susannah Caroline Delany 12/21/1831
Margaret Elizabeth Delany 1/23/1833
Sarah Adeline Delany 12/2/1834
John Landrum Delany 2/22/1837
Delilah Julia Delany 4/11/1839

Thomas Newport Delany 2/7/1841
William Green Delany 6/21/1843
Rebecca Frances Delany 2/14/1847

John McMillan Delany died 11/21/1864

MICHAEL A. WASHBURN BIBLE
Owner: Ms. Marilyn Wilson
310 Winterberry Drive, Athens, GA 30606

MARRIAGES:
Michael A. Washburn to Catharine L. Fisher 3/27/1861

BIRTHS:
Michael A. Washburn 10/8/1819
Catharine L. Fisher 6/13/1838
Elisabeth A. Washburn 6/14/1865
William K. Washburn 12/28/1867

NATHANIEL HARRIS COWAN BIBLE
Owner: Dr. Zach S. Cowan
1179 Clifton Road, N. E., Atlanta, GA This Bible belonged to James Jones Cowan (1812-1898)
From: A History of Cowan Family by Dr. Zachary S. Cowan

BIRTHS:
Nathaniel Harris Cowan was born Feb. 17, 1791.
Margaret McCalvey Cowan was born June 1, 1791.
Mary Carolina Harris born July 30, 1811.
Rebecca Adaline Harris was born April 1, 1813
Charles Pinckney Harris was born Oct. 21, 1815
James McCalvey Harris was born Sept. 8, 1817
Samuel Jackson Harris was born Mar. 24, 1821.

James Cowan was born Nov. 14, 1775
Agnes Cowan, his wife, was born Mar. 5, 1791
James Jones Cowan was born April 8, 1812.

John Woods Cowan was born Dec. 19, 1813
Robert Frazier Cowan was born Mar. 17, 1816.
Mary Harris Cowan was barn Dec. 24, 1818
Elizabeth Baskin Cowan was born Feb. 11, 1821
William Harris Caldwell Cowan was born May 15, 1825
Daniel Bird Cowan was born Nov. 7, 1827.

Daniel B. Bird was born Jan. 29, 1803. Mary Jones Bird was born Mar. 27, 1806.
Sarah Ann Cook, Wife of James Jones Cowan was born June 7, 1816.

Nancy Elizabeth Cowan was born Sept. 3, 1834.
Mary Bird Cowan was born Feb. 8, 1836
Thomas Franklin Cowan was born Oct. 10, 1837
Zachariah J. Cowan was born Dec. 10, 1839
John Jordan Cowan was born Jan. 8, 1842
Robert A. Cowan was born Dec. 7, 1844
Joseph LaFayette Cowan was born Mar. 7, 1847
James William Cowan was born May 9, 1849
Hiram Darnell Cowan was born June 4, 1851
Martha Joyce Cowan was born May 7, 1853.
M. J. (Smith) Cowan, 2nd wife of James Jones Cowan, was born Jan. 30, 1845.

MARRIAGES:
Nathaniel Harris and Margaret McCalvey were married July 26, 1810.
James Cowan and Agnes Jones were married July 27, 1811.
Daniel B. Bird and Mary Jones were married Sept. 27, 1811.
James Jones Cowan and Sarah Ann Cook were married Oct. 24, 1833.
Joseph LaFayette Cowan and Fannie Rhodes married in 1874.
Nancy Elizabeth Cowan and Stephen Simmons were married in 1856.
Mary Bird Cowan and Joseph Tanner were married in 1856.
Thomas Franklin Cowan and H. E. Smith were married in 1860.
John J. Cowan and Frances Wingate were married in 1865.
Zach J. Cowan and Saleta Reagan were married in 1869.
Martha Joyce Cowan and G. W. Martin were married in 1874.
James W. Cowan and Annie Bailey were married in 1877.
Hiram Cowan and Dilla Crowley were married in 1877.

DEATHS:
James McCalvey Harris died Oct. 21, 1822.
Infant deceased Nov. 2, 1822.
Margaret Harris deceased Dec. 23, 1825.
Agnes Cowan, deceased Jan. 18 1833, Age 42.
Robert Frazier Cowan deceased Nov. 16, 1835, Age 17 yrs. 8 months, lacking one day.
James Cowan died July 10, 1849. Age 73.
Sarah Ann Cook Cowan, deceased 1887.
Dr. James Jones Cowan departed this life July 10, 1898.
Mattie Cowan Buckalew died 1919. First husband, George W. Martin.
Joseph L. Cowan died in 1925.
Annie Bailey Cowan died 1926. (Wife of James W. Cowan who d.1901)

"Dr. Z. S. Cowan has in his possession the following:

1. A New Testament published in London 1863. On the fly-leaf is the notation "Confederate States Bible Society, W. N. Reeves, Pastor Baptist Church, Eufaula, Ala. James H. Jones, his Testament bought for one dollar in Eufaula, Ala., Sept. 3, 1864.

2. Collection of "Hymns of the Methodist Episcopal Church principally from the collection of Rev. John Wesley, late fellow of Lincoln College, Oxford. This was published in New York in 1833. Inside the back cover is written "Mary Cowan:- present by Lewis Jones"

3. "Christian Psalmody", comprising "Dr. Watts Psalms Abridged", and Dr. Watts Hymns, Abridged and "Select Hymns from other authors. This was edited by Samuel Worcester, D. D., Pastor of the Tabernacle Church, Salem, published in Boston 1821. The names written on the inside of the front cover are: Nancy Cowan, James Cowan and Mary H. Cowan.

4. A New Testament published in New York In 1823. On the fly-leaf is written "James Cowan, Aug. 17, 1827--by Daniel Bird."

5. Bible published in Dublin in 1780. On the fly-leaf is written "James Jones, his book, bought September 1791, price 6s. This Bible contains the following record:

James Cowan was born Nov. 14, 1775
Agnes Cowan his wife was born Mar. 31, 1790
James Jones Cowan was born April 8, 1812.
John Woods Cowan was born Dec. 19, 1813.
Robert F. Cowan was born Mar. 17, 1816.
Mary H. Cowan was born Dec. 24, 1818.
Elizabeth B. Cowan was born Feb. 11, 1821.
William H. C. Cowan was born May 15, 1825.
Daniel B. Cowan was born Nov. 7, 1827.

James Cowan and Agnes Jones were married on June 27, 1811
On the inside of the back cover is written "Agnes Cowan's book, $1.43, June 27, 1811."

JESSE POPE's BIBLE of Warren Co.

Written in the back of the Bible on an empty page was "my mother's father was Louis Wright, my brothers were John, Dick, and Stephen. My sisters Elizabeth, Caroline and Martha." The Bible is raw-hide leather bound, and now belongs to Jessie Rando Pope. The Bible was published by Kimber and Sharpless in Philadelphia, probably 1835.

MARRIAGES:
Jesse Pope and Nancy Wright his wife was married Oct the 22th 1818
Frances M. Pope and Peter Mosely was married the 17th Dec 11; 1837
William A. Pope and Nancy Turner was married 27th March 1842
Frances M. Mosly and William H. Franks was married 11th of Aug 1844
James Pope and Martha Brinkley was married the 2 day of Nov 1848
Saml. A. Jones and L.S.A. Pope was married the 9th Dec. 1852
N. Lewis and Mrs. F.M. Franks was married April the 10th 1857

BIRTHS:
Jesse Pope was bornd the 8th August 1796
Nancy Pope his wife was bornd October 22th 1802
Frances Marion our daughter was bornd August 5th 1819
William Allen our son was bornd August the 8th 1821
James Lewis our son was bornd April the 2?th 1824
Pinkney Hill our son was bornd Aug 28th 1826
Martha Ann our daughter was bornd November the 6h 1828
Joseph Cunagm our son was bornd March the 8th 1831
Robert Jabez, our son, was born May 9th 1833
Lydia Shadyan our daughter was born June the 11th 1835
Jesse Wright our son was born July the 22th !838
Elick Zander Pope was born the 9 December 1849
William Pope was born July the 17 1852
Newton Lewis born August the 28th 1814
Rufus Darling Moseley was bornd September the 1st 1839
Nancy Turner was bornd March the 30th 1823
Frances Jane was bornd the 19th July 1843
John Oliver was bornd the 19th April 1845

Isaac L. Franks was born ---------------
Hannah Calidona was born August 22d 1872 Fuller
Mary Alles Fuller born December the 9th 1869
Isaac Lewis was born the 25th July 1845
Joseph ? was born January 2nd 1849
Louisa M. Jones, daughter of S.A. and F.S.A. Jones his wife was born Sept. the 15th AD 1857?
Eliza Jane Franks was born January the 25th A.D. 1852
William James Lewis was born August the 12th A.D. 1858
Samuel P. Lewis was born the 28th of Jan. 1862

DEATHS
Joseph C. Pope dyed the 31st October 1832
Peter Moseley Dyed 5th August 1840
Jesse Pope Departed this life Aug. 11th 1848 in full hope of eternal life aged 52 years and 3 days. He was a professer of Religion about 26 years.
Rufus D. Moseley dyed March the 8 1849
Robt. J. Pope Departed this life 29th Aug 1852 Aged 19 ys 2 mos 18 das
Martha Ann Pope Departed this life Jany 12th AD 1850 ,22 ys, 2 mos 6 da
William James Lewis departed this life 9th of Sept. 1868 Age 10 yrs 27 da
Samuel P. Lewis departed this life 9th Sept. 1868 Age 6 yrs, 7 mos 16 das.
Pinkney H. Pope departed this life November the 3th 1882.

WILSON CONNER BIBLE
Owner: Mrs. W. C. McAllister, Hawkinsville, GA (1920)

Wilson Conner born 7/7/1768 Craven Co., S. C., married 10/8/1789 in Marlboro Co., S. C. To Mary Cook, born 8/1/1774 Cheraw District, S. C.

BIRTHS:
James Gassaway Conner 8/20/1790
Nancy Conner 4/20/1792
Harriot Elizabeth Conner 9/1793
Lucy Ann Conner
Mary J. Conner
Thomas Benton Conner 8/21/1798
Betsy Conner 3/9/1801
Polly Godwin Conner 1/25/1804
Eliza Tarpley Conner 7/29/1807

Mariah McDonald Conner 6/13/1810
Wilson Conner Cooper 9/16/1812, son of George Cooper
Wilson Walker Conner 4/19/1813
Mary Ann Elizabeth Cooper 12/4/1813
Samuel Conner Griffin 9/23/1814, son of John Griffin
Penelope Luvancy Cooper 6/14/1815
Elizabeth Griffin 10/19/1815
William DeWitt Clinton Conner 9/23/1819
George Washington Cooper 4/21/1821
Thomas Benton Conner 8/29/1821, son of James Conner
Thomas B. C. Cooper 12/26/1824
Louisa Ann Conner 10/25/1815
Eleanor Cook Cooper 2/10/1817
Martha Lucy Conner 3/30/1818
James Conner Griffin 2/18/1818
Penelope Ryals 9/11/1798
Luvancy Cooper 2/16/1819
Mary Ann Sullivant 11/10/1825

MARRIAGES:
Nancy Conner 12/20/1810 to George Cooper
Harriot Conner 5/25/1813 to John Griffin
James Gasaway Conner 10/1/1818 to Penelope Ryals
Lucy Ann Conner 3/31/1822 to Joseph Ryals
Mary J. Conner 1/2/1824 to Thomas C. Sullivant

DEATHS:
Thomas Conner Sr. 8/4/1768, aged 90 years
Margaret, wife of Thomas Conner, 17---, aged 60 years
John Beverley 1786, aged 80 years
Ann, wife of John Beverley, 1787, aged 81 years
Eleanor Cook 9/15/1793, aged 50 years
Ann Conner 9/1791, 60 years (nee Ann Beverley, mother of Wilson 1768)
Lewis Conner 8/30/1793, aged 37 years
William Conner 7/1797, aged 32 years
Bethe Conner 1820, aged 27 years
James Conner 1805 by a fall from a horse
Thomas Conner, Jr. 9/12/1802, aged 75 years ("Jr." in Bible)
Samuel C. Griffin 10/21/1814, aged 27 days
Annias Lang 7/21/1807

Betsy Conner 2/4/1809 in her 8th year
Elizabeth, widow of Annias Lang, 5/10/1809

ARCHELEUS CONE DUGGAN BIBLE of N. C., Barnwell Co., S. C., Warthen, Washington Co., Ga.
Owner: Sam Duggan, Sandy Run Plantation, RFD 4, Moultrie, GA

Archeleus Cone Duggan born 4/29/1808, died 8/27/1877, son of John and Mary Duggan
Married 3/17/1829 to Miss E. A. Walker born 8/8/1808 "Mrs. Elizabeth Ann Duggan" died 8/10/1861
Daughter of John and Rebecca Walker
Married second 11/27/1862 to
Miss N. R. Maddux "Mrs. N. R., wife of A. C. Duggan, died 2/1879"

Children by first wife:
Rebecca Kelly Duggan, daughter, born 1/4/1830
Ivy Walker Duggan, son, born 12/22/1831
James Barnes Duggan, son, born 11/1/1833, died 9/29/1915
Martha Elizabeth Duggan, daughter, born 9/7/1835
Chloe Ann Duggan, daughter, born 7/23/1838, died 8/27/1864
Joseph Franklin Duggan, son, born 10/10/1840, died 4/7/1865
Thomas Green Duggan, son, born 10/28/1842, died 8/24/1850? (1880?)
Clarissa Ann Duggan, daughter, born 1/25/184--
Benjamin R. Duggan, son, born 1/9/1850, died 5/18/1865
Children by second wife:
Elizabeth Nancy Duggan, daughter, born 10/7/1863, died 10/22/1864
Georgia Margaret Duggan, daughter, born 4/19/1865
Georgia M. Trawick died 1/6/1954
Archeleus Maddux Duggan, son, born 5/30/1867
Susan Frances Duggan, daughter, born 7/24/1869, died 9/5/1869
Mary N. Duggan, daughter, born 7/9/1870
David Edmund Duggan, son, born 10/10/1872, died 5/5/1954
J. W. Duggan died 9/6/1917
E. F. Jordan married 12/17/1846 to R. H. Day
Slave Amanda born 5/6/1833 and her children:
Leo born 8/2/1849
Isaac born 5/5/1851

Slave Celia born 11/5/1827 and her children:
Mary born 6/7/1843
Lucinda born 2/27/1846
Sarah born 3/26/1848
Seaborn born 5/10/1850

NICHOLAS OVERBY BIBLE of Abbeville Co., S. C. and Stewart Co., Ga.

From: Leonardo Andrea Collection
In possession of Miss Connie Andrea, Columbia, S. C. (1974)

Nicholas Overby born 1/20/1784 in Virginia, died 3/1868 in Gwinnett Co., Ga. Married 1/10/1812 in Abbeville Co., S. C. To Mary Hallum born 2/3/1783 in Laurens Co., S. C., died 11/4/1862 in Abbeville Co., S. C.

Basil Hallum Overby, son, 11/19/1814-11/27/1859 married 5/18/1837 to Asenath Thrasher; married 6/27/1854 to E. S. Harrolson

Ann Elizabeth Overby, daughter, born 1/12/1816, married 6/3/1845 to B. Allen
Benjamin Mitchell Overby, son, 9/18/1818-11/17/1891, married 8/18/1841 to Lucy C. Seay
John Bayliss Earl Overby, son, 1/8/1821-5/14/1854 at Thomasville, Ga.
Nicholas G. Overby born 10/16/1826
Nimrod W. Overby born 10/8/1827

"I raised three sons to manhood".
Births of Children of B. Allen and A. E. Allen (all born Abbeville Co., SC.):
Bannister Bowling Allen 12/13/1847
Basil Barion Allen 5/11/1849
Mary Aseneth Allen 10/1/1850
E. S. Harrolson Allen 11/29/1852
Caroline Gilmore Allen 4/20/1855
Ginnie Taburn Allen 8/2/1859

On flyleaf of Bible:
"I came to Abbeville County, S. C. from Virginia in 1789. I moved to Georgia in November of 1863."

Meshack Overby 1753-1841 lived to be past 90 years...He married Mary Mitchell. I am aged 84.
My brother Nimrod Overby lived to be 85
My brother Benjamin Overby lived to be 84

My first American ancestor was Nicholas Overby 1622-1732 who lived to be 110...He came to Virginia from Paris, France and raised 3 sons, Nicholas, Obidiah and Peter. The Bristol Parish records in Virginia have some records of my family."

WILLIAM THREADGILL BIBLE
Owner: Mrs. T. A. Anderson (nee Lois Threadgill)
Houston, TX (1931)

"Presented to her by her husband, William Threadgill, 8/11/1857"
Martha E. A. Jelks, daughter of Robert Jelks and his wife, Mary Nicholson, born 8/25/1808
Martha E. A. Jelks married first time to Green W. Drake who died 1838
Green W. Drake born 12/7/1806
Children of Green W. Drake and his wife, Martha Jelks Drake:
BIRTHS:
Mary Elizabeth Drake 12/16/1832
William Green Drake 6/10/18333
Louisa M. Drake 10/15/1836
S. T. Drake 3/12/1838
Tempie Lula Drake 1/18/1839
Martha Drake married William Threadgill 12/24/1843. Births of their children:
James R. Threadgill 7/6/1845
Rebecca Threadgill 4/6/1847
Thomas Jelks Threadgill 9/27/1848
George A. Threadgill 8/10/1851

MARRIAGES:
Mary Elizabeth Drake to John Alexander James Phillips 5/19/1852
William Green Drake m. 1st V. A. Turner, born 4/15/1838, 12/8/1858
Tempie Lula Drake-J. F. Tate 11/8/1860
Thomas Jelks Threadgill-S. F. Davis 1/2/1873

WILLIS GORHAM BIBLE
Owner: W. Henry Cobb II
3134 Shadow Walk Lane, Tucker, GA 300

MARRIAGES:
Willis Gorham and Mary J. Anderson married July 2d 1818
L.S. Mitchell and Mary E. Gorham were married May 4th 1847
James A. Gorham and Ally T. Truitt were married April 8th 1851
Robert B. Gardner and Susan B. Gorham were married July 27th 1854
John Murphy and Cornelia L. Gorham were married October 1854
George C. Gorham and S.A.E. Pope were married 1864
Willis J. Gorham and Mary E. Pope were married January 27th 1870
John L. Harp and Georgia V. Mitchell were married May 14th 1872
W.J. Gorham and Mary C. Crawl were married Dec. 31th 1878.

BIRTHS:
Willis Gorham was born Oct. 27th 1793
Mary J. Gorham was born May 12th 1800
George C. Gorham was born Sept. 15th 1823
Mary E.A. Gorham was born February 16th 1825
Cornelia L. Gorham was born Oct. 25th 1827
Jos. J. Gorham was born January 8th 1829
James A. Gorham was born July 28th 1830 (33 beside it)
Sarah R. Gorham was born Nov. 7th 1831 (39 beside it) Susannah B. Gorham was born Aug. 8th 1833 (41 beside it)
Willis J. Gorham was born February 5th 1835 (43 beside it)
Anne F. Gorham was born Feb. 8th 18--

BIRTHS:
Wiliis Jackson Mitchell born 17th March 1849
Mary Elizabeth Gorham Daughter of Jos. A. and Ally T. Gorham, born on the 14th February 1852
Georgia Virginia Mitchell born July Ist 1852
John Willis Gorham born July 3d 1853
Claude L. Mitchell born June 14th 1854
William Anderson Gorham born Oct. (blank) 1855
Walter Gorham Gardner born Oct. 29th 1855

Mary P. Murphy born March 6th 185(?)
Sarah Neal Gardner was born November 14th 1856
Mary Ethel was born Mach 8th 1871
Florence Agnes was born November 10th 1872

DEATHS:
Polina C.F. Gorham Died Oct. 6th 1822 aged one Year and six days
Willis Gorham, Sr. Died May 22d 1851 aged 57 years, 6 months, 22 days
Joseph J. Gorham died January 2nd 1856
James A. Gorham wounded in front of Petersburg defending the Confederate Capital -- supposed to have died in Hospital of wounds after the fall of Richmond and the death of the Confederacy April 1865
Cornelia L. Murphey died July 27th 1873
Mary J. Gorham died Nov. 2nd 1879 aged 79 years 3 months and days
Mary E. Gorham died Jan. 13th 1877 aged 28 years (possibly 88: months and 7 days
W.J. Gorham, Junior died Dec 26th 1881
Robert B. Gardner died Oct. 9th 1882
Anna Fannie Gorham died Dec 12st 1884
Mary E. Mitchell died Jan 10th 1887 aged 62 (1888 written below)

ANDERSON GREEN MICHAEL BIBLE of Walton Co., GA
Owner: Elder Foster Michael
RFD No. 1, Monroe, GA
From: Leonardo Andrea Collection

Anderson Green Michael born at Good Hope, Ga. 9/16/1847
Died at Mt. Carmel, Ga. 5/14/1917, son of
Catherine Johnston and David Michael, Was married 1/5/1866 in
Anderson Co., S. C. To Rachel Mary Ann LaBoon
Born in Anderson Co., S. C. 11/29/1834, died in Walton Co. 8/19/1896, daughter of Elizabeth Tripp and Joseph LaBoon.

Children:

Elizabeth Catherine Michael, daughter, 12/18/1866-3/23/1893 married 12/15/1886 to Redmond Leonardo Andrea of Greenville Co., S. C. (My parents...Leonardo Ardrea)

Sarah Michael, daughter, 3/26/1868-2/2/1934 (tombstone has born 1869) married 1/6/1887 to Charles Thurston Snow of Walton Co., Ga.

Mary Emma Michael, daughter, 1/10/1870-12/30/1907 married 12/26/1893 to Moses Edward Moon of Greenville Co., S. C.

Joseph LaBoon Michael, son, 1/8/1873-6/11/1948. He never did marry.

David Franklin Michael, son, 4/13/1875-4/28/1953 married 12/29/1901 to Ada Jane Harper of Walton Co., Ga.

John Anderson Michael, son, 8/6/1877-7/28/1951 married 8/24/1902 to Frances Aycock of Walton Co., Ga. (Tombstone has Fanny), married 10/16/1910 to Minnie Estelle Johnson of Oconee Co., Ga.

Comments by copist, Leonardo Andrea.

"The three daughters were called Bettie...Sallie...Mollie.

The Bible of the father, David Mikel, is not spelled Michael."

Deaths of In-Laws listed in the Bible:

Fanny Aycock-Michael died 12/27/1909
Redmond Leonardo Adrea died 7/11/1921
Charles Thurston Snow died 1/16/1934
Moses Edward Moon died 11/11/1942
Ada Jane Harper Michael died 11/16/1952

Joseph LaBoon died 10/1/1871 in Anderson Co., S. C....Father-in-law
Elizabeth Tripp LaBoon died 5/27/1872 in Anderson Co., S. C....Mother-in-law

"Anderson Green Michael enlisted in Co. A 4th Georgia Militia Regt., in 1864...Private. I received a Confederate Cross of Honor on this record for my service in the U. S. Navy in World War I...Andrea."

DAVID MIKEL BIBLE of Walton Co., Ga.
Owner: Misses Annie and Mary Love
Good Hope, GA, From: Leonardo Andrea collection

David Mikel born in Oglethorpe Co., Ga. 12/20/1815, died in Walton Co., Ga. 2/12/1896 Married 1/1/1835 to Catherine Hughes Johnston, born in Caswell Co., N. C. 4/13/1812, died in Walton Co., Ga. 9/27/1895

Children:
John W. Mikel, son, 3/24/1836-11/19/1881 married 10/1/1865 to Nancy Clark Johnston
Martha Ann Mikel, daughter, 1/25/1839-6/7/1842
William D. Mikel, son, 11/30/1841-11/24/1887 married 11/15/1869 to Mary C. McGaughey
James K. Mikel, son, 10/23/1844-4/22/1937 married 2/14/1867 to Mollie D. Hale of Clarke Co.
Anderson Green Mikel, son, 2/16/1847-5/14/1917 married 1/5/1866 to Rachel Mary Ann LaBoon of Anderson, S. C. *("These are my maternal grandparents...Andrea")*
Samuel H. Mikel, son, 8/24/1850-6/28/1853
Elizabeth Fendron Mikel, daaaughter 9/19/1853-9/21/1940 married 1/19/1871 to John Elder Lowe
Elizabeth, wid. of Jacob Mikel, Mother, d. 7/29/1853 (She was nee Kelly)
John Elder Lowe, son-in-law, 12/16/1845-8/24/1917

Comments by Leonardo Andrea:
"Catherine H. Johnston, wife of David Mikel, was a daughter of Elizabeth Hemphill and Richard Johnston of Caswell Co., N. C. to Walton Co., Ga. *In the Johnston Bible David Mikel is spelled Michel...In Oglethorpe Co., Ga. in all records of land and his estate the father of David Mikel is spelled Michel...The tombstone of David Mikell and all of his sons are Michael.

One son of David Mikel was a Union soldier while all the other sons were Confederate soldiers and David Mikel was in Confederate Home Guard of Walton County...All the Union and Confederate records spell all sons as Michael...David Mikel/Michel/Michael was literate and wrote his own Bible...His father was French Michel and my idea is that David Mikel wrote his Bible as the French pronunciation sounded for Michel. The sons continued to spell their surnames as Michael as in the spelling used by clerks in Union and Confederate Armies. *The Richard Johnston Bible is in the collection of Bibles in my files....L. A."

JOHN WALKER BIBLE of Orangeburg Dist., S. C., Washington Co., Ga.

Owner: Mrs. Walter Harris
R. F. D., Warthen, Sandersville, GA
From: Leonardo Andrea Collection

John Walker was born 1/31/1777, died 8/19/1848, married 12/16/1800 to Rebekah Kelly born 9/30/1780, died 4/30/1823
Married second 7/15/1824 to Elizabeth Little born 1/19/1802 died 9/1/1880

Births of Children by first wife:

Allen Walker 10/27/1801
William H. Walker 2/5/1804
Fanna May Walker 2/23/1806
Elizabeth Hobb Walker 8/8/1808
John Daniel Walker 8/14/1813, died 6/1816
John Ivy Walker 7/26/1815, died 6/1816
Joseph Franklin Walker 7/22/1817, died 1817
Absley K. Walker, son, 3/1/1819
Henry Buleker Walker 10/6/1820
Kinchen W. Walker 5/25/1821
Virgil Green Walker 4/26/1825, died 2/11/1859

Births of Children by second wife:

Clarissa L. J. Walker 3/24/1827 married 4/3/1851 to Curtis Hooks
Freeman F. Walker 12/16/1828, died 6/22/1863 married 4/22/1857 to Nancy Hooks
Ann L. Walker 9/6/1830
Susan T. Walker 8/27/1832-8/19/1906
Martha G. Walker 9/13/1834
Wilson D. Walker 12/24/1836-3/23/1892 m. 6/12/1856 to Julia A. Mills
Mary Walker 6/15/1838
Trecey E. Walker 8/31/1840
Harriet Olivia Walker 3/12/1843-5/28/------, married 8/9/1869 to Macon Warthen
Nancy Walker born 6/5/1780
Dorset Walker born 2/22/1782
Sarah Ann Butcher born 1/17/1822
Henry Butcher born 10/6/1820

Henry Wilson Walker died 8/28/1866
Sarah Ann Palmer died 8/29/1899, aged 77 years, 9 months, 12 days
Sarah Frances Vandella Hooks born 8/20/1855

Comments by Andrea: "Copied from a photostat owned by Mrs. Sam Duggan, Sandy Run Plantation, R. F. D. #4, Moultrie, Ga.

JAMES COBB BIBLE
Owner: W. Henry Cobb II
3134 Shadow Walk Lane, Tucker, GA 30084

DEATHS:
Mary Ann Cobb July 16th 1838
James Henry Cobb Nov. 12th 1861 In the War
William Johnston Cobb November 1862 In the War
James Cobb February 24th 1876
Mary E. Cobb May 23rd 1876
Ida E. Cobb Oct. 27th 1877
Exie F. Cobb May 23rd 1883
John P. Cobb Jan. 31st 1896
Sarah Ann McConniel Nov. 15 1887
Alfert? J. Teasley June 22 1896
Mary? F. Teasley May 29th 1899
Alice A. Craft Dec. 27 1897
Allie Irwin Craft May 9, 1898
Eliza C. Cobb (Young) June 6, 1923
George V. Young ------

BIRTHS:
James Cobb Novr. 12th 1799
Mary J. Cobb May 14th 1805
Emily Cobb January 11th 1822
Ransom A. Cobb October 19th 1824
Malinda C. Cobb January 11th 1826
Frances E. Cobb January 28th 1828
Mary Ann Cobb March 1st 1830
Martha J. Cobb May 6th 1833

Sarah Ann Cobb January 11th 1836
Elmira Cobb Deer 7th 1839
James Henry Cobb Oct 21st 1842
William Johnston Cobb July 2nd 1845
John P. Cobb April 30th 1850
Eliza C. Cobb Jan 16, 1854
Mary Essie Cobb March 6th 1875
Ida Elmira Cobb Feby 4th 1877
James Alfred Cobb Sept 19th 1878
Exie Francis Cobb May 21st 1881
Neta Jane Cobb Aug. 19th 1883
William H. Cobb April 18th 1886
Ransom M. Cobb June 14th 1888
Allie Irwin Craft (no month) 21st 1897

MARRIAGES:
James Cobb and Mary J. Sullivan Dec 26th 1820
Reuben T. Wansley and Emily J. Cobb 1843
Job W. Burden and Frances E. Cobb 1845
Ransom A. Cobb and Lucy A.E. Brown
Milton McConiei and Sarah A. Cobb Dec 22nd 1857
William Phillips and Malinda C. Cobb Jany 27th 1859
Joel Crawford and Elmyra Cobb Oct 29th 1863
James F. White and Martha J. Cobb Sept 15th 1870
John P. Cobb and E.C. Teasley April 24th 1874.

(Clippings glued into the back of the Bible:)

OBITUARY - *Died February 22. 1886, Mrs. Mary Cobb wife of James Cobb, deceased, aged 8 1 years. She had been a faithful member of the Baptist Church for sixty years....*

OBITUARY - *Died on the evening of the 23d of May 1883, Exie Frances, only daughter of John P. and Eliza C. Cobb, aged two years and two days. Little Exie was the object of the most tender parental affection. The bereavement of the fond parents in this affliction is rendered more severe, being the third one which has been called away..../s/ M.J. Lewis.*

A poem dedicated to "Little Mamie Teasley", written by a devoted friend, as a memorial.

"Lines Dedicated to Mr. and Mrs. H.F. Hailey on the Death of their daughter Lizzie" dated May 30, 1889, by "an old friend".

McGEHEE BIBLE
Owner: Mrs. Pearl Baker, Thomson, Georgia

MARRIAGES:
John Megehee and Emily Carroll 1-7-1830
James Megehee and Martha [blank] 10-22-1856

Births of Children of Robert Megehee:
Mary (?) Lovler born 11-8-1867
Ida Isebell 4-20-1870
John M. ?-29-1872
William 4-16-1873
Sarah 4-18-1879
Georgian 8-6-1858
James Lee 7-26-1862

Births of Children of John Megehee:
William 5-20-1831
*James 4-9-1833
**Michael 3-1-1835
Elizabeth Louisa 12-27-1836
John 9-29-1838
Nancy 11-29-1844
Robert 10-29-1845
Jasper 10-29-1849
Georgia 1-12-1851
Virginia 8-16-1854

Births of Children of Michael Megehee:
Mary Jane 8-9-1862
John, son of Michael and Jane Megehee. 10-21-1843
Mary L. Megehee 11-8-1867

DEATHS:
John Megehee senior was bornd the 21st November 1772 and died the 2 day of August 1845
Elizabeth Megehee 23 December 1858
William Megehee 17 October 1857

John Megehee 9 January 1861
Michael Megehee was born the 26th October 1804 died the 12 of June 1844
James R Lee Megehee was borned the 26th of July 1862
An infant of James Megehee was borned the 26 of November
Georgia Ann Megehee died 6 April 1860 age 1 yer 8 months

Infant of James Megehee departed this life 11 January 1861, age 6 weeks
John Megehee was born --/4/1802
Michael Megehee was borned October 1804
Betty was borned November 25 1862

*James Megehee was wounded on 2 July 1862 and lived about six weeks.
**Michael Megehee was wounded 19 Oct 1864 and was reported dead
Michael Megehee, Sr., married Jane Jenkins 6-28-1841.

JEREMIAH FRANKLIN of N. C., Franklin Co., Ga., Dallas Co., AL
Copy from: Ms. Helen Franklin Starnes, Route 1, Box 332, Oakwood, TX 75855, Published Family Puzzlers, No. 1032

Jeremiah Franklin, son of Bernard Franklin and Mary, his wife, was born 9/2/1754
Barnard Franklin, Jur. Was Born 4/28.1756
Jesse Franklin Was Born 1758 March ye 3d
Jesse Franklin died 1759 May ye 14th Day
Betty Franklin Was Born 1762 March ye Ioth
Abner Franklin Was Born 1764 April ye 28th
Shadrach Franklin Was Born 1769 April ye 20th
Mary Franklin Was Born 1771 May ye 14th
Meshach Franklin Was Born 1773 Sept. 17th?
Abednego Franklin Was Born 1774? May? 29th?
Sythea Cleveland Daughter of Reubin Cleveland and Elizabeth His Wife was Born in the Year of our Lord 1776? Febry? ?
Bernard Franklin Senr. born 1731 May 26
Bern'd Franklin died January the 2 1828
Shadrach Franklin born 20th April 1769
Judith Franklin born 27th Feby. 1762
Bernard Franklin born 22nd Sept. 1788

Sarah Franklin born 20 Novr. 1789
Lucinda Franklin born 4th August 1793
Mary H. Franklin born 5th October 1794
Patsey Franklin born 18th Augst. 1797
John T. Franklin born 4th Jan'y 1799
Benjamin Franklin born 9th May 1800
Wylie Franklin born 25 Dec. 1801
Bryson Franklin born 24th Augst. 1803
Bryson Franklin Died 10th Jany 1804
Betsy Franklin born 26th March 1805
Benjamin Franklin died 28th July 1824
Judith Franklin died 28th September 1850
Ambrose Johnson born 14th May 1793
Ambrose Johnson died 13th June 1858.

JAMES CALHOUN BIBLE of Washington and Baker Co.'s, Ga.
Owner: Miss Charlotte Bush, Colquitt, GA

MARRIAGES:
James Calhoun to Elefair Metts 12/20/1840 by G. Dickin, Justice of Peace, Washington Co., Ga. Wits: Wright Metts, William Calhoun
James Wright Calhoun and Louise Sylvania Adams were married November 4th 1866

BIRTHS:
James McCoy Calhoun, son of James and Sarah Calhoun, born July 28th 1821 at Augusta, Ga.
Elefair Metts, dau. of Wright and Martha Elizabeth Metts, born August 5th 1820, Washington Co., Georgia
Nancy Medford Calhoun, daughter of James and Elefair Calhoun, born October 6th 1841 at Washington County, Georgia
Jane Catherine Calhoun, daughter of James and Elefair Calhoun, born December 2nd 1842 at Washington County, Georgia
James Wright Calhoun, son of James & Elefair Calhoun, b. Sept 25th 1844
Martha Vashti Calhoun, born Febrary 18th 1846
Mary Elizabeth Calhoun born April 15, 1848
Virginia Ellen Calhoun born January 28, 1950
Elvira Covender Calhoun born October 22, 1851
Saluda Anna Calhoun born April 12, 1853

Sarah Ann Calhoun born July 11th, 1855
Thomas Wade Calhoun born September 6th 1858
Georgia Ella Calhoun born September 6th 1868
Caroline Blackshear Calhoun born Febrary 23, 1861
Alice Capitola Calhoun born September 30th, 1862

DEATHS:
Nancy Medford Calhoun died October 6th, 1841
Jane Catherine Calhoun died September 8th, 1846
Mary Elizabeth Calhoun died October 22, 1851
Thomas Wade Calhoun died November 15, 1858
My devoted wife Elefair Calhoun died on this day of Our Lord October 4th in the year Eighteen Hundred Seventh Three. May she rest in peace forever.
James M. Calhoun died at his home February 2, 1883
Elvira Ray died December 19, 1886
Georgia Ella Riley died January 13, 1891
Sarah Ann Riley died December 1, 1912
James Wright Calhoun died November 30, 1927
Alice Capitola Bush died Colquitt, Georgia, November 7, 1929.

SIDON H. HARRIS BIBLE of Burke and Madison Co.'s, Ga.
Owner: Mrs. Gary Bronson
1518 Weeks Lane, Ft. Smith, AR 72903

MARRIAGES:
Sidon H. Harris to Amanda Caroline Atkinson 8/9/1842
Samuel Washington Harris to Rachel Jane Wilson 2/28/1866

BIRTHS:
Samuel Washington Atkinson 3/5/1797
Nancy Atkinson 3/12/1792
Sidon H. Harris 11/2/1820
Amanda Caroline Atkinson 2/26/1822
Samuel Washington Harris 11/29/1843
Rachel Jane Wilson 10/16/1848
----Clay Harris 8/1/1846
Nancy Margarit Harris 8/1/1846

Thomas Jefferson Harris 4/6/1848
William Alfred Jones Harris 5/27/1850
Melinda Harriet Harris 3/24/1852
Wesley Smith Harris 9/23/1854
John Applewhite Harris 11/22/1856
Minor Harris 12/9/1858

FREDERICK SCHUMPERT BIBLE, Newberry Co., SC & Hartwell, Ga.
Owner: Ophelia C. Norris, Hartwell, GA (1932)
From: Leonardo Andrea Collection

Frederick Schumpert 11/23/1783-1/28/1846 married 3/19/1805 to
Mary Kinard 12/18/1787-12/29/1873
Catherana Schumpert, dau., b. 1/28/1806 m.1/4/1827 Bailey Conwill
Jacob Schumpert, son, born 10/10/1807 m. 4/1/1834 to Harriet Abney
Elizabeth Schumpert, dau., b.11/3/1809 Newberry Co., SC 4/16/1854
William K. Schumpert, son, born 4/1/1811, died in MS 4/16/1851
married 18-- to Catherine Long
Magdena Schumpert, daughter, born 4/14/1813, died Edgefield Co., SC.
1/9/1903 married 10/21/1830 to Jacob Long
Amos Schumpert, son, b.11/19/1815, d. Americus, Ga. 6/9/1902 m.
2/24/1839 to Eliza Gray
Rhoda Schumpert, daughter, born 3/22/1818, died Newberry, S. C.
4/30/1835 married 3/13/1834 to Robert Y. Brown
Sarah Schumpert, daughter, born 2/6/1820, died Moreland, Ga.
2/13/1903, married 11/2/1837 James Cureton;moved to Coweta Co., Ga.
John Frederick Schumpert, son, born 18---, died 11/27/1854, married
10/20/1853 to Rachel Welch
Elisha K. Schumpert, son, born 18---, died 11/27/1854 married
10/20/1853 to Rachel Welch
Elisha K. Schumpert, son, born 18---, died 9/10/1877 married 18--- to
_____ Morgan, married 18--, to Martha Stone

Comments by Andrea:
"Mary, wife of Frederick Schumpert, was a daughter of a Revolutionary Soldier from Newberry Co., S. C. Named Michael Kinard and his wife, Catherine Swittenberg. Frederick Schumpert is a son of Peter Schumpert and his wife, Eliza Schaffer and a grandson of Jacob Schumpert and his wife, Anna Christian...immigrants from Germany."

LEONARD FORSYTH GREER BIBLE of Monroe Co., Ga.
Owner: Mrs. J. G. Sherrer, 39 Parkwood, Charleston, S. C.

Holy Bible, Rochester, NY, published by Wanzer, Foote and Co. 1851

MARRIAGES:
Leonard Forsyth Greer to Martha Caroline Thrasher 2/4/1852
Leonard P. Greer to Addie E. Card 11/30/1880 in Jones Co., Ga. By Rev. George Bonner
David H. Sawyer to Leanna Greer
Sallie Clyde Greer to Frand Pierce Heifner 3/27/1883 in Oxford, AL.
Gussie M. Greer to William T. Lee 11/6/1833 in Oxford, AL

BIRTHS:
Leonard Forsyth Greer the 2nd 5/10/1828
Martha Caroline Thrasher Greer 3/11/1837
Elizabeth Leanna Moore Greer 3/7/1853
Augusta Matella Greer 6/4/185---
Thadeous Ethelbert Greer 3/18/1857
Sallie Clyde Greer 9/17/1861
Leonard Forsyth Greer the 3rd 8/24/1863
Frank Pierce Heifner 8/18/1890 in Anniston, Alabama

DEATHS:
Martha C. Greer 9/1/1863
Leonard F. Greer the 2nd 12/14/1896 in Atlanta, Ga.

BIRTHS:
Mary Leonard Heifner 1/9/1884
Willa Virginius Heifner 5/20/1886
Lillie Adaline Heifner 10/20/1887
Frank Pierce Heifner, Jr. 8/18/1890
Martha Clyde Heifner 8/24/1898

DEATHS:
Martha Thrasher Greer 9/1/1863
Leonard Forsyth Greer the 3rd 12/14/1896
Sallie Clyde Heifner 5/15/1922
Martha Clyde Heifner 6/2/1900

Frank Pierce Heifner, Jr. 8/17/1911
Sallie O. Greer Heifner 5/13/1922
Mary Leonard Hardwick 1/1/1952
Willa V. Markley 11/5/1959

ELIZABETH SOPHIA SPANN NICHOLSON BIBLE
Owner: Mrs. Juanita S. Brightwell
1307 Hancock Drive, Americus, GA 31709

Melson Nicholson married 1/22/1880
James J. Nicholson b. 8/7/1838
Ellona Mildred Nicholson and Green Whiddon Tanner m. 9/26/1931
Martha Jane John Nicholson b. 1/8/1819
N. N. Nicholson b. 1811
Ellona Mildred N. Tanner d. 10/21/1961
Martin L. Nicholson b. 9/16/1840
D. M. Nicholson b. 3/20/1848
C. R. Nicholson b. 1/3/1858
Mr. L. Nicholson
Miss L. M. Nicholson b. 2/26/1862
Elizabeth S. Nicholson b. 5/22/1858
Mamie Ivera Nicholson b. 3/25/1883
Ellona Mildred Nicholson b. 10/28/1884
William Louther Nicholson b. 5/6/1886
Eula May Nicholson b. 5/1/1888
Vernard Nathaniel Nicholson b. 9/27/1889
Jessie Remous Nicholson b. 2/23/1891
Bertha Lillian Nicholson b. 1/12/1893
N. N. Nicholson d. 7/--/1891
Martha Jane John Nicholson d. 10/16/1869
Miss L. R. Nicholson d. 1/30/1862
W. J. Nicholson d. 9/6/1862
Miss L. M. Nicholson d. 1/12/1866
Vernard Nathaniel Nicholson d. 11/5/1890
Luther Nicholson
Bertha Lillian Nicholson d. 6/26/1893
D. M. Nicholson d. 9/23/1904
Elizabeth S. Nicholson d. 2/18/1926
Jesse R. Nicholson d. 4/20/1930
Eula May Nicholson Farmer d. 2/4/1949

MERCK BIBLE
Owner: Mrs. Howard Mintz
Maysville, GA 30558

J. R. Mitchell was married 1/25/1874 to Miss Annie LeMaster
William E. Merk b. 8/20/1869 and was hurt 2nd day of Christmas 1873
M. J. Patrick was ---------------

Ages of George Marks and Elizabeth children:
Nancy Mark b. 8/9/1821
Andy Mark b. 2/25/1823
Elizabeth Mark b. 4/25/1828
George Elbe and -----------------
Andria Mark b. 5/27/1832
Mary Jane b. 1 first 1834
Henry Merk b. 5/15/1826
Elizabeth Merk b.-----------------
Catherine Mark b.---------------(1824 written underneath)

JAMES STRICKLAND BIBLE
Published in a periodical, "Our Heritage"
and in Vol. 6, No. 2, "Strickland Scene"
Owner: Mrs. Raymond Palmer Whitfield
207 East Mulberry, San Antonio, TX 78212

Bible published by G. Lane and P. P. Sandford for the Methodist Episcopal Church, New York, 1841

MARRIAGES:
James and Elizabeth Strickland 10/30/1836
Augustus R. Newsome to Victoria O. Newsome 8/17/1858
James and Ann Jane Strickland 6/23/1859
James Strickland to Mary E. Bennett 8/25/1846
A. P. Watson and Elizabeth D. Strickland 8/28/1873
Zacary Taylor and Jennie Strickland 2/21/1878
J. M. Green and Sarah L. Strickland 6/20/1889

R. C. Roos and Mary Strickland 12/27/1893
Marshall Moreland and Annie Strickland 7/3/1898
Andrew Pickens Watson, Jr. and Lelia Perkins 2/25/1903
BIRTHS:
James Strickland, son of Benjamin and Elizabeth Strickland, 6/13/1813
Elizabeth B. Strickland, dau. of William and Elizabeth Wall, 1/4/1817
William B. Strickland, son of James & Elizabeth B. Strickland, 10/6/1838
Obedience Victoria Strickland, dau of Jas & Elizabeth B. Strickland, 1/28/1841
James Franklin Strickland, son of Jas & Elizabeth B. Strickland, 10/29/1849
Elizabeth Dillon, daughter of James Strickland and Elizabeth, 7/4/1851
Stephen A. D. Strickland, son of Elizabeth B. & Jas Strickland,8/4/1854
Ann Jane Strickland, dau. of Jeremiah and Nancy Fortenberry, 2/7/1831
Talitha Jane Strickland, daughter of James and Jane Strickland, 6/9/1860
Sarah Louisa Strickland 2/3/1870
Mary Elizabeth Strickland 7/4/1872
Annie Mariah Strickland 10/19/1874
Peter Larkin Strickland 10/3/1861, son of James and Jane Strickland
James Bennett Strickland 7/26/1865
Elizabeth Lavinia Newsome, daughter of Augustus R. Newsome and Obedience Victoria Newsome, 9/13/1862
Joe S. Newsome 3/4/1864
Mary M. Watson, dau. of Elizabeth and Andrew Watson, 11/28/1874
Andrew Pickens Watson, son of Elizabeth & Andrew P. b. 9/27/1876
James Herman Lenoir, son of Johnnie & Sallie Lenoir b. 9/10/1876
Willie Charleton Taylor was born July 23, 1879
Jennie Belle Taylor was born June 16th, 1881
Mary Strickland Taylor was born Dec. 10, 1887
Zachary Taylor was born Oct. 2nd, 1890
Annie Lee Green was born Dec. Ist, 1890
James Bennett Taylor was born August 3, 1892
Louise Green was born Feb. 9th, 1893
Belle Green was born Nov. 20, 1894
Sarah Green was born Oct. 21, 1896
Charles Roos was born March 27, 1897
Gray Green was born Aug. 11, 1899
Howard Green was born July 1, 1901
Mary Bennett Roos was born June 13, 1902

Arthur Green was born Apr. 29, 1904
Jane Waverly Green was born Sept. 1, 1908
Mary Moreland was born Oct. 30, 1902
Sallie Green Moreland was born Aug. 6th, 1904
Margaret Moreland was born 1906
Robert Moreland was born July 1910
Harry Perkins Watson, son of Andrew F. Jr. & Lelia, b. July 2nd 1904
Elizabeth Strickland Watson, dau. of Andre P. Jr. & Lelia b. 4/10/1906
Baptisms:
James Strickland was Baptized February the 27th 1842
Elizabeth B. Strickland was Baptized June the 10th, 1842
William B. Strickland was Baptized Juce 10th 1842
Obedience V. Strickland was Baptized June 10th, 1842
James F. Strickland was Baptized May the 13th, 1847
Elizabeth D. Strickland was Baptized May 23rd, 1852
Stephen Arnold Douglas Strickland was Baptized September 3rd, 1855
Lizzie L. Newsome was emersed June 14th, 1877
Jennie Strickland was Baptized June 14th, 1877
DEATHS:
Elizabeth B. Strickland, the wife of James Strickland died 3/11/1858
Wm. Benjamine Strickland Departed this life July 28th, 1859
Ann Jane Strickland, the wife of James Strickland died 9/13/1862
Peter Larkin Strickland departed this life August 31st, 1863
James F. Strickland departed this life Dec. 21st, 1863
Victoria Obedience Newsome departed this life Nov. 25, 1865
James Bennett Strickland died Jan. 27th, 1867
Jas. Strickland departed this life May 15th, 1874
Mary Eliza Strickland, wife of James Strickland, d. March 21st, 1907 Yoakum, Texas
Jane Waverly Green died on Aug. 7, 1912 at Cuero, Texas
Sallie L. Strickland Green (Mrs. John M. Green) died 11/16/1932
Sarah Green died 2/22/1921
Helen Roos died 1895
Robert C. Roos died 1933
Mrs. Robert C. Roos died 1942
John M. Green died 8/30/1939
Marshall Moreland died 1934
Annie M. Strickland Moreland died 1951
Gray Green Campbell died 7/29/1943

John Green Ellzey, son of Belle Green Ellzey and M. P. Ellzey, died 8/17/1944 in the European Theater War, 2nd Lt. 9th Inf. Division AUS.

JOSEPH EATON BIBLE
G. W. Eaton Walhalla through, J. K. Mendenhall, Greenville, S. C. (1962)

BIRTHS:
Joseph Eaton 7/2/1802
Lewis Eaton 7/22/1804
Dorcas A. Eaton 12/31/1808
Mary Eaton 5/24/1814
Mary M. Eaton 2/12/1834
James M. Eaton 10/20/1835
Elizabeth A. Eaton 7/9/1837
Nancy E. Eaton 10/21/1839
Eleanor C. Eaton 11/11/1841
Sarah F. Eaton 3/26/1843
John L. Eaton 8/6/1845
Susan E. Eaton 7/27/1847
Martha L. Y. Eaton 6/14/1848
George W. D. Eaton 7/25/1849
William H. Eaton 1/6/1851

LITTLETON CLEAVELAND EDWARDS BIBLE
Owner: Mrs. George E. Simmons
2274 Sharon Avenue, Charlotte, N. C. (1960)

Littleton Cleaveland Edwards born 2/1812
Narcissa Brooke Edwards born 3/15/1817 and married to Littleton C. Edwards 3/31/1836

BIRTHS:
Nancy Eveline Edwards 4/17/1837
Islan William Edwards 11/8/1838
Mary Amanda Edwards 3/16/1840
Alfred Edwards 12/30/1841
Sarah Florence Edwards 5/17/1843
Alfred Edwards was married his 2nd wife, Cordelia Hanes in 1888

MARRIAGES:
Littleton C. Edwards to Narcissa Brooke 3/31/1836 (our father and mother)
Nancy E. Edwards to Willburn Petree 10/8/1854
Mary Amanda Edwards to William George March or April 1859
Sarah T. Edwards to ?(smudged) Waray Brooke 3/1865
Alfred Edwards to Sousan R. Wesley 1867
Islan W. Edwards to Amanda Chandler nee McCleskan, a widow, 2/20/1898? (Smudged)
Nancy Evoline Edwards Petree to Robert House? McMillan 4/9/1889, being 52 years of age and he 60 years of age.

BIRTHS:
William Theodore Petree 9/29/1834
Nancy Eveline Edwards Petree (smudged)
John Charles Petree 1/1856 (smudged)
Villa?_____Petree 1/1/1852 or 1858
_____? 1860

William T. Petree died 9/4/1860
Villa V. Petree died 2/8/1867
Littleton Cleaveland Edwards died 9/19/1843
Narcissa Edwards died 6/2/1894
They married 3/31/1836

Julia Francis Petree married to Agustus Lovely Rogers 3/31/1880
John C. Petree married to Elizabet J. Smith 11/14/1883

ANTHONY DE WOLF BIBLE
Owner: Janice McKinnan
P. O. Box 285, Cuthbert, GA 31740 (1980)

Parents Names:

Anthony DeWolf born 12/9/1843
Wife: Agness DeWolf born 1/30/1844
Married 12/25/1866

Childrens Names: (Births)
Lyllian Jane DeWolfe 10/24/1862
William Gorden DeWolfe 7/25/1865
Charles Byron 8/5/1871
Everd Warden 3/12/1874
Milton Milburne 7/17/1878
Corrie May 2/17/1882
Mossen Clark 12/4/1883
George V. DeWolfe 12/30/1885
Ford W. DeWolfe 10/9/1888
Borned to Mossen Clark DeWolfe and Annie Jordan DeWolfe, Sara Agnes DeWolfe, 2/13/1920

MARRIAGES:
William G. DeWolfe 10/4/1893
Lyllian J. DeWolfe 12/25/1906
Mossen C. DeWolfe 5/21/1913
Annie B. Jordan

DEATHS:
Everd Warden 12/8/1882
Charles Byron 12/11/1882
Milton Milborn 12/11/1882
Corra May 12/19/1882
Anthony DeWolfe 10/7/1894
William Gordon DeWolfe 2/23/1908
Lyllian Jane Armstrong 4/17/1951
Mossen Clarke DeWolfe 3/7/1954

DAVID DAY BIBLE
Owner: Raymond Roberts
Brookhaven, MS

"David and Mary Johnson Day were both born in the State of Georgia. They married in Clarke Co., Ga. 11/22/1807. With the possible exception of the first child, the children were born in the State of Mississippi. Mary Johnson was a daughter of Caleb Johnson who immigrated to Amite Co., Miss., served in the Minute Militia from the State of Georgia in the American Revolution, and was born in Chester Co., Pennsylvania."

"The following "Family Record" was printed by the request of Bluford B. Day and he had it framed. This record hung on a wall of the home of my aunt, Mrs. Ida Belle Price Smith for many years. Bluford B. Day willed all of his land and possessions to her....Mrs. Edwina Price."

David Day was born 4/20/1787
Mary Johnson, wife of David Day, was born 5/15/1787
Mary Day, daughter of David and Mary Day, was born 3/20/1809
Frances A. Day, daughter of David and Mary Day, was born 2/7/1811
Lemenda K. Day, daughter of David and Mary Day, born 11/22/1812
Saletha R. Day, daughter of David and Mary Day, was born 11/14/1814
Aaron B. Day, son of David and Mary Day, was born 1/14/1817
Zilpha Day, daughter of David and Mary Day, was born 1/6/1819
Martha Ann Day, daughter of David and Mary Day, born 12/24/1821
Eliza Day, daughter of David and Mary Day, was born 8/17/1824
Emily Day, daughter of David and Mary Day, was born 6/21/1826
Bluford B. Day, son of David and Mary Day, was born 12/29/1828
Adaline Day, daughter of David and Mary Day, was born 12/30/1832

WILLIAM THOMAS DENHAM BIBLE
Owner: Mrs. Betty Denham Vicknair

BIRTHS:
Josiah C. Denham 9/15/1821
Elizabeth Jane Singleton 4/22/1827
Nicy Ann F. Denham, oldest child of J. C. and E. J. Denham, 12/27/1846
Mary Elizabeth Denham, daughter of J. C. and E. J. Denham, 4/24/1848
Mariah Louisa Denham, daughter of J. C. and E. J. Denham, 11/27/1850
William Thomas Denham, son of J. C. and E. J. Denham, 7/28/1852
Josiah Singleton Denham 4/12/1863
Louisa Atlilla Fudge 2/16/1853
Guy Otto Denham 11/10/1875
William Edwin Denham 12/8/1877
Maggie May Denham 5/9/1880
Paul Denham 7/28/1883
Oscar Fudge Denham 3/17/1886
Leroy Denham 2/13/1888
Minnie Elizaabeth Denham 3/29/1895
Ruth Denham 4/12/1892
Alva David Denham 5/13/1894
Earnest Willie Denham 7/24/1897

JOHN WESLEY COLQUITT BIBLE of Pike Co.
Owner: Miss Sara Colquitt, Barnesville, GA

This certifies that The Rite of Holy Matrimony was celebrated between John W. Colquitt of Upson Co., Ga., and Rebecca E. Stafford of Pike Co., Ga. on the 21st of Dec; 1869 at the residence of the bride's father by Rev. Wesley F. Smith.
John W. Colquitt was born July 20th 1849
Rebecca E. Colquitt was born Feb. 26th 1854
Wesley F. Colquitt was born Jan. 26th 1871
Frances Antionette Colquitt was born Oct. 29th 1872
Franklin A. Colquitt was born Dec. 24th 1876
James L. Colquitt was born April 15th 1878
Mary Emma Colquitt was born March 3rd 1883
Edward G. Colquitt was born April 19th 188~.
Addie May Colquitt was born March ?st 1886
Otis Lindsey Colquitt was born July 14th 1888
Florence Odessa Colquitt was born Aug. 27th 1890
John Marvin Colquitt was born Oct. 6th 1895
Paul Gibson Colquitt was born May 2nd 1898
Sarah Anna Colquitt was born June 8th 1900
Pierce Kemp Colquitt was born April 2nd 1904.
Charlie Glen Colquitt was born July 21st 1906
Albert Candler Colquitt was born Sept. 26th 1909
MARRIAGES:
John W. Colquitt and Robecca E. Stafford were married Dec. 21st 1869
Wesley F. Colquitt et Octavia C. ColLier were married July 12th 1892
John W. Colquitt and Alice E. Gibson were married July 12th 1894
George W. Moore and Frances A. Colquitt were married Jan. 31st 1894
DEATHS:
Mary Emma Colquitt died April 10th 1883
Edward Gray Colquitt died Sept. 11th 1885
Rebecca E. Colquitt died Aug. 17th 1892
Florence Odessa Freeman died Dec. 22,1912
John Marvin Colquitt; died Oct. 10, 1918
Alice E. Colquitt died Aug. 19, 1911
Franklin A. Colquitt died Feb. 25, 1933
John Wesley Colquitt died Sept. 20, 1935
Wesley F. Colquitt died Feb. 10, 1936
Sara Frances Colquitt died Feb. 27,1936

JOHN COLLEY BIBLE

BIRTHS:
John Colley 9/14/1752
Gabriel Colley 2/23/1782
Francis Colley 2/20/1785
Eliza Colley 5/12/1788
Mary Colley 5/26/1790
Nancy Colley 1/2/1792
Spain Colley 1/22/1794
Louisa Colley 9/23/1801
Lieusinday E. Tindall 4/26/1809
Demaris Goolsbe 4/25/1814
Sarah Colley, daughter, was born 6/4/1763
John C. Fanning 1/19/1821
Mary Fanning 7/5/1824
Nancy Fanning 3/9/1827
Martha Fanning 2/1/1829
Webster Fanning 3/25/1831
Parks Fanning 3/9/1833
Sabrina Ellen Fanning 13th July or August 1835
Charles Ann Fanning 9/23/1838
Victoria A. Fanning 11/16/1840
Bryan Fanning 10/18/1842
Frances Fanning 1/6/1845
Samuel D. Fanning 7/4/1862
Alace Estelle Fanning 4/23/1864

DEATHS:
Parks Fanning 8/4/1835
Frances Fanning 10/1/1846
Abina Victoria Fanning 12/4/1846
Charles Ann Fanning 12/28/1850
Mrs. Louisa Fanning 10/1/1853
Welcome Fanning born 7/14/1799, died 10/3/1873
William S. Brown 1/16/1855?
Rev. A. J. Orr 7/12/1860
John C. Fanning 4/19/1870
Sarah F. Fanning 11/30/1869

DEATHS:
Webster Fanning 4/24/1903
I. A. Brown 1/10/1903
Mary P. Johnson 3/29/1904
Sabrina Ellen Fanning Brown 6/23/1905
Nimrod Colley
Lieusinday Colley
Lewis Colley
John Colley 6/9/1815
Sarah Colley 12/21/1833
Thomas B. Tindall 20th or 27th of Nov. 1809

JAMES McDANIEL BIBLE
Owner: Jim Edwards, P. O. Box 32631, Decatur, GA 30032 (1972)

BIRTHS:
James McDaniel 1/20/1812, baptised 8/1832
Elvina C. Johnston 3/6/1813, baptised 9/26/1840
John J. McDaniel 7/24/1831
Milda McDaniel 4/8/1833
William L. McDaniel 4/6/1835
Mary L. McDaniel 7/15/1837
Sarah S. McDaniel 4/2/1839
Daniel R. McDaniel 2/19/1841
Elizabeth E. McDaniel 6/1/1843
James W. McDaniel 10/29/1845
Imand C. McDaniel 3/8/1848
Eli C. McDaniel 8/14/1850
Darling E. McDaniel 8/16/1853

MARRIAGES:
James McDaniel to Elvina B. Johnston 7/22/1830
John J. McDaniel to Martha Wills 10/27/1855
Mary L. McDaniel to W. S. Seaton 12/5/1858
Daniel R. McDaniel to Virginia Minor 1/1/1865
Elizabeth E. McDaniel to John B. Williams 8/3/1865
Sarah S. J. McDaniel to John A. Jordan 8/30/1866

James W. McDaniel to Marget Nash 9/9/1866
Imanda C. McDaniel to John M. Arnold 12/12/1867
Eli C. McDaniel to Mary E. L. Shell 8/3/1871
Milda McDaniel to James C. Carroll 8/16/1887

DEATHS:
Elvina B. McDaniel 10/28/1880
William L. McDaniel 4/29/1841
Darling E. McDaniel 8/7/1862
James McDaniel 11/5/1894
William McDaniel, Sr. 9/29/1848
Sarah McDaniel, Sr. 11/11/1862

CHARLES DEVEREUX BIBLE of Baldwin and Hancock Co.'s

"Copied from an old family Bible"

MARRIAGES:
Charles Devereux and Nancy Woods in Virginia 10/7/1776
Elizabeth Devereux and Samson S. Steele 10/18/1784
Samuel M. Devereux and Anna Loyd Dixon about 1820

BIRTHS:
Elizabeth Devereux in Virginia 12/7/1767
William Devereux in Virginia 3/15/1769
James Devereux in Virginia 10/7/1771
Samuel M. Devereux 10/7/1773
Archibald Devereux 8/20/1775
John Devereux 9/7/1777
Nancy Devereux 11/16/1779
Charles Devereux, Jr. 3/7/1782

DEATHS:
Elizabeth Devereux Steel in Baldwin Co., Ga. 10/22/1830
Samuel M. Devereux at Devereux, in Hancock Co., Ga. 10/23/1840

THOMAS ELKINS BIBLE
Owner: Miss Irene Arden
404 Hilldale Drive, Decatur, GA (1963)

MARRIAGES:
Thomas Elkins to Ann Simson 10/1808
Thomas Elkins to Sarah Powers 8/22/1811
Thomas Elkins to Moriah P. Tondee Patterson 10/14/1830
Moselle Elkins to Robert H. Bourquins 10/13/1831
Julia Elkins to Ebenezar Jenckes 7/21/1836
Charles C. Elkins to Ann E. Caarle 11/11/1857
L. L. Elkins to Ellis Card 4/5/1853
Sarah E. Elkins to Kollock Harrison 11/4/1849
Selina V. Elkins to Morgan Rawls 10/22/1851
Caroline M. Elkins to James G. Watts 5/31/1855

BIRTHS:
Thomas Elkins 10/25/1783
Sarah Powers 5/3/1793

Simson Elkins 7/1809, son of Thomas Elkins and Ann, his wife.
Moselle Elkins 1/10/1814, daughter of Thomas Elkins and Sarah, his wife.
Phares N. Elkins 4/1/1815, son of Thomas and Sarah, his wife.
Julia Elkins 10/3/1816, daughter of Thomas and Sarah, his wife.

DEATHS:
Ann Elkins, wife of Thomas Elkins, 11/1809
Sarah Elkins, wife of Thomas Elkins, 12/29/1829
Wiley Elkins, son of Thomas and Sarah, his wife, 2/3/1824
Augustus R. Elkins, son of Thomas and Moriah, his wife, 9/12/1842
Phares Nepolian Elkins, son of Thomas Elkins and Sarah, his wife, 9/27/1846

BIRTHS:
Wiley Elkins, son of Thomas and Sarah, his wife, 6/12/1818
Lydia Ann Elkins, daughter of Thomas and Sarah, his wife, 1/6/1821
Thomas P. Elkins, son of Thomas and Sarah, his wife, 10/16/1822

BIRTHS:
Sarah E. Elkins, daughter of Thomas and Sarah, his wife, 5/7/1829
Caroline M. Elkins, daughter of Thomas and Moriah, his wife, 12/12/1831

DEATHS:
Thomas Elkins 2/19/1854
Maria P. Tondee Elkins, wife of Thomas Elkins, 2/17/1878
Julia Jencks 5/20/1877
Thomas P. Elkins 6/1/1886
Caroline M. Watts 2/19/1887
Selina V. Rawls 6/22/1891

BIRTHS:
Selina V. Elkins, daughter of Thomas and Moriah, his wife, 2/27/1833
Charles C. Elkins, son of Thomas and Moriah, his wife, 5/20/1835
Leander L. Elkins, son of Thomas and Moriah, his wife, 1/10/1837
Augustus R. Elkins, son of Thomas and Moriah, his wife, 5/23/1839

Maria P. Tondee 11/5/1797
Ann E. Carle 5/14/1839

DEATHS:
Charles C. Elkins 11/25/1863, killed in war at Lookout Mountain
Sarah E. Harrison, daughter of Thomas Elkins, 6/10/1858. She died in Texas.
Leander L. Elkins 10/29/1904 at St. Augustine, FL, the house of Dr. L. C. Elkins, his son.

Morgan Rawls was born 6/29/1829, died 10/18/1906

JOHN SHERWOOD THOMAS BIBLE of Baldwin Co.
Owner: John Greenberry Thomas
Decatur, GA

Mary New (or Neuse) Thomas was born 5/10/1831 near Milledgeville, Ga.
John Greenberry Thomas was born 3/28/1833 in Milledgeville
Eliza Neyle Thomas was born 8/7/1834 at Clifton
Bryan Morel Thomas was born 5/8/1836 at Clifton

Mary Bryan Neyle and John T. Thomas were married 6/24/183-- in Christ Church, Savannah, by the Rev. Mr. Goforth.

Elizabeth Neyle Thomas entries in the hand of Anna Drayton (Mrs. John Greenberry Thomas), died 4/16/1910 Milledgeville.

BIRTHS:
In Dooly Co., Ga. On 11/30/1866 Catharine Drayton Thomas.
In Dooly Co. On 3/31/1868 Edith Carson Thomas
In Dooly Co. On 12/10/1870 Bessie Neyle Thomas
M6/21/1873 John G. Thomas, Jr.
In Midway 9/14/1876 Martha Gadsden Thomas
In Scottsboro, Ga. 10/28/1880 Thomas F. Drayton Thomas

MARRIAGES:
In Midway, Baldwin Co., Ga. 12/7/1864 John G. Thomas, elder son of J. S. Thomas to Anna M., eldest daughter of Thomas F. Drayton of S. C.

DEATHS:
In Dooly Co. 9/25/1867 Catharine Drayton Thomas
In Midway on 9/12/1881 Edith Carson Thomas

JOHN HARRISON BIBLE
Owner: Mrs. J. E. Harrison
1402 E. 40th Street, Savannah, GA 31404

BIRTHS:
Mildred Harrison, daughter of John Harrison and Ann ----9/2/1776
Benjamin Harrison 10/30/1778
Henry Harrison 2/10/1781
The twins 2/4/1783
Martha Harrison 9/16/1784
Nathaniel Harrison 4/5/1787
Emelers Harrison 10/15/1789
Margaret Harrison 2/2/1792
John Harrison 8/26/1794
Temperance Harrison 2/20/1797
James Harrison 8/31/1799

Written at bottom of page:
"Benjamin Harrison, signer of Declaration of Independence James Harrison and others."
Harrison Allmand was married to Louisa Kule 12/1/1785

BIRTHS: (corner torn off of page)
----------------1/12/1703
----------------9/15/1705
----------------10/30/1707
----------------1/21/1710
Mildred Harrison 10/15/1713
Susana Harrison 5/2/1716
John Harrison 9/5/1718
Ann Harrison 8/10/1720
Henry Harrison 5/1/1723
Sarah Harrison, daughter of William Harrison and Mary, his wife, born 9/23/1725
Mary Harrison born 2/14/1729
Benjamin Harrison born 10/24/1730
William Harrison born 4/29/1733
Ann Harrison born 4/3/1735

Mildred Harrison born 10/19/1738
Elizabeth Harrison born 12/24/1740
Henry Harrison born 1/13/1742
Lucy Harrison born 2/19/1745
John Harrison born 8/11/1750

Fitt, a negro, was born 12/1759
Tom, a negro, was born 10/1759
Venus, a negro, was born 8/1767

Benjamin M. Roberts was married to Patsey Mc------- 5/13/1802
Caroline A. Roberts, daughter of Benjamin H. Roberts and Patsy, his wife, born 4/4/180--
William H. Roberts, son of Benjamin H. Roberts and Patsey, his wife, was born 5/18/---

BENJAMIN SLATON DICKINSON BIBLE of Prattville, Alabama and Atlanta, Ga.
Owner: Mrs. C. R. Cannon
4779 Adams Road, Chamblee, GA 30341 (1973)
Purchased in a book store

Parents:

Benjamin Slaton Dickinson born 12/22/1846 in Jefferson Co., Alabama
Sarah J. Ledbetter born 5/28/1849 in Talladega Co., Alabama

BIRTHS:
Benjamin Roburtus Dickinson 10/12/1870 in Prattville, Alabama
Craven Payton Dickinson 8/15/1872 in Prattville, Alabama
Martha Elizabeth Dickinson 4/6/1874 in Prattville, Alabama
Sarah Dickinson 9/20/1876 in Prattville, Alabama
Edna Earle Dicksinson 8/22/1878 in Cottondale, Alabama
Maggie Belle (Margaret) Dickinson 4/23/1881 in Atlanta, Ga.
Leonora Dickson 8/21/1883 in Elmore Co., Alabama
Gilbert McDuffie Dickinson 9/11/1885 in Atlanta, Ga.
Bertha Mae Dicksonson 9/11/1889 in Atlanta, Ga.
Ruby Estelle Blocker 7/30/1892 in Atlanta, Ga.

MARRIAGES:
Benjamin Slaton Dickinson and Sarah J. Ledbetter 9/30/1869 in Cottondale, Alabama
Oscar J. Blocker and Martha Elizabeth Dickinson 1/14/1891 Atlanta, Ga.
Benjamin R. Dickson and Zadie Buice 6/12/1893 Atlanta, Ga.
Ralph Deane Dickinson 8/5/1896 Atlanta, Ga.
Edna C. Dickinson and Robert E. Keen 12/28/1906 Atlanta, Ga.
Bertha Mae Dickinson and Norris Walton Warren 12/13/1913, St. Phillips Cathedral, Atlanta, Ga.
Bertha Mae Dickinson Warren & Henry Colquitt Johnson 5/21/1939 in Atlanta, Ga.
Gilbert M. D. Dickinson and Emma Butler 5/24/1941 in Rome, Ga.

DEATHS:
Craven Payton Dickinson 1/14/1874, aged 1 year, 11 mos., 30 days
Sarah Dickinson 10/17/1877, aged 1 year, 27 days
Mrs. Sarah Jane Ledbetter Dickinson 6/8/1915, aged 66 years, 11 days
Oscar J. Bocker, husband of Martha Elizabeth Dickinson, 1/15/1956, aged 86 years, 11 months, 27 days
Benjamin Slaton Dickinson 3/23/1930, age 83 years, 3 months, 1 day
Edna Earle Dickinson Keene 9/30/1932, age 54 years, 1 month, 8 days
Norris Walton Warren, husband of Bertha M. D. Warren, 1/11/1938, age 49 years, 3 months, 27 days
Margaret (Maggie Belle) Dickinson 12/6/1944, age 63 yrs, 7 mos, 13 days
Albert McDuffie Dickinson 10/9/1949, age 64 years, 28 days
Leonora Dickinson 2/14/1956, age 72 years, 5 months, 24 days
Martha Elizabeth Dickinson Blocker 5/9/1956, age 82 yrs, 1 mo., 3 days
Benjamin Robertus Dickinson 3/1959, age 88 years, 4 months.

W. R. DANCER BIBLE of Dougherty Co., Ga.
Owner: Mrs. Lillian S. Ryder
605 E. Brevard, Tallahassee, FL 32303 (1970)

W. R. Dancer of Dougherty Co., Ga. and M. J. Clifton of Dougherty Co., Ga. Married 12/29/1864 at Albany by Rev. Daniels. Wits: N. A. Scarborough, J. S. Clifton

MARRIAGES:
S. E. Grimes-Anna Leonorie Dancer 9/6/1883

A. J. Cowart-Minnie Lee Dancer 8/8/1888
W. C. Dancer-Rannie Lou Boykin 1/18/1893
J. S. Sheffield-Theodosia A. Dancer 12/20/1893
W. I. Geer-Ada Dancer 6/10/1899

BIRTHS:
W. R. Dancer 6/12/1839
M. J. Clifton 11/27/1842
A. L. Dancer 10/3/1865
W. C. Dancer 9/30/1867
--L. Dancer 9/14/1870
T. A. Dancer 4/28/1875
A. M.? Dancer 2/9/1880
Infant son of J. S. and D. A. Sheffield 8/8/1894
Audrey Mary Sheffield 8/5/1895
Ada Lee Sheffield 2/12/1897
Reuben Sheffield 9/19/1899
Burney Steed Sheffield 11/14/1900
Lillian Lucile Sheffield 8/23/1903
J. S. Jr. and W. R. Sheffield 7/13/1908

DEATHS:
Infant son of W. R. And M. J. Dancer was born 3/31st and died 4/7/1874
Infant son of J. S. And T. A. Sheffield died 8/8/1894
Audrey Mary Sheffield died 3/3/1896
Reuben Sheffield died 10/31/1899
W. R. Dancer died 9/1/1900
J. S. Sheffield died 7/1913
Mary Jane Clifton (faded)
-----Sheffield 1930 (faded)
Nora 8/13/1930
Ada Gill 8/25/1910
Seab 8/26/1910
Burney Steed Poole 7/1951
Theodosia A. S. Rick 11/8/1955
William R. Sheffield 5/7/1967

WILLIAM S. COWAN BIBLE of Newton Co.
Owner: Dr. and Mrs. Alva M. Gregg, Box 499, Franklin, LA 70538

William S. Cowan of Newton Co., Ga. and Georgia V. Morgan of Newton Co. Married 12/13/1870 at Horme Morgan Plantation by Rev. William McMichael.

MARRIAGES:
S. Morgan Cowan-Ella Cornelia McCowan 12/24/1879
Frances Letitia Cowan to Asbury Cleveland Wellborn 7/31/1907
Crystal Hope Wellborn to Rev. Alva Mayes Gregg 6/27/193--
Mary Margaret Cowan to Columbus Jefferson Hollingsworth 8/7/19---
Edwina Nell Cowan to Israel D. Bennett
S. Morgan Cowan, Jr. to - blank
Asbury Wellborn Gregg to Sandra Louise George 4//17/----
Alva Hope Gregg to William Michael Spillane 6/22/1968

BIRTHS:
William S. Cowan 9/11/1850
Georgia V. Cowan 9/23/1849
Henrietta C. Cowan 11/5/1871
Mary Margaret Cowan 10/18/1874
Samuel Morgan Cowan 7/29/1877, died 7/16/1954
Willie J. Cowan 2/21/1880
Fannie Lettie Cowan 11/4/1882

Children of S. Morgan Cowan and Elea ----as follows:

Ellie Evelyn 6/7/1901-9/26/1902
Morgan Cowan, Jr. 9/26/1902
Edwina Nell Cowan 3/22/1905

DEATHS:
William S. Cowan 11/5/1887
Georgia V. Cowan 5/11/1937
Willie Evelyn Cowan 12/23/1901
Samuel Morgan Cowan, Sr. 7/16/1954
Willie Jack Cowan 9/6/1956

DEATHS:
Mary Margaret Cowan Hollingsworth 7/15/1957
Henrietta Clementine Cowan 9/23/1962
Frances Letitia Cowan Wellborn 11/25/1965
Asbury Cleveland Wellborne 7/3/1971

BIRTHS AND MARRIAGES:
Sandra Louise George Gregg 9/5/1943 Thomaston, Ga.
Wife of Asbury Wellborn Gregg married 4/17/1965 Thomaston, Ga.
Amanda Carlisle Gregg, Shreveport, La 6/4/1967
Margaret Letitia Gregg, Shreveport, La 6/20/1969
William Michael Spillane Holbrook 10/29/1940, husband of Alva Hope Gregg married 6/22/1968, Columbia, S. C.
Elizabeth Page Spillane, S. C. 1/18/1973, adopted 3/2/1973

JAMES COOK BIBLE
Owner: Mrs. Jim Matthews
Pelican, LA (1965)

"James Cook Book
Price 5.00
Bought the year 1831"

On a flyleaf of Bible, owned by James Cook, born 2/16/1807 in Clarke Co., and his wife, Eliza Barton, born 1811 in Georgia, were listed the names and birthdates of their slaves.

BIRTHS:
Simon 1815
Tom 1816
Nancy 1823
Charity 1924
Mariah 1836
Sarah 1844
George 1848
Nathan 11/18/1850
Henry 5/10/1852

DEATHS:
Mary Cook 7/25/1838 (Mother)
Martha Sherman 6/11/1839
John Cook 9/25/1843 (father)
James Cook 5/20/1877, age 70 years, 3 months
James Willey Cook 8/16/1873
Eliza Cook 9/19/1893
John Pease Cook 8/29/1895
Julian Cook 6/29/1828, age 62 years
William H. Thomas Cook 8/1841 and deceased 11/1843, age 14 years, 5 months
Lovic Pierce Cook 2/22/1860, age 7 years, 3 months, 21 days
R. F. Cook 2/18/1868, age 31 years, 5 months, 22 days
Tamer C. Cook 9/4/1863, aage 23 years, 2 months, 12 days
Elizaaabeth A. Thornton, daughter of R. F. And M. A. Thornton, 1/18/1877, age 22 months, 11 days

MARRIAGES:
James Cook 2/16/1807-Eliza 7/12/1827
Eliza Barten born 1811
Eliza professed religion in 10/1820
James Cook professed religion in 1827 at Camp Meeting in Newton Co.. 11/1st
C. F. Thornton married M. A. Cook, daughter of James and Eliza Cook 3/19/1874
N. J. Thornton married to M. E. Cook, daughter of James and Eliza Cook 12/21st in the
Centennial year of our Lord 1876.
Robert F. Cook 6/14/1866
N. O. Cook 9/28/1867
C. A. Cook 8/20/1868
J. W. Cook 12/22/1870
M. A. A. Cook 3/19/1874
J. W. Cook 3/28/1895

BIRTHS:
John Cook 3/26/1765 (Father)
Mary Cook 5/18/1771 and was married 11/1786
John Cook deceased 9/25/1843
Elizabeth A. Thornton, daughter of C. F. and M. A. Thornton was born 3/7/1875
James J. Thornton, son of C. F. and M. A. Thornton, 9/18/1876
Thelma Mathews born 12/3/1901
Olivia Mathews born 11/26/1903
LaVern Mathews born 1/12/1906
Son of C. A. Cook
James William Cook born 8/1/1869

(Different handwriting)

J. W. Cook born 5/20/1839
Eliza Killgore born 9/10/1842
John Pierce Cook born 11/15/1871
James Willey Cook born 6/1/1876
C. E.? Cordelia Eliza Cook born 6/7/1880
Iris Mathews born 2/12/1920
Dorothy Mathews born 4/22/1917

BIRTHS:
William Thomas Cook 6/2/1829
Robert Francis Cook 8/2/1831
John Wesley Cook 5/20/1834
Columbus Asburry Cook 8/3/1837
James Collinsworth 6/23/1840
Mary Ann Amelia Cook 8/15/1842
Oliver Neal Cook 6/6/1845
Morning Elisabeth Cook 1/15/1849
Julian Cook 6/19/1828 deceased at 6 days old
Lovic Pierce Cook 11/1/1852
John Davis Cook 5/16/1861, son of P. F. Cook
Mary Eliza Cook 7/--/1868, daughter of O. N. and. M. Cook
John Pierce Cook 11/14/1871

JOSEPH DARSEY BIBLE
Owner: Mrs. Alex Carswell
1423 Olive Street, Santa Barbara, CA (1965)

MARRIAGES:
Joseph Darsey, born 11/24/1762
Mary Darsey, wife of Joseph Darsey, born 2/2/1772

Joseph and Mary Darsey were married 10/13/1791

Nancy Darsey to Marcus? Wheat 1811
William Darsey to Elizabeth Mathews 1815
Fetney Darsey to Washington W. Stone ---/30/1816
Harriet B. Darsey to John Barnes 12/28/1823
James M. Darsey to Mary Sutton 12/28/1828
Mary M. Darsey to Alfred Sturgis 10/19/1830

DEATHS:
Joseph Darsey 1/11/1823
Mary Darsey 5/24/1830

BIRTHS:
William Darsey, son of Joseph and Mary Darsey, 7/28/1792
Nancy Darsey, daughter of Joseph and Mary Darsey, 4/5/1794, died 7/24/----
Fetney Darsey, daughter of Joseph and Mary Darsey, 7/6/1796, died 5/21/1838
Margaret? Darsey, daughter of Joseph and Mary Darsey, 6/7/1798
Hariot Darsey, daughter of Joseph and Mary Darsey, 1/6/1800, died 1/31/1835
Thomas Darsey, son of----------------, 1802 (blurred), died 11/10/1822

DEATHS:
William Darsey 10/12/1817, aged 25 years, 2 months, 11 days
Moriah Darsey 11/1808

BIRTHS:
-------J. Darsey, daughter of Joseph and Mary Darsey, born 9/29/1804
Joseph B. Darsey, son of Joseph and Mary Darsey, born 12/12/1806
James Madison Darsey, son of Joseph and Mary Darsey, born 5/19/18--- (torn off)
Mary Moriah Darsey, daughter of Joseph and Mary Darsey, born 6/13/---(torn off)

DEATHS:
Louisa Darsey 6/1805
Joseph G. Darsey 8/1830

Births of Joseph and Mary Darsey grandchildren:
Maryann Wheat was born 1815, died 11/24/1837
Mary Ann ---- Sturgis, daughter of A. and M. Sturgis, born 10/30/1831
Georgia Carolina McDuffie Sturgis, daughter of A. and M. Sturgis, born 11/13/1834
Thomas Bowdre Darsey born 1816
Louisa Darsey Stone born 10/12/1817

HENRY W. DARSEY BIBLE of Bainbridge
Owner: Jane Darsey Humphrey, Rt. 4, Box 1519, Bainbridge, GA 31717

MARRIAGES:
Henry W. Darsey of Concord, FL and Lenna L. Johnson of near Amsterdam, Ga. on 2/8/1919 at Bainbridge, Ga. By the Ordinary, Berry Maxwell. Wits: Tom N. Darsey, Lois Johnson.

Henry Woodruff Darsey to Mamie S. Butler 3/25/1897
Henry Woodruff Darsey the second time to Lenna Lee Johnson 2/8/1919
J. H. Darsey and Julia F. Shelfer 7/1865

BIRTHS:
Henry W. Darsey 12/5/1868
Mamie E. Darsey 11/18/1871
Mamie Hellen Darsey 3/26/1898
Lenna Lee Johnson Darsey 9/8/1882
Joab H. Darsey 1/21/1837
Julia F. Shelfer Darsey 2/25/1847

DEATHS:
Mamie E. Darsey 4/10/1898
Mamie H. Darsey 5/26/1898
Leannia L. Darsey 6/10/1929
Joseph H. Darsey 7/29/1918, he was 81 years, 6 months, 8 days
Jane Elizabeth (Darsey) Henly 1/22/1928, she was 93 yrs, 3 mos, 9 days
Henry W. Darsey 4/22/1958
Children's Register:
Jamie Rufus Darsey 11/7/1910 East Point, Ga. - 11/8/1910 East Point, Ga.
Marian Elizabeth Darsey 12/14/1912 St. Augustine, FL m. 1/12/1929 Ft. Lauderdale, FL, Claud Alfred Campbell
Frances Axie Darsey 9/10/1915 Homestead, FL m. 11/11/1937 Homestead, FL Bowling G. Dye
Virginia Nell Darsey 10/1/1921 Homestead, FL m. 11/24/1940 Homestead, FL William Edward McMichael.

ALBERT GREEN DOZIER BIBLE of Columbia Co.

Given to family by Jane Margaret Gilmer Powers' father, Nicholas Powers, on her marriage to Albert Green Dozier (1819-1862)

MARRIAGES:
8/170/1837 Albert G. Dozier to Jane M. Powers by Rev. George W. Powers
6/11/1818 the Rev. Nicholas Powers to Mrs. Mary M. Taliaferro by Rev. James R. Turner
7/29/1813 Green Jones Dozier to Constantia Hunt by the Rev.----
11/1/1841? George Powers to James L. Williams by Rev. Joshua N. Glenn.
11/2/1841? Mary C. Powers to William C. Williams by Rev. L. Benning.
5/10/1849 Dr. Nicholas H. Powers to Henrietta Morgan, Rev. J. W. Reid
8/183-- Frances Dozier to William Hardwick by Rev. James B. Turner
8/14/---, William H. Dozier to Martha S. Staples by the Rev. Dawson.
5/23/--- John E. Dozier to Mary Ann Adkins, Rev. W. P. Arnold in 1847
--/27/1851 Miss Elizabeth Dozier to Rawlin? Peoples, Rev. Panels?.
7/1/1851 M. G. Lowe, my youngest brother, to M. Parton?
7/9/1851 James J. Dozier to Miss Rebecca Lindsey by Rev. John Knight.
9/1855 John Dozier to ------------------

BIRTHS:
Nicholas Powers, son of John and Elizabeth Powers, 1/1/1753 in Ireland
Mary Meriwether Powers, dau. of Thomas & Elizabeth Gilmer, 6/23/1786
Gree0n Jones Dozier, son of John and Frances Dozier, 9/7/1793
Constantia Hunt Dozier, dau. of Thomas and Isabella Hunt, 9/25/1794
Albert Green Dozier, son of Green S. and Constantina W. Dozier 6/4/1819 Columbia Co., Ga.
Jane Margaret Dozier, dau. of Nicholas and Mary M. Powers, 7/5/1812
Nicholas Green Dozier, son of A. G. and J. M. Dozier, 9/12/1832
Mary Constantina Dozier, daughter of A. G. and J. M. Dozier, 7/2/1840
Elizabeth Fanning Dozier, daughter of A. G. and J. M. Dozier, 6/9/1843
Jane Alberta Dozier, daughter of A. G. and J. M. Dozier, 2/8/1845
-------Frances Dozier, daughter of A. G. and J. M. Dozier, 9/8/18--?
John George Dozier, son of Albert Dozierr, 1/11/1850
Thomas Henry Hunt Dozier, son of Albert and Jane M. Dozier, 11/07/1852
Benjamin Lewis Gilmer, son of G. And J. W. Dozier, 2/11/1854
William Albert, son of Jane M. Dozier 6/29/1856
Carrie Lee Jackson Dozier, last child of A. G. And J. N. Dozier, 8/1/1862

DEATHS AND MARRIAGES:
Jane Albert Dozier Collier died Thomson, Ga. 3/8/1918. She married Dr. W. A. L. Collins 5/10/1871. Her little girl, Lizzie, born 4/3/1872. Little Lizzie died 9/10/1883
Dr. William A. L. Collins had formerly been married to Miss Dora Allen 4/16/1844
Sara Allen Collins died 2/17/1869
Dr. William A. L. Collins died 4/28/1884 a short time after---Lizzie died.

DEATHS:
Rev. Henry Hurt Dozier, son of Albert Green and Jane M. Dozier, died 12/16/1913
The Rev. Nicholas Powers, father of Jane M. Dozier, died 6/14/1843.
My dear beloved husband, Albert, departed this life 12/31/1863 (1862 written under it)
1/29/1876 Green J. Dozier, my grandfather, died, near Shiloh Church, Columbia Co., 83 years. His wife, Constance, died in 1858.
-----------------------------------1875
-----------------------------------1879

Bud Willie A. Dozier died at the Sutton Place 1881.
Mary C. Dozier died 2/9/1918?
Jane Alberta Dozier Collins died 3/8/-----------
Sarah Frances Dozier died 5/12/1929
Albert Dozier Kean died 2/20/1937
Carrie Lee Jackson Dozier died 3/26/1943, Thomson, Ga.
The youngest and last member of the immediate family.

Obituaries in Bible:

"NICHOLAS GREEN DOZIER, son of A. G. and J. M. Powers Dozier, who died 7th Dec. 1858, was born 12th Sept. 1838....His body rests not far from his home and place of decease, with those of his fathers maternal ancestors--the Hunts' of Columbia Co., Georgia."

"Obituary. Died at her residence in Columbia County on morning of 16th instant, Mrs. Constantia H. Dozier, consort of Green J. Dozier, in the sixty-fourth year of her age...."

Parents:
Albert Green Dozier was born 6/8/1819 Columbia Co. was married 8/17/1837, died 12/31/1862
Jane Margarett Dozier born 7/5/1819 at Pleasant Grove in Oglethorpe Co., died 11/18/1875

Children:
Nicholas Green Dozier born 9/12/1838 Columbia Co., died 12/16/1853
Mary Constantia Dozier born 7/20/1840 Poplar Grove, Columbia Co., died 2/8/1878 Thomson
Elizabeth Fanning Dozier born 6/8/1842 Columbia Co., died 12/13/1879, married 11/30/1867 by Rev.---------
Jane Alberta Dozier born 2/8/1845, died 3/8/1918 Thomson, married 5/10/1871 by Rev. F. Dozier
Sarah Frances Dozier born 9/8/1847, died 7/12/1934 Thomson, married 10/7/1868 by Rev. Steed
John George Dozier born 1/10/1850, died 2/8/1937
Thomas Henry Hunt Dozier born 11/7/1852, died 12/15/1913, married 10/22/1873
Benjamin Lewis Gilmer Dozier born 2/11/1854, died 1/3/1868
William Albert Dozier born 6/29/1856, died 2/23/1881 Sutton Place
Carrie Lee Jackson Dozier born 8/1/1862, died 3/26/1943 Thomson

GREEN JONES DOZIER BIBLE
Owner: Robert W. Lane, Winfield, GA (1987)

"For Ida C. and T. H. Dozier. Presented by their Motherr, J. M. Dozier, Oct. 22nd."

MARRIAGES:
Thomas Henry Dozier & Ida Cunningham Wilkes 10/22/1873 by Rev. L. P. Neese
Albert Darsey Dozier and Loula Agnes Humphreys 11/12/1902 by Dr. Yarbrough and Dr. Quillian
Walter Powers Dozier and Carrie McLean Smith 11/11/1903 by Rev. John Little
Claude Wilkes Dozier and Sarah Balkes Fannin 2/16/1904 by Rev. B. A. Jackson of Alabama
Ida Camille Dozier & John Edward Smith, Jr. 12/18/1907,Rev. J. R. Allen
Jane Alberta Dozier & Robert Willie Lane 11/17/1909 by Rev. F. R. Seaby
Thomas Henry Dozier, Jr. & India Heath Ham? 6/14/1911, Rev. R. E. L. Harris

BIRTHS:
Thomas Henry Dozier 11/7/1852
Ida Cunningham Dozier 10/18/1852
Claude Wilkes Dozier, son of Thomas H. and Ida C. Dozier, 1/3/1875
Albert Darsey Dozier, son of Thomas H. and Ida C. Dozier, 6/21/1877
Walter Powers Dozier, son of Thomas H. and Ida C. Dozier, 7/26/1879
Edgar Collins Dozier, son of Thomas H. and Ida C. Dozier, 9/16/1881
Jane Alberta Dozier, daughter of T. H. and Ida C. Dozier, 2/9/1884
Ida Camille Dozier, dau. of Thomas H. and Ida C. Dozier, 8/11/1886
Thomas Henry Dozier 9/20/1888, son of Thomas H. and Ida C. Dozier
Laurena Gilmer Dozier, son of T. H. and Ida C. Dozier, 10/17/1893

DEATHS:
Dr. J. L. Wilkes 2/23/1882
Edgar Dozier, son of T. H. and I. C. Dozier, 5/12/1883
Sarah Frances Dozier, daughter of C. N. and Sara B. Dozier, 7/1/1905
William Allen Dozier, son of C. W. and S. B. Dozier, 1/7/1907
Walter Herbert Dozier, son of W. P. and C. M. Dozier, 6/23/1910
Ida Camille Dozier Smith, daughter of T. H. and I. C. Dozier, 12/26/1911, wife of Edward Smith
Thomas Henry Dozier, Sr., husband of Ida Wilkes, 12/18/1914

Ida Camilla Lane, dau. of R. W. and B. J. Lane, 10/27/1913, age 1 year
John Laurens Lane, son of R. W. and B. J. Lane, 6/7/1925, age 2 years
Albert (Allie) Dorsey Dozier, wife of Lauren? Humphreys Dozier, 3/10/1936
Ida Wilkes, wife of Thomas Henry Hunt Dozier, 6/21/1937

DEATHS:
Philip Thomas, son of C. W. and S. B. Dozier, 7/8/1937, age 27 years
Claude Wilkes Dozier, son of T. H. and Ida C. Dozier, 12/20/1938
Thomas Henry Hunt Dozier, Jr., son of T. H. and Ida Wilkes Dozier, husband of India Hawes Dozier, 3/11/1943
Walter Powers Dozier, son of T. H. and Ida Wilkes Dozier, husband of Carrie Smith Dozier, 12/1/1959
Robert Wilkes Lane, Sr., son of Dr. George M. and Mary Frances Lane, husband of Jane Alberta Dozier Lane, 7/10/1943?

MARRIAGES:
Green and Constance Dozier 7/29/1873
Frances J. Dozier 8/9/1832 by Rev. J. B. Turner
Als Dozier 8/17/1837 by Rev. G. W. Person
Walter M. Dozier 8/11/----- by Rev. Thomas H. Dawson
John E. Dozier 555/23/1847 by Rev. W. P. Arnold
Martha A. E. Dozier 3/27/1857 by Rev. F. F. Reynolds
Ignatius J. Dozier 7/9/1851 by Rev. J. W. Huie
Wilson W. Dozier 2/12/1859? By Rev. J. B. Hanson
Sallie C. Dozier and Charles C. Smith 8/10/1855 by Rev. R. A. Conner

BIRTHS:
William W. Dozier 6/23/1814
John A. Dozier 11/25/1815
Frances J. Dozier 4/1--/1817
Albert Dozier 1819
Erasmus J. Dozier 5/18/1821
Isasbellus A. Dozier 2/18/1821
Leonard T. Dozier 9/21/1825
Ignatius James Dozier 12/2/1828
----------------Dozier----------------
-----------------5/10/1836

BIRTHS:
Green J. Dozier 9/7/1773
Contance Dozier, wife of Green J. Dozier, 9/25/1794

DEATHS:

Mrs. Constance W. Dozier, wife of G. J. Dozier, 3/16/1858, in the 64th year of her age
John A. Dozier 2/2/1816, aged 2 months, 8 days
Leonard T. Dozier 10/28/1826, aged 13 months, 7 days
Isabellah A. Dozier 10/16/1827, aged 3 years, 8 months
Mary Ann Dozier, wife of John E. Dozier, 8/22/1848, aged 22 years

(In different handwriting)

Bennie Green Peeples, son of Reuben P. and Elizabeth Peeples, died 19th March, aged 2 months, 19 days, 1852

(In different handwriting)

Johnnie Dozier born 1882 but record changed 1883 as told to son. Annie born 1877

MARRIAGES:

L. E. Dozier of Wilkes Co. and S. E. Patterson of the same married by Rev. G. A. Simpson 3/28/1872.

BIRTHS:

Annie A. Dozier, daughter of L. E. Dozier and Sallie E. Dozier, 12/31/1872
Willie L. Dozier, son of L. E. Dozier and Sallie E. Dozier, 1/19/1873
-----------------------Dozier, 9/2/1877
Johnnie W. Dozier 7/4/1883
Claud Carreca Dozier 10/13/1885
Floyd Truman Dozier 11/1/1888

ABERCROMBIE
E. 45
Edmund 45
Malinda Booth 45
Mary 45
Robert 45
Sarah Watts 45
ABNEY
Harriet 161
ADAMS
Amarintha E. 12
Amarintha E. Duggan 13
Archelas B. 12, 13
Calvin Emmett 13
Clara C. 12, 13
Elizabeth 137
Irvin H. 12, 13
Johnnie May 13
Lacora E. 12, 13
Lillie Clyde 13
Louise Sylvania 159
Martha G. 12
Mary Elefare Barwick 13
Mary Winifred 13
Nathan Joseph 12 (2)
Oscar James 13 (2)
Sarah Ardelia 13
W. T. 11
William Luther 12
William T. 13
William Tanner 12, 13
ADAMSON
Martilla Ellen 94
ADKINS
Mary Ann 188
ADOLPHUS
Crocket 122
AGNEW
Waco 98
AKENS
Samuel G. 133
AKIN
Kenneth Judson 102
Owen 102
AKINS
Sherod Sheffield 130(2)
ALEXANDER
Araminta Autorrietta 31
Elizabeth R. 32
Leonidas B. 32
Louisa 124
ALLEN
A. E. 148
B. 148(2)
Bannister Bowling 148
Basil Barion 148
Caroline Gilmore 148
Dora 189
E. S. Haralson 148
Elizabeth 38
Ginnie Taburn 148
J. R., Rev. 38
Mary Aseneth 148
Matilda Louisa 6(3)
Nancy A. 6
Nancy W. 38
W. P. 6
William 38
ALLIN
Mary L. G. 21
ALLMAND
Harrison 178
ALLMON
E. E. 124
John 34
Mark 34
Cynthia Jane 74
Eliza 26(2), 27
Nancy E. G. 124
R. T. 124
Reuben T. 124
Rubon T. 124
Sarah S. A. 124

ANDERS
Annacaona Hantippe 52
Tipp 5(2)
ANDERSON
Bessie Lara Catherine 85
Hypatia Virginia Bowdoin 85
Josephus Emina 85(2)
Mary J. 150
ANDERSON
Sarah V. 89
ANDREA
Leonardo 151
Redmond Leonardo 151
ANDREW
Ellie 78
Redmond Leonardo 152
ANDREWS
Ave 34
Elizabeth 34
Hannah 34
Jesse 34
Mark S., Rev. 35
Mary 34, 39
Susanna 34
Thomas 34
William 34
ANN
Thomas 34
APPLING
James 126
ARCHER
Nora Lenna Turk 77
ARMSTRONG
Lyllian Jane 169
Samuel, Rev. 35
ARNOLD
John M. 174
W. P., Rev. 188, 192
ARRINGTON
Frances A. 21
Francis Amanda 20
James 19, 20(2), Jane 20
Jane B. 19

ASH
Charles Burnsides 26
Charles K. 26
Cinthia Jane 76
Eugenia R. 26
Eugenia Rosemond 27
George 27
George A. 26, 27
George Adair 26
ASH
George Adam 26
George Henry Wyer 26
Georgia Ann Gorham 26
Georgia Anna Gorham 26
John Hergan 26
Mary E. 27
Mary Eliza 26
Susannah B. 27
Susannah Burnsides 26
William Rahn 27
ASTON
Mary 135
ATKINSON
Amanda Caroline 160(2)
Nancy 160(2)
Samuel Washington 160
ATKISSON
Annie 22
Brazos 22
Victoria 22
Vinnie 22, 60
AVERILLA
Caroline 22,23
Dairy 22
Edith 22
Ellis 22
Eva 22,23
Frances 22
Frances A. H. 22
G. E. 22
George 22
George Baber 21,23
George Ellis 21,22,23

George McDonald 22
George Stanhope 22,23
Grace 22
Henry 22
Horace 22(3)
Horace Gunnel 22
Horce L. B. 23
Horace W. 21
J. 22
Joab 21,22
Jude 21
M. E., Mrs. 22
Marcella 22
Maud 22
Michael 22
Olivia 22(2)
AUBREY
Chandler 64
AUSTIN
Byron Kirksy 60
Clifford Glenn 60
Gwernia Inez 60
Ivan Chester 59
J. Caesar 60
J. P. 59
J. T. P. 59
Jack Carlton 60
John 59
Loy Parker 60
Luan Chister 60
Margerete Elminy 60
Mary G. 59
Robert J. M. 60
Robert Matha 60
Robert Pennington 59
Solomon K. 60
Solomon Kirksy 59
Verna 59
Viola 60(2)
W. H. M. 59
Walter Manning 60
William Pierce 60
AVRET

Alexander 18m 29*2(m 21
Alexander, Rev. 19
Amanda 20(2)
Barbry H. 20
C. C. 20,21(2)
Christopher C. 21
Christopher Columbus 20
Cornelia A. L. 20
E. Ann 21
Elizabeth 20
Elizabeth W. 19
Frances Ellen 20
Frances Tobiah 20
Hove 20
Jane B. 21
John 20
John G. 21
John Glen 19
John W. 21
John Wesley 20
Joseph 20(2)
Joseph B. 21
Joseph Benson 20
Lavenia 20
Levings 21
Louie K. 20(2)
Louisa Manerva 20
M. 21
Margaret A. 20,21
Mary 20,21
Mary Jane 20,21
Mary L. Z. 20
Robert C. 20
Samuel Alexander 21
Sarah 19
Sarah Mariah 20
William A. 20
AVRETT
Alex Samuel 21
Clifford A. 21
Edmon T. 20
Edmund T. 19
Fannie B. 20

George E. 19
Jane 20
John 186(2)
John G. 19
John Luther 19,21
Lillie Mae 21
Magie 20
Sallie 20
William L. 20
AYCOCK
Eva J. 19
Fanny 152
Frances 152
Joel 18,19
Joel Jr. 19
Joel Sr. 19
M. D. 18,19
M. D. Sr. 19
Margaret E. 19
Martha R. 19
Mary Ann 86
Mary C. 19
Middleton D. 19
Neaty 18,19
Pheriaby E. 19
Rebecca 19(2)
Virginia 19
W. H. 18
William 19
AYERS
Francis 85
BABER
George 22
Thomas 22
BACCUS
A. H. 23
Hamilton 23
Bertha Leona Studdard 23
Cleophus A. 23, 24
Doris Elizabeth 23
E. H. S. 23
Eler O. 24
Elick 24

Ellick 23
Estellar J. 24
Francis C. M. 24
Hulda Ellen 23
Huldy 24
Joseph 23
Joseph T. 24
Mahulda 23
Mary 23
Mary A. E. 24
Mary W. 23
Sarah Francis 23
Thurmond J. 24
Thurmond Joseph 23
W. B. F. 24
BAGWELL
L. R. 78
BAILEY
Annie 142
Caroline 2
Caroline Bird 1, 118
Carrie E. 2
Edmund Washington 1,2
Eliza A. E. 1
Eliza Ann 2
Eliza Ann Ellen 1
George G. 25(2)
Henry May 1,2
James Blackstone 1,2
John 1,2(2)
John Jackson 1,2
John Sr. 2
Judah 2
M. C. 1
Mary 1,2
Mary A. Gates 2
Robert Neal 1,2
BAKER
Stella Viola 31
BALEY
James 106
BALL
Catherine Candler 119

Catherine Warren 118,119
David Ashley 119
Lamar Q. 119
Lamar Q., Jr. 118
Lamar Quintero, Jr. 118
Lamar Quintero III,118
William Warren 119(s)
BALLEW
Amanda S. 77
BALLOW
W. S. 51
BANISTER
A. M. 102
Eliza Carline 102
M. M. 102
BANKS
Anna Hamilton 17
Anna Josephine Virginia 25
Catherine 6
Coleman 17, 18
Dunslan 24
Dunston 17
Edward Sims 25(2)
Elbert 24
Elbert Augustin 25
Eliza 26
Eugene 25(2)
Francis Scott 17(2)
George Young 16, 17, 25
George W. 25
Gilmer R. 25
Hannah Kimbrough 6
Henry 24
J. O. 16
James 6
James F. 24
James O. 16
James Oliver 16(4), 17, 18
James Watkins 25
Jennie 16
John 24,25(2)
John Coleman 17
John James 17(2)

John Oliver 17
John Troup 25(2)
John, Co. 26
Josephine A. J. 25
Lemuel 24
BANKS
Lucy Ann 17(2)
Lucy Young 17
Marion 24
Martha 25
Mary Bacon 16
Mary Gray 17
Mary Oliver 16,17
Mary Winfredy 17
Mitchell 25
Mattie 25
Rachel 24(2)
Ralph 24(3)
Reuben Raymer 17
Ricchard 24
Robert H. 26
Rockingham Gilmer 25
Sarah 24,25
Sarah Lucy 25(2)
Sophia 26
Susan 25
Susan Martha 25
Thomas A. 24
Thomas Gray 16,17
Watkins 25(2)
Wiley Coleman 17
William Kelly 25(2)
William Lemuel 17(2)
Willis 16(5),17,24
Willis Dunstan 25(2)
Willis Dunston 17
Wilson 18
Wylie Coleman 20
BARNETT
A. Seth T. 38
Ann 36(2)
Ann E. 35
Ann Eliza 36

Anna 37(2)
Ave G. 38
Betsy 36
Clara 38
Clarissa 37(2)
Edwin 37(2)
Fanney 28
Fanny 28
Hamilton 37
Harriet 37
Harriett 38
J. B. 35
J. G. 35
James 27,28,36
James H. 37
Job 36
John 27(2),28(2),36(3)
John Adams Griffin 35
John G. 35,38
John Hirart 37
John Sr. 36
Joseph 37(4),38
Joseph Sr. 37
Joseph Martin 37
Joseph Mathis 27
Lewessy 36(2)
Lucy W. 38
Mary 36(2)
Mary A. 38
Mary Elizabeth 35,38
Nathan 38
Nathan Thomas 35
Nathaniel 36
Polly 27
Rebkah 27
Richard Davis 27
Robert 36(2)
Susan J. 38
Thomas 34,36
Thomas G., 35,38(2)
William 27(2), 28,36,37(2)
William Boyd 37,38
William F. 38

William Jr. 28
William Sr. 27,28
Zalsey Davis 28
BARNEY
R. C. 107
BARRETT
Cornelius Dupre 14
E. D. 14
Edward Benjamin 14
Edward Benjamin, Rev. 15
Elizabeth Massey Graves 14(2)
Ellen 14
Eudelle Agnew 15
Francis Stanton 15
James Legh Richmond 15
John 15
John Isaiah 15
John Roger 15
Lyman Elmer 15
M. P. 13
Margaret Anna 15
Martha Alice 14
BARRETT
Mary Lenora 14
Mary Leonora 14
Massey G. 15
Massey Goodwin, Mrs. 14
Minnie Megee 15
Paul Stanton 15
Peter Birdrian 15
Rosa Waneta 15
Sarah Boardman 14
Sarah Lavenia Gready 15
Sarah Levenia 14
Thomas Henry 14
W. G. 13, 14(2)
William G. 15
William Goodwin 13,14
William Samuel Ferdrian 14
BARRINGTON
Albert Maranda 102
Anne Zember 102
John Matterson 102

Marion Hen 102
Sarah Seliel 102
William Agustus 102
Willis Garber 102
BARRON
Susan Pearl 89
BARTEN
Eliza 184
BARTON
Amarintha 11
Ann Davis 12
Ayres 12
Elizabeth 12
Elizabeth Ava 11(2)
John Davis 11
Joseph Johnson 11
Marg E. 11
Margann 11
Marintha 12
Marja Ann 11
Martha Ann Susan 11
Martha H. S. 11
Mary E. 12,13
Mary Elefare 11
Nancy 12
Nancy Cornelia 11
Nannie C. 11
Nathan 11,12
Nathan Zackariah 11,12
Sara Ann 12
Sarah A. E. 11,12
Sarah Ann 11
Sarah Catherine 11,12

BARWICK
Ruth Alston 52
Sophia Malinna 52
Stancel 11
William Eason 12
William Easton 11
Winford Frances 11
BATES
A. J. L. 53

A J. L. J. 53
Anthony W. 53
Anthony Whitfield 52,53
Diedmonda 53
Emma L. 52
Hariet 53
Howard W. 53
Ida Martin 53
M. H. 52
M. W. 53
Marion H. 53
Marvin Terece 52
Mary J. 53
Mary Jane 52
Mollie Martin 53(2)
Molly Martin 53
Mona 52
N. B. 53
Octasco Lucinda 53
Susie Elizabeth 53
T. Q. 53
W. A. 52(2), 53(2)
W. C. 53
Wilhelminia 53
Wilhemina 52
BATTLE
Lazarus 124
Margaret 124
Marian Louise 2
BAUGHN
Bouley, Col. 137
BEACH
Benjamin Amzi 69
BEALL
E. H. 102
BEATTIE
Sarah 104
BEDENBAUGH
S. W. 41
BEDSOLE
Carol 88
Catherine Louise 88
Terry 88

BELCHER
Abraham, Rev. 51

BELL
Carry Eva 50
Dorothy Jeane 51(2)
Elliss 50
Eva 51
Florence 87
George 50
George Pearce 50
George Virginia 50(2)
Henry Thomas 50
Iola 50(3)
James J. 50(2), 51(2)
James Samuel 50
Lavina 71
Mattie Ruth 50
Pierce 51
Samuel 50
Sarah Adline 50
Sarah Ellen 51
William Ruburthus 50
BENNETT
Israel D. 1182
Mary E. 164
BENNING
L., Rev. 188
BENTON
Judith 20
BERRY
Emily Ford 55
BEVERLEY
Ann 146(2)
John 146
Wilson 146
BIBBER
Ann Mary Van 79(2),80
BILES
David 95
BIRD
Daniel B. 142(2)
Ella 15,16
Gertrude 15,16
H. V. 15,16
Homver V. 15
Horace C. 16
Horace V. 16
J. Philip 16
John 15
John F. 16
John F. (Jack) 16
John S. 15
Mary Jones 142
Terral 15
BIRDRIAN
Massey 13

BIRDSEY
Albert Hiram 55(2)
Angus Bell 55(2)
George Thomas 55(2)
Green 55
Herbert Ford 54
Hiram 54
John Sandford 54,55(2)
Kate Lunsford 55
Katherine Landford 54
Katherine Sanford 55
Margaret Sanford 54,55(3)
Marion Jones 55
Myra Hubbard 55
Ralph Talmadge 54,55(3)
Ralph Talmadge II 54
Rosaland Davis 55
Samuel R. 55
Samuel Robinson 54(3),55(2)
Samuel Robinson Jr. 55
BLACKBURN
John W. 21
Thompson A. 20
Mary M. 68
BLACKMAN
C. W. 87
BLACKMON
Thomas J. 98

BLANKS
Dottie 35
Fred A. Mrs. 35
BLOCKBURN
Sarah 68
BLOCKER
Oscar J. 180(2)
Ruby Estelle 179(2)
BLOOMER
Isaac 112
BLUE
Annie 46,47,81(2)
Archie Elide 47,82
Caroline L. 47,81
Carrie 46,81
Charles Edwin 47,81
Charlotte 82
D. P. 46
Dan 82
Daniel A. 81
Edna 47(2), 82(2)
F. A. 46,47(2),81(3),82(2)
Francis Archibald 47,81
John 46,47(2)
John Edwin 47,82
John Thomas 82
Katie Adell 47,82
M. E. 47(2),81,82(2)
Mary 47(2),81
Mary E. 82
Mary Virginia 47,82
Stephen Agustus 47,82
Willie Edgar 82(2)
BOATRIGHT
Susan M.
BOLEYN
Charles, Dr. 118
BOND
Ann Mary Van Bibber 79
Carry Delute 80
Charity 77
Charlie Lafayette 80
Dudley 79

E. F. 78
E. J. 78
Easom 77
Eleza J. 78
Elizabeth M. 78
Essie Meridith 80
F. A. 79
Fanny E. 78
Flavious Augusta 79
Flavius A. 79
Flavius Augusta 79
Francie E. 78
Gabriel 77
Henry 79
Henry Clifford 80
Herman 80
J. L. 78
J. R. 78
James T. 78(2)
Janie 78
Heney 77
Jenney 77
Jessie Lorina 79
Jessie Lourine 80
John Anderson 80
Johnnie A. 79
Joseph 77
Joseph L. 78
Lavinia 77
Leo Nora 78
Leonard 78
M. R. 78(2)
Mae Foster 79,80
Marcus R. 78
Martha C. 79
Mary E. 78
Mavisra Ida 78
Milley 77
Nathan 77
O. H. 78
Omer H. 78
Pollers 77
Robert J. 78

Susanna 77
Tandie Dudley 80
W. F. 78
W. L. Dr. 85
William 77
William Dudley 79
William F. 78
William Wallace 80
BONDS
Alexander Lumpkin 81
Caroline 80
Carye Deluta 80
Charley Dafoot 80
Charlie 81
Dudley 79,80
Elsey 81
BONDS
Essi 79
Essie Meredith 80
F. A. 79
Flavious A. 80
Flavious Augusta 80
Flora 81
Flora Lutch 81
Henry V. 80
Herman 80,81
Hillary 80
J. A. 81
Jessie 81(2)
Jessie Loorine 80
John A. 81(2)
John Anderson 80
John J. 80
Laura 81
Martha Jane 79,80
Martha M. 79
Martha Meridith 80
Mary Elizabeth 80
Mary Foster 80
May Foster 81
Thomas M. 80
William 80
William Dudley 80

William Wolis 80
Zemily 80
Tandy Dudley 80
BONNER
George, Rev. 162
BOOKMAN
Leona 69
BOON
Bollin 130
BOONE
Jennie 57
BOOTH
Adeline P. 84
Albert Dewey 83
Alexander S. 85
Arrenia Ellen 85
Cathrinas Clifford 85
Dewey Otis 84(2)
Elisabeth C. 83
Elizabeth C. 84
Elizabeth Catherine 84
Ellen Bert 83,84
Elmer Hoyt 85
Essie Cathrine 85
George Conners 85
Henry Grady 85
Homer O'Neil 84
J. R. 83
Jamerson Vaanburen 84
James Melvin 83,84(2)
Jameson Van Buron 83
John Lee 85
John R. 84
John W. 85
John Wiley 84
Katherine Aderline 85
Leona 83(2),85
May Belle 85
Mildred 83,84
Ray Edwin 84
Rossie Bideau 83
Susie Lee 83,84
T. A. 83,84

Thomas Atkins 82,83
Thomas Carl 83,84
BOREN
John 116
BORGAN
Esther 139
BORT
Wilhelm
BOURQUINS
Robert H. 175
BOWDOIN
Basheba 85
Elizabeth 85
Frank Dewitt 85
Hypatia Catharine 85
Joseph D. 85
Josephus Patman 85
Joshua 85
Ross 85
BOWLING
C. J. 87
Elizabeth O'Neill 86
Emily 86,87
George 86,87
Harriet Hewel 86,87
Harry 86,87
James 86
James Thornberry 86
John Newton 86
BOWLING
Joseph C. 87
Joseph Smith 86
Lucy Ann 86
M. Elizabeth 87
Martha Watkins 86
Mary Ann 86, 87(2)
Matthew 87
Matthew Rainey 86
Penelope 86
T. J. 86
T. T. 87
Thomas 87
Thomas Thornberry 86,87(2)

Thornberry Jackson 86,87
Walter Grogan 86
Will 87
William 86,87
William Franklin 86
BOWMAN
Spicey 129
BOYD
Fanny 132
James T. T. 132
John 132
Mary 37(2),132
Nancy 37
Richard 132(2)
Richard Jr. 132
Samuel 132
William Sr. 37
BOYKIN
Rannie Lou 180
BRANCH
W. S. 87
BRANTLY
Susan 69
BRAY
Bessie C. 87
BREMMER
Elizabeth 52
BRENT
Carl Howard 99
Howard Cumly 88
Louise Forrest 88
BREWER
F. D. 33
BRICE
Phebe 29
BRIDGES
Henrietta 73
BRINKLEY
Martha 144
BRINSON
Bonnie 58
Bonnie Patricia 58
Elizabeth Gray 58

Hendrick 58
Julia 58(2)
Julia G. 58
Julia Goodall Williams 58
Julia W. 58
Mary Louise 58
Pete Mills 58
R. H. 58(2)
Robert H. 58(2)
Robert Hendrick 57,58(2)
Robert Hendrick Jr. 58(2)
Sally Mills 58
Sara 58
Sara Elizabeth 58(2)
Sarah E. 57
Sharrell Ann 58
Sherrel 58
BRITT
Priscilla 24
BROOKE
Narcissa 168
Waray 168
BROWN
Elizabeth A. J. 73
Elizabeth Ann 73
Elizabeth Ann Jane 74
George A. 73
I. A. 173
J. A. 128
James V. 127
Lorens Sucky 57
Lucy A. E. 156
Robert Y. 161
Sabrina Ellen Fanning 173
Sarah 31
BROWN
W. A. 78
William S. 128,172
BRUTON
Delilah 140
BRYANT
Ellis 10

BUCK
Capt. L. 50
Lois Margaret 60
BUCKALEW
Mattie Cowan 143
BUCKNER
Fatima 134
BUFFINGTON
Caroline 21
Joseph 135
Mary Few 135
BUICE
Zadie 180
BUIE
Alzens Baden 89
Daniel 89(2)
Daniel B. 89
James A. Mrs. 89
John C. 89
Mary Eunice 89
Sarah A. 89
Sarah V. 89
William D. 89
BULL
Alice 89
Alonzo T. 89,90(2)
Annie V. 90
Edgar A. 90(2)
Elmira V. 90(2)
Ida S. 90(2)
James A. 89,90
James S. 90
Jessie A. 90
Jessie Annie 89
Martha A. 90
Mary E. 9-
Mary Estella 90
Mattie T. 90
Milton F. 90
Milton S. 89
Virginia Anne 89
Walter H. 90(2)
Willie A. 90(2)

BULLOCK
David 130
Edward 130
Elizabeth 130
Elizabeth Oliphant 129
James 130
John 130
Loretta Elizabeth 54
Sally 130
Susanna 130
William 129
William O. 130
Winifred 129
Zachariah 130
BURCH
A. (Andrew) J. 100
Aeolain L. 99
Albert 100
Benjamin 98(2)
Clyde Lanier 99
Duquesne 100
Elizabeth 98, 100
Eunice 98
James J. 98
Jane 98(2)
Jincy 100
John 100
John Adrain Roy 99
John B. 100
John P. (Pinson) 100
Keziah 98
Lafayette 100
Margie Anna 99
Marjorie 99
Marshall 100
Mortimer 100
Nancy E. 100
Raul W. 100
Roland Brown 99
Ruth 98
Sarah 98, 110
Thomas 98
W. D. 99

William Dapesney 99
William Stapleton 98
Willie Stokes 99
BURDEN
Job W. 156
BURGE
Adolphus Green 101
Allen 101
David 101
Dorer Jane 101
Eliza Ann 101
Elizabeth 101
Elizabeth Ann 101
James Robert McFee 101
Jane Adeline 101(2)
John Pinckney 101
Joseph Green 101
Judith 101
Judy 101
Mary 101
Mary E. 101
Mary Elizabeth 101
Milly Texaner 101
Nancy 101
Nancy Elizabeth 101
Nathaniel 101(3)
Priscilla 101
Sarah 101
Sarah Susan 101
William 101
William T. 101
William Twilly 101
Woody 101
BURKE
E. W. 57
BURKS
Charles H. 102(2)
Charles Henry 102
Dorie Edwin Emmet 102
Fannie Lou 102
James M. 102
James Madison 102
Martha Jane Eunice 102

Mary C. 102
Mary Catherine 102(2)
Minnie A. 92
Narcissa J. M. 102
Narcissa James M. 102
Narcissa Jane 102
Robert Emmett 102
S. W. 91
Stella Elizabeth Goulding 102
BURNEY
Catherine 25
BURNS
Narcissa J. Burks 104
Narcissa J. M. 104
Robert Holmes 102
Salmon Holmes 104
Samuel A. 102,104
BURNSIDES
Susannah 26
BUSCH
Virginia Bell 50
BUSH
Alice Capitola 160
BUTCHER
Henry 154
Sarah Ann 154
BUTLER
Annie E. 62
Emma 180
Inez 57
BYRON
Charles 169(2)
CAARLE
Ann E. 175
CADDENHEAD
Edmond 33
Lucey H. 33
CALDWELL
Allen 34
Amanda P. 33
Amanda Permelia 33
Andrew James 104,105
Andrew T. 104

Betsey 32,33
Betseyan 33
Betseyann 32
Betsy 34
Catharine Parks 105
Catherine P. 104
Creed 32,33,34
David 32,33(2),34
David A. 33(2)
David Allen 32
Elizabeth 33,34
Elizabeth F. 104
Elizabeth Freelove 105
Harriet 104,105
Harriet B. 104
Helen Demeray 105
CALDWELL
Helen Dmanery 104
James M. 33
John 32,33,104(2)
John F. 33
John Floyd 32,34
Julia M. 33
Julia Marion 33
Lucey H. 33
Lucey Haskins 32
Martha 33
Martha A. 34
Martha A. E. 33
Martha Ann 32
Martha Ann Elizabeth 33
Mary Freelove 105
Mary M. 33
Mary Melissa 33
Matthew, 32,33,34
Nancey 31,33
Patsy 32
Polley 32,33,34
Richard 104,105
Robert F. 33
Robert F. 33
Salley 33
Sally 32

Samuel Brewster 104,105
William H. 33
William Hurley 32
CALHOUN
Alice Capitola 160
Caroline Blackshear 160
Elefair 160
Elvira Covender 159
Georgia Ella 160
James 159(3)
James M. 160
James McCoy 159
James Wright 159(2),160
Jane Catherine 159,160
Martha Vashti 159
Mary Elizabeth 159,160
Nancy Medford 159,160
Salida Anna 159
Sarah 159
Sarah Ann 160
Thomas Wade 160
Virginia Ellen 159
William 159
CALIDONA
Hannah 145
CALLAWAY
Apsilla Ann 114
Ardecoe G. 114
Beniter A. 114
DeLamaster 114
Eliza E. 114
Elizabeth 114,116
Elizabeth Clark 114
Elizabeth Shivers 114
Ellen Wilie Jourdan 114
Jacob King 114
James M. 114
James Madison 114
Jesse 114
John 114
John H. M. 114
John Sr. 116
Joseph 114

Joseph M. 114(2)
Joseph Sr. 116
Joshua 114,116
Joshua S. 114
Joshua Sanford 114
Luke J. 114,116(2)
Lydia 114,116
Lydia Ann 116
Mary 114
Mary Catherine 116
P. M. Milnor 114
Polley 114
Polly Milner 114
Sabrina 114,116
Samuel M. 114,116
William 114,116
Willis Joshua 114
Woodson 114
CALLOWAY
Cynthia Catherine 133
Rebecca 85
CALVIN
Tinie 69
CAMPBELL
Alfred 188
Archibald 112,113,114(2)
Betsey Hays 113,114
Duncan G. 113
Duncan Green 113
Edwin 112
Edwin Eliza 113
Elina 113
Fina McQueen 113
Flora MacQueen 113
CAMPBELL
Frances A. 112
Frances Alexander 113(2)
Gray Green 166
James Archibald 113
Jason Griffin 113
John 112
John M. 113
John Wesley 113

Lillie 85
Margaret Jane 113
Mary Ann 113
Nancy Mansfield 113,114
Rebecca 113
Rebecca Caroline 113
Rebecca Kirk 114
Sarah Q. 113
Sarah Quinten 113
Susan 112
Susan G. 113
Walter Lewis 113
William Archibald 113
CANDER
Beth D. 119
Douglas Harper 119
Richard Alden 119
Samuel 119
CANDLER
Asa G. 121(2)
Asa G. IV 121
Asa G. Jr. 120(4)
Asa Griggs Jr. 121
Asa Griggs 116,120,121
Asa Griggs III 120
Berrie 121
Beth Denny 119(2)
Beth Meredith 119
C. H. 121
C. H. Jr. 120
Catherine McGregor 119
Catherine 116,117,121
Catherine Claire 119
Charles Howard 116(2),117,118,120
Charles Howard IV 118
Charles Howard Jr. 116,117(2),118,119(2), 120
Claire Clements 119
Eugenia 121(2)
Eugenia Bigham 121
Flora 121
Flora Glenn 116,117,118(2),120

Helen 120,121(3)
Helen Magill 121
Henry Charles Jr. 121
Howard III 119
John Howard 121(2)
Laura 121
Lucy Beall 120
Lucy E. 120
Lucy Elizabeth 116,121
Luvy Magill 120
Martha 121
Mary 121
Mary Louisa 116,117,121
Rena Elizabeth 121
Ruth 117,118
Ruth Ozburn Jr. 117
Samuel 119,121
Samuel Glenn 119
Samuel O. 119(2)
Samuel Ozburn 118,119
W. A., Bishop 116
W. T. 121
Walker Tolbert 118
Walter T. 121
Walter Turner 120
Walter Jr. 121
William 120,121
William Berrie 121
William Jr. 121
CANNON
Russel Hunter 101
CARD
Addie E. 162
Ellis 175
CARLE
Anne E. 176
CARLTON
Alen 111
Allen Burton 110
Benjamin F. 111
Daniel Milton 111
Eveline 110,111
Henry 111(2)

James 110
James M. 111
James Sr. 111
Jane 110,111
Joelander 111
John 110,111,112
John F. 112
John T. 111,112
John W. 112
John Wesley 112
CARLTON
Lorenzo D. 111
Margaret 112
Margarett W. 112
Marthy 111
Mary A. R. 112
Mary Ann Elisabeth 111
Mildred C. 112
Mildred Corine 112
Rebecca Girtrude 110
Rebekah G. 111
Richard G. 111
Ruth 110(2),111(4)
Sally Leanerah 110
Susan M. 110
Thomas 110,111(3)
Thomas C. 111
Travis H. 111
William L. 111
William T. 112
CARROLL
Emily 157
James C. 174
Sarah Elizabeth 60
CARSON
Elizabeth Jane 110
Joseph 110(2)
Joseph J. 110
Mary A. 110(2)
Mary M. 110
Sarah F. 110
W. H. G. 110
William 110

CARTER
Britt 71
E. R. 71
Francis P. Barlow 71
Lucinda 71
CASSADAY
Elbert Sevier 95
Elizabeth Jane 95(2)
Elizabeth L. 96
Hannah L. 95
Hannah Louca 95
Lula 97
Martha E. 95
Martha Emelia 95
Mary 95
Mary Lamanda 95
Mary Lamly 95
Nancy Ann 95
R. M. 95
Richard 95
Richard W. 95(2)
Romney M. 95
Russell Marimore 95
Russell Merriman 95
CASSADAY
Nancy Ann 95
CATER
Amelia E. 6
Catherine Virginia 6(2)
Thomas J. 6
CAUDWELL
Ed 24
CAUKER
Thomas Glenn 27
CHAMBERS
Margaret M. 76
William 89
CHAMBLESS
Lovicy 114
CHAMLEE
J. W. 99
Jacob 99
James 99

CHANDLER
Amanda 168
CHAPEAU
Armand L. 5
Austin Chazal 5
Eleanor 5
Elise 5
Ellen 5(2)
Pauline 5
Thomas 5
Thomas T. 5
CHAPMAN
Emma Bert 83
James Booth 83
James O. 83
James Otis 85
Mary Louise 83(2)
William Thomas 83
CHEEK
James Bynum 84
Thomas Angus 84
CHENEY
A. J. 44
CHRISTIAN
Anna 161
William J. 106
CLARK
Mossen 169
CLAYTON
Rachel 33
CLEMENTS
Katherine Claire 118
CLEVELAND
Elizabeth 158
Reubin 158
Sythea 158
CLIFTON
Elva R. 58
J. S. 180
M. J. 180,181
Mary Jane 181
CLOSEYMORE
Ann M. 37

COBB
A. E. 105
Abby R. 106
Aby B. 106
Anzlet Burges 107
Charles K. 106
Charles R. 106
D. H. 106(2)
David H. 105,106(2)
Edwin Parker 107(2)
Eliza C. 156(2)
Elmyra 156
Emily 105,106,155
Emily J. 156
Exie F. 155
Exie Frances 156
Exie Francis 156
Frances E. 155,156
Green C. 107
Eda E. 155
Ida Elmira 156
Ida Ophelia 106
J. C. 107
J. H. 107
James 155(3),156(2)
James Alfred 156
James C. 107
James E. 107
James Edmund 107
James H. 107
James Henry 155,156
James R. L. 107
John H. 106
John N. 105
John P. 155,156(3)
John R. 107
John W. 106(2)
Malinda C. 155,156(2)
Marila L. 105
Martha A. 106
Martha J. 155,156
Martha L. 106
Mary 156

Mary A. E. 106(2)
Mary Ann 155(2)
Mary E. 155
Mary Essie 156
Mary J. 155
Mary K. 105
N. M. 105
Nancy M. 105
Neta Jane 156
R. C. 107(2)
Ransom A. 155,156
Rebecca C. 107
Rebecca Sugar 107
Robert 107
Rosa P. 106
Rosy L. 106
S. S. 105
S. T. 105
Sam Rev. 118
Samuel 105(2)
Samuel N. 106
Sarah A. 156
Sarah Ann 156
Sarah F. 105
Thomas H. 107(2)
Thomas H. D. 107
Thomas H. Sr. 107
W. J. 107(5)
William H. 156
William J. 107(2)
William Johnston 155,156
William S. 105,106
COCHRAN
Calvin W. 51
Sarah Kathryn 51
COLE
Paul Wilson 84
Paul Wilson Jr. 84
COLEMAN
Julia 16
Martha J. 16,17
Sarah 49
COLEY
Lucinda 139
COLLEY
Eliza 127,172
Elizabeth 127
Francis 127,172
Gabriel 127,172
John 127,128,172(2),173
Lieusinday 128,173
Louisa 127(2),172
Mary 127,172
Nancy 127,172
Nimrod 128,173
Sarah 127,172,173
Spain 172
COLLIER
Frances 56
James 56
Nancy Elizabeth 56(2),57
COLLINGSWORTH
James 185
COLLINS
Angeline 29
Anna Maria 28
Annie 3
Benjamin J. B. 28,29
Charles 3
Creed 28,29
Jane Alberta Dozier 189
Jerry Lind 29
John 28,29(2)
Judah Bailey 3
Lizzie 189
Phebe 28,29
Robert 3
Sara Allen 189
Sarah B. 28,29
Sidney 3
COLQUITT
Addie May 171
Albert Candler 171
Alice E. 171
Charles Glen 171
Edward G. 171

Edward Gray 171
Florence Odessa 171
Frances A. 171
Frances Antionette 171
Franklin A. 171(2)
James L. 171
John Marvin 171
John W. 171
John Wesley 171
Mary Emma 171(2)
Otis Lindsey 171
Paul Gibson 171
Pierce Kemp 171
Rebecca E. 171(2)
Sara Frances 171
Sarah Anna 171
Wesley F. 171
COLQUOHOUN
Ann Elizabeth 134
Archibald 134
Archibald Sr. 134
Calvin 134
Duncan 134
Isabel 134
James Gamble 134
John C. 134
Malcolm 134
Margaret Ann 134
Mary 134
Rachel 134
Richard Marks 134
CONKLE
Alice Bull 90
John H. 89
CONNER
Ann 146
Bethe 146
Betsy 145,146
Eliza Tarpley 145
Harriot 146
Harriot Elizabeth 145
James 146
James Gasaway 146
James Gassaway 145(2)
Lewis 146
Louisa Ann 146
CONNER
Lucy Ann 145
Margaret 146
Mariah McDonald 146
Martha Lucy 146
Mary J. 145,146
Nancy 145,146
Polly Godwin 145
R. A. Rev. 192
Thomas 146
Thomas Benton 145,146
Thomas Sr. 146
William 146
William DeWitt Clinton 146
Wilson 145
Wilson Walker 146
CONWILL
Bailey 161
CONYERS
Daniel B. 101
COOGLE
Billie 43
George Herbert 43
Laura 43(3)
Robert Leo 43
Roy 43
Roy Allen 41,44
Sarah Elizabeth 43
T. L. 43(3)
Thomas Leslie 41,44
W. B. 43
Willia 43
COOK
C. A. 184,185
C. E. Cordelia 185
Charity 183
Columbus Asburry 185
E. C. 91
Eleanor 146
Eliza 184

George 183
Henry 183
J. W. 184(2),185
James 183,184(2)
James S. 94
James Willey 184,185
James William 185
John 184,185
John Davis 185
John Pease 184
John Pierce 185(2)
John Wesley 185
Julian 184,185
Lovie Pierce 184,185
M. 185
M. A. 184
M. A. A. 184
M. E. 184
Mariah 183
Martha 19,94
Mary 19,123(2),124,145,184,185
Mary Ann Amelia 185
Mary Eliza 185
Morning Elizsabeth 185
N. O. 184
Nancy 183
Nathan 183
O. N. 185
Oliver Neal 185
P. F. 185
R. F. 184
Robert F. 184
Robert Francis 185
Sarah 183
Sarah Ann 142
Simon 183
Tamer C. 184
Tom 183
William 98
William H. Thomas 184
William Thomas 185
COOPER
Eleanor Cook 146

George 146
George Washington 146
Luvancy 146
Mary Ann Elizabeth 146
Penelope Luvancy 146
Thomas B. C. 146
Wilson Conner 146
COWAN
Agnes 141,143(2),144
Annie Bailey 143
Daniel B. 143
Daniel Bird 142
Edwina Nell 182(2)
Elea-- 182
Elizabeth B. 143
Elizabeth Baskin 142
Ella Cornelia 182
Ellie Evelyn 182
Fannie Lettie 182
Frances Letitia 182
Georgia V. 182
Henrietta C. 182
Henrietta Clementine 183
Hiram 142
Hiram Darnell 142
James 141,142,143(3),144
James Jones 141,142(3),143
James Jones, Dr. 143
James W. 142,143
James William 142
John W. 142
John Jordan 142
John Woods 142,143
Joseph L. 143
Joseph LaFayette 142(2)
M. J. (Smith) 142
Margaret McCalvey 141
Martha Joyce 142(2)
Mary 143
Mary Bird 142(2)
Mary H. 143(2)
Mary Harris 142
Mary Margaret 182(2)

Morgan Jr. 182
Nancy 143
Nancy Elizabeth 143(3)
Nathaniel Harris 141
Robert A. 142
Robert F. 143
Robert Frazer 142
S. Morgan 182(2)
S. Morgan Jr. 182
Samuel Morgan 182
Sarah Ann Cook 143
Thomas Franklin 142(2)
William H. C. 143
William Harris Caldwell 142
William S. 182(2)
Willie Evelyn 182
Willie J. 182
Willie Jack 182
Z. S., Dr. 143
Zach J. 142
Zachariah J. 142
COWART
A. J. 180
Jackson S. 138
COX
John 140
CRAFT
Alice A. 155
Allie Irwin 155,156
CRANFORD
Ellen 87
CRAWFORD
Flavius Henry 81
Hester Ann 81
Joel 156
Martha Jane 79
Martha Maria 79(2)
Martha Marie 80
CRAWL
Mary C. 150
CRAWLEY
Margaret 116
CRITTENDEN

E. J. 78
CROFT
C. W. 138
CROSLAND
Charlotte 123
CROSS
H. R. 105
William H. H. 105
CROWLEY
Dilla 142
CRUMBY
M. F. M. D. 43
CRUMRINE
Jennie L. 29
CULPEPPER
Maryann 12
W. 11
CUMMING
Thomas J. 108
CURETON
James 161
CURRAN
Charles Marion 30
Holland Kinon 30
CURRIN
Mary 139
CURTH
Thomas Gastin 129
CURTIS
Edward 43
Emma 42
Silas 42
Silas W. 42
CUTHBERT
James, Rev. 13
DAHL
Ruth 60
DALBO
Anne E. 52
Anthony Bates 53
Emil Jens 53
Emil Peter 52(2)
Johnna Lorensen 53

Mona Samaria 53
DANCER
A. M. 181
A. L. 181
Ada 180
Anna Leonorie 1180
L. 181
M. J. 181
Minnie Lee 180
T. A. 181
Theodisia A. 180
W. C. 181
W. R. 180,181(3)
DANIEL
David 112
James Edward 30
Margarett W. 112
Mary 112
Mary H. 30
Susannah 26
DANIELS
Rev. 180
DARSEY
Fetney 186(2)
Frances Axie 188
Hariot 186
Harriet B. 186
Henry W. 187(2), 188
Henry Woodruff 187
J. 187
J. H. 187
James M. 186
James Madison 187
Jamie Rufus 188
Joab H. 187
Joseph 186
Joseph B. 187
Joseph G. 187
Joseph H. 188(2)
Julia F. Shelfer 187
Leannia L. 188

Lenna Lee Johnson 187
Louisa 187
Mamie E. 187,188
Mamie Hellen 187
Margaret 186
Marian Elizabeth 188
Mary 186(2),187
Mary M. 186
Mary Moriah 187
Moriah 186
Nancy 186(2)
Thomas 186
Thomas Bowdre 187
Tom N. 187
Virginia Nell 188
William 186(3)
DAVIS
Dottie 35
S. F. 149
W. A. 52
DAWSON
Annebelle 124
Rev. 188
Thomas H. Rev. 192
DAY
Aaron B. 170
Adaline 170
Bluford B. 170(2)
David 169,170
Eliza 170
Emily 170
Frances A. 170
John McMillan 140,141
Margaret 170
Minnie Elizabeth 170(4)
Lemenda K. 170
Martha Ann 170
Mary 170
Mary Johnson 169
R. H. 147
Saletha R. 170
Zilpha
DEER

Elmira Cobb 156
Mary J. Sullivan 156
DELANY
Alexander 140
Daniel 140
Delilah Julia 140
Elizabeth 140
Esther 140(2)
George Durham 140
James 140
John 140
John Landrum 140
Maryann 140
Matilda Moroney 140
Rebecca Frances 141
Rosannah M. 140
Sarah Adeline 140
Susannah Caroline 140
Thomas Newport 141
William Green 141
DENHAM
Alva David 170
E. J. 170
Earnest Willie 170(2)
Guy Otto 170
J. C. 170
Josiah C. 170
Josiah Singleton 170(2)
Leroy 170
Maggie May 170
Mariah Louisa 170
Mary Elizabeth 170
Nicy Ann F. 170
Oscar Fudge 170
Paul 170
Ruth 170
William Edwin 170
William Thomas 170(2)
DENNIS
Jacqueline Brent 99
Jacqueline Elaine 99(2)
DENNY
Beth Graham 118

Beth Gresham 119
DERRICK
H. C., M. D. 43
DEVANE
Elizabeth J. 60
DEVEREUX
Archibaldn 174
Charles 174(2)
Elizabeth 174
James 174
John 174
Nancy 174
Samuel M. 174(2)
Williamn 174
DEWOLF
Agness 168
Annie Jordan 169
Anthony 168,169
Craven Payton 179,180
David 64(2),65(2)
Ford W. 169
George V. 169
Lyllian J. 169
Lyllian Jane 169
Mossen C. 169
Mossen Clark 169
Mossen Clarke 169
William G. 169
William Gorden 169
William Gordon 169
DEWOLFE
Sara Agnes 169
DICKIN
G. 159
DICKINSON
Albert McDuffie 180
Benjamin R. 180
Benjamin Robertus 180
Benjamin Roburtus 179
Benjamin Slaton 179,180
Bertha Mae 179,180
Edna C. 180
Edna Earle 179

Gilbert M. D. 180
Gilbert McDuffie 179
Leonora 179,180
Maggie Belle 179
Margaret (Maggie Belle) 180
Martha Elizabeth 179,180
Ralph Deane 180
Sarah 179,180
Sarah Jane Ledbetter 180
DICKSON
Amer Saphrona 66
Anna 65
Anne Allen 65
Annie Allen 65(2)
Annie E. 63
Benjamin H. 63
C. C. 62
Charles A. 65
Charles D. 63
Charles Robert 65,66
Christopher Columbus 65
David Harris 65
David Manson 65
David Monro 64
David Sumpter 65
Davis Jr. 65
E. J. 62
Elisabeth Ann Riley 65
Elisabeth C. 65(2)
Elisabeth 64,65
Elizabeth Jane 62
Elizabeth Posy 64
Emer Saphrona 66
Eugene Bee 62
Eugenia Elizabeth 62
Henry Bee 62
Howard H. 63
James 64
James Otterson 64
John Landers 65
John Marshal 65,66
John O. 64,65(2)
John Orr 64(2)

John S. 63(3)
Julia Maria 64
Loriann O. 65
Manson 65(2)
Martha 64,65
Martha 64,65
Martha Jane 65
Martha Letitia 65
Martha Louisa 65
Mattie T. 89
Mrs., M. D. 41
Mary 65,65
Mary Ann 65(2)
Matheny 65
Michael 64(3)
Nancy Campbell 64
Nancy Eliza 64,65
Patrick Henry 62
Patsey Ealse 64
Pearl 63
Robert D. 65
Robert David 64,65
Robert L. 63
S. L. 62
Samuel Cans 62
Sarah 65,65
Sherman Glass 65
Stephen 62
Stephen L. 60,62
Stephen Light 62
Thomas G. 62
Thomas Green 62
Thomas Hyde 64
Thornton S. 64
Thornton Smith 65
W. Hugh 64
W. W. 62
Walter J. 63
William 64(3)
William Hugh Crawford 64
William W. 62,63
William White 62
William Wyatt 65(2)

Wylie P. 62
Eylie Peyton 62
Wylie Pope 62
Zebulon Montgomery Pike 64
DILLINGHAM
Absalom 100(2)
Hiram 100
Janette Carolyn Burch 100
DILLON
Corley Hall 89
DIXON
Anna Loyd 174(2)
D'LANUACY
Pauline 25
DOMESLY
Marion 21
DONALD
Edna 46,81
DOSTER
Hannah 121
DOZIER
A. G. 189,190
Albert 189,192
Albert Darsey 191
Albert Dorsey 191
Albert Green 188,189(2),190
Als 192
Ann 136
Annie 193(2)
Benjamin Lewis 189
Benjamin Lewis Gilmer 190
Bud Willie A. 189
Claud Carreca 193
Claude Wilkes 191,192
Constance 192(2)
Constance W. 193
Constantia 190
Constantia Hunt 189
Constantia W. 189
C. M. 191
C. N. 191
C. W. 191,192
Carrie Lee Jackson 189(2),190

Edgar 191
Edgar Collins 191
Elizabeth 136,188
Elizabeth Fanning 189,190
Erasmus J. 192
F., Rev. 190
Floyd Truman 193
Frances 188,189(2)
Frances J. 192(2)
G. J. 193
Green 192
Green J. 192
Green Jones 188,189,191
Green S. 189
Henry Hurt, Rev. 189
Hunt 189,190
I. C. 191(2)
Ida C. 191,192
Ida Camille 192(2)
Ida Cunningham 191
Ida Wilkes 192
Ignatius J. 192
Ignatius James 192
Isabellah A. 193
Isabellus A. 192
J. M. 189,191
J. M. Powers 190
James 136
James J. 188
James M. 189
Jane Alberta 189,190,1911(2)
Jane M. 189(2)
Jane Margarett 190
Jemina 136
John 136,188
John A. 192,193
John E. 188,192,193
John George 189,190
John S. 63(3)
Johnnie 193
Johnnie W. 193
Julia Maria 64
Keziah 136

L. E. 193(2)
Lauren Humphreys 191
Larena Gilmer 191
Leonard 136
Leonard III 136
Leonard T. 192,193
Martha A. E. 192
Mary Ann 193
Mary C. 189
Mary Constantia 189,190
Nicholas Green 190(2)
Philip Thomas 192
Richard 136
S. B. 191,192
Sallie C. 192
Sallie F. 193
Sara B. 191
Sarah Frances 189,190,191
Susannah 136
T. H. 191(3), 192
Thomas 136
Thomas Henry 191
Thomas Henry Hunt Jr. 192
Thomas Henry Jr. 191
Thomas Henry Sr. 191
W. P. 191
Walter Herbert 191
Walter M. 192
Walter Powers 191,192
William 136
William Albert 189,190
William Allen 191
William H. 188
William W. 192
Willie L. 193
Wilson W. 192
DRAKE
Green W. 149
Louisa M. 149
Martha 149
Martha Jelks 149
Mary Elizabeth 149(2)
S. T. 149(2)

Tempie Lula 149(2)
DRAPER
Lucy 123
DRAYTON
Anna 177
Anna M. 177
Thomas F. 177
DRINKARD
Eugene Dr. 117
DUGGAN
A. C. 147
Amarintha 13
Archeleus 147
Archeleus Maddux 147
Benjamin R. 147
Chloe Ann 147
Clarissa Ann 147
David Edmund 147
Elizabeth Ann 147
Elizabeth Nancy 147
George Margaret 147
Ivy Walker 147
J. W. 147
James Barnes 147
John 147
Joseph Franklin 147
Mary 147
Mary N. 147
N. R. 147
Rebecca Kelly 147
Susan Frances 147
Thomas Green 147
DUGGAN (Slave)
Amanda 147
Celia 148
Isaac 147
Leo 147
Lucinda 148
Mary 148
Sarah 148
Seaborn 148
DUNCAN
Sallie 78

DUNLAP
Jeanie 16
DURHAM
Delilah Bruton 140
Delilah 140
George 140
Susannah 140
DURWELL
---aisy 21
DYE
G. 188
DYKES
Hulda Ann 101
Mary M. 167
Mary Amanda 167
EARP
Caleb 139
Caleb Asbury 140
Caswell 140
Catherine 140
Caty 140
Daniel 140
David D. 140
James M. 140
Lavonia 140
Llewellen 140
Margaret 139
Matthew 140
Matty 140
Statiba 140
EASTIN
Christiana 35
EATON
Dorcas A. 167
Eleanor C. 167
Elizabeth A. 167
George W. D. 167
James M. 167
John L. 167
Joseph 167
Lewis 167
Marthaa L. Y. 167
Mary 167

Nancy E. 167
Rev. 4
Sarah F. 167
Sarah E. 167
William H. 167
EBERHART
Elizabeth 91
ECHOLS
Elizabeth 65
ECKFORD
Charles Gates 45
EDENS
R. L. 52
EDGE
Martin
EDISON
George Towns, 113
EDMUNDSON
M. L. 50
EDWARD
J. W. 106
EDWARDS
Alfred 167(2),168
Islan W. 168
Islan William 167
Lee 117
Littleton C. 168
Littleton Cleaveland 167,168
Nancy E. 168
Nancy Evaline 167,168
Narcissa Brooke 167
Rhoda 130
Sarah Florence 167
Sarah T. 168
ELBE
George 164
ELDREDGE
Alfred Stewart 116
Alfred T. Jr. 119
Alfred Turner 116,117(3),118
Alfred Turner III 119
Ann Glenn 117,118
Claire M. 119

Claire Middlebrooks 119
David Read 56
Janie Bell Turner 116
L. C. 120
Louisa 117
Louisa Candler 117,119
Mary Candler 119
Simson 175
ELIZABETH
Thomas 189
ELKINS
Ann 175(2)
Augustus R. 175,176
Caroline M. 175,176
Charles C. 175,176
Julia 175(2)
L. L. 175
Leander L. 176(2)
Lydia Ann 175
Maria P. Tondee 176
Moriah 176
Moselle 175
Phares N. 175
Phares Nepolian 175
Sarah 175(2),176
Sarah E. 175,176
Sekuba V, 175,176
Thomas 175(3),176(3)
Thomas P. 175,176
Wiley 175
ELLIOTT
Frances 138
ELLIS
James McLevi 140
ELLZEY
Belle Green 166
John Green 166
M. P. 166
ELMORE
J. S., Rev. 41
Jacob, Rev. 41
ENGLISH
Bethia 43

H. 41
Mathew 41
ESTES
Elbert 98
EUBANKS
Bessie 97
Corrine Elizabeth 138
EVANS
Ardin 66(2)
Ardin B. 66
Casst A. 66
Cornelius Jefferson 66(2)
David Reid 66
Davy 56
Elizabeth Acadia 66(2)
Elizabeth Martha Sophia 56
Emely 56
Evann 66
G. B. 66
George Brown 66
Joseph 56
Josephine 66
Josephine McMichael 66
Louisa Francis 66
Louvenia 66
Mary 56(2)
Mary Cuella 66
Sarah Augusta 66
Seaborn Ardin 66(2)
William 56
FAIN
J. G. 51
FAMBROUGH
Anderson 132
Byrd 132
FANNIN
Abram 112
Ann M. 124
Isham S. 124(2)
Jepthah 124
Sarah Balkes 191
FANNING
Abina Victoria 127,172

Alace Estelle 128,172
Bryan 128,172
Charles Ann 127,128,172
Frances 128,172(2)
Francis 127
John C. 127,128,172(2)
Louisa 127,172
Martha 127, 172
Mary 127,172
Nancy 127,172
Parks 127,128,172(2)
Sabrina Ellen 128(2), 172
Samuel D. 128,172
Sarah F. 127,128,172
Victoria A. 128,172
Webster 128(2),172,173
Welcome 127(2)
FANNY
Richard, Jr. 132
FAUCETTE
Annie 15
FEARS
James 124
FERRELL
Adeline Elizabeth 70
George Arch Sr. 70
George Archer 69
George Archer Jr. 70
Toon Fletcher 70
FEW
Hannah 135
Joseph 135(3)
Joseph II 135
Mary 135
FISH
Calvin 128,129
Clarasha 128
Clarisa 129
Eliza 129
Naomi 129(2)
Nathan 128,129,
Poley 128
Rusel 129

Russel 129
Sarrina 129
Susan 128
Theren Happwah 128(4)
Thomas Gastin 129
FISHER
Catharine L. 141
FITCHETT
John 130
John K. 130
FLETCHER
Hannah Loueva 96
Lewis R. 95
Lewis Rowland, Mrs. 95
Osker Alonzo 96
Romney Atticus 96
Talullah Alphonso 96
Williamson Montgomery 96
FLOWERS
Sophian Malinda Barwick 12
FLUKER
Mrs. 113
FOOT
Bro. 60
FORA
Emily Harcell, 55
FORTENBERRY
Ann Jane, 165
Jeremiah, 165
Nancy, 165
FOY
Lula, 27
FRANK
Henry, Jr., 127
FRANKLIN
Abednego, 158(2)
Abner, 158
Barnard, Jr., 158
Benjamin, 159(2)
Bernard, 158
Bernard, Sr., 158
Betsy, 159
Betty, 158

Bryson, 159
Jeremiah, 158
Jesse, 158
John T., 159
Judith, 158, 159
Lucinda, 159
Mary, 158(2)
Mary H., 159
Meshach, 158
Patsey, 159
Sarah, 159(2)
Shadrach, 158
Talighta Loretta, 10
Wylie, 159
FRANKS
Eliza Jane, 145
F. M., Mrs., 144
Isaac L., 145
FREEMAN
Florence Odessa 171
Mary 38
FRIEND
Benjamin Few, 135
Edward 135
Eliza Buffington 135
Fanny Buffington 135
John Ozburn 135
Joseph 135
Mary Few 135
Matilda 135
Phoebe Ozburn 135
Thomas 135
FROST
Eugene 109
William J. 109
FUDGE
Louisa Atlilla 170
FULLER
Glenn C. 120
Mary Alles 145
Thomas III 118, 120
Thomas IV 120

FURLOW
Nancy 133

GARDNER
C. W., 59, 60
Robert B., 151
Sarah Neal, 151
Walter Gorham, 150
GATES
Mary A., 2
GAYLE
Anne, 136
GEER
W. I., 180
GEORGE
Sandra Louise, 182
GIBBO
Nevada, 69
GIBSON
Alice E., 171
Arthur Van, Rev., 118
GILBERT
A. O., 71
C. F., 71
Estelle, 71
J. D., 71
Laura Bell, 71
Lena M., 71
Lilla G., 71
M. V., 71
Mante L., 71
Mary F., 71
O. C., 71
Robert E., 71
V. B., 71
W. E., 35
W. O., 71
W. S., 71(2)
GILL
Ada, 181
GILMER
Thomas, 189

GILSON
  T. W., 99
GLASS
  Johathan H., 65
GLEATON
  Effie, 138
GLENN
  Flora 116
  Floreall Harper, 116
  Florella Harper,
    27
  Joshua N., Rev.,
    188
  W. F., 35, 116
  W. F., Dr., 116
  W. F., Rev., 35
  William Fiske,116
GODSON
  T. W., 11(15)
GOFORTH
  Rev. Mr., 177
GOODALL
  Julia, 57
  Sarah, 57
  Sarah Weeks, 57
GOOLSBE
  Darmaris, 127
  Demaris, 172
  Kirby, 127
GORDON
  William D., 122
GORHAM
  Ally T., 150
  Anna Fannie, 151
  Anne F., 150(2)
  Cornelia L.,
    150(2)
  Florence Agnes,
    151
  George C., 150(2)
  James A., 150(2),
    151
  John Willis,
    150(2)
  Joseph A., 150
  Joseph J., 150,
    151
  Mary E., 150, 151
  Mary E. A., 150
  Mary Elizabeth,
    150(2)
  Mary Ethel, 151
  Mary J., 150, 151
  Polina C. F., 151
  Sarah R., 150
  Susan B., 150
  Susannah B.,
    150(2)
  W. J., 150, 151
  William Anderson,
    150
  Willis, 150(2)
  Willis J., 150(3)
  Willis, Sr., 151
GRACY
  Mary, 16
GRAVES
  M. S., 15
  Sallie Porter, 126
GRAY
  C. M., Rev.,
    54(2)
  Eliza, 161
  Mary, 16, 17
  Rob. B. M., 54
GREEN
  Annie Lee, 165
  Arthur, 165
  Belerina, 101
  Belle, 165
  Grace Caroline,
    54
  Gray, 165
  Howard, 165
  J. M., 164
  Jane Waverly,

165, 166
John M., 166(2)
Joseph, 101
Louise, 165
Nancy, 101(2)
Sallie L.
  Strickland, 166
Sarah, 165, 166
GREER
Aden, 43(2)
Aden Lovell, 41, 44
Allen H., 41
Angusta Matella, 162
C. A., M. D., 43
Elizabeth Leanna, 162
Elvie Ann, 43
Gussie M., 162
Larry, 58
Leanna, 162
Leonard F., 162(2)
Leonard Forsyth, 162
Leonard P., 162
Martha C., 162

Martha Caroline
  Thrasher, 162
Mary Ruth, 43
Ruth, 43(2)
Sallie Clyde, 162(2)
Thadeous
  Ethelbert, 162
GREGG
Alva Mayes, Rev., 182
Amanda Carlisle, 183
Asbury Wellborn, 183
Margaret Letitia, 183
Sandra Louise
  George, 183
W. A., Rev., 50
GRIFFIN
Aby B., 106
Ave Garnet, 39
Blonde, 69
David C. Jesse
  Andrews, 39
Elizabeth, 146
George
  Washington, 39
James, 39
James Conner, 146
John, 35, 38(2), 39(3), 146(2)
Mary, 39(2)
Mary Caroline, 38
Ruth Athlove, 6
Sally, 38
Samuel C., 146
Samuel Conner, 146
Sarah C., 38
Susannah, 39
Thomas, 39
Thomas Mitson, 38
Wiat Andrews, 39
William, 38, 39
GRIGGERS
Alice, 41
McAllen, 41
GRIGGS
Henry, 8(2)
Nancy Marinda, 8
GRIMES
S. E., 180
GRISSELL G.

M. F., 53

M. H., 53
O. S., 53
W. A., 53
GROGMAN
Clarisa, 96
GROVENSTEIN
Benjamin, 27
GUILFORD
J. E., 2
GUILLAN
Hannah, 56
GUINN
Martha R., 18
GWIN
W., 120

HAILEY
H. F., 156
HAISTEN
Elizabeth, 73(2)
William, 73
HAISTONS
Elizabeth, 73
HALE
Mollie D., 153(2)
HALLUM
Mary, 148(2)
HALSEY
Alexander
 Campbell, 1
Anna Harris, 1
David Parkman, 1
Eugenia Campbell, 1
Henry Freeman, 1
Lachlan McIntosh, 1
S. Parkman, 1
William Harris,
 1(2)
HAM
India Heath, 191
HAMILTON
James, Dr., 133
John, 133

Mary, 74
HANES
Cordeala, 167
HANSFORD
George B., 22
Jesse, 21

Maude, 22
Maude Atkisson,
 23
Stephens, 22
Wise, 22
HANSON
J. B., Rev., 192
HARDEN
Frances Ann, 22
HARDWICK
Mary Leonard, 163
William, 188
HARP
William H., 11
HARPER
Ada Jane, 152
Bee, 60(3)
Flora, 116
Florella A., 35
Florella C., 35
George B., 35(2), 36
George W., 35, 36
George William, 35
James P., 35
James R., 36
John J., 35(2), 36
John Jackson, 36
Joseph, 62
Lucy F., 35(2)
Robert F., 35
Susie, 85
William F., 35
William T., 36
HARRIS
Anna, 1
Benjamin, 41

Charles Pinckney, 141
Clay, 160
Eliza Ann Ellen Bailey, 2
Emily, 87
Hartmell, 71
James McCalvey, 141, 143
Jeptha V., 16
John Applewhite, 161
Lena, 45
Margaret, 143
Mary Carolina, 141
Melinda Harriet, 161
Minor, 161
Nancy Margarit, 160
Nathaniel, 142
R. E. L., Rev., 191
Rebecca Adaline, 141
Samuel Jackson, 141
Samuel Washington, 160(2)
Sidon H., 160(2)
Susannah, 73
Thomas E. R., 87
Thomas Jefferson, 161
Wallace, Mrs., 1
Wesley Smith, 161
William Alfred Jones, 161
William Gay, 1, 2(2)
Willis, 25

HARRISON
Ann, 178(2)
Benjamin, 178
Elizabeth, 179
Emelers, 178
G. H., 55
Henry, 178(2), 179
James, 178
John, 178(3), 179
Kollock, 175
Lucy, 179
Margaret, 178
Martha, 178
Mary, 178
Mildred, 178(2), 179
Nathaniel, 178
Sarah, 178
Sarah E., 176
Susana, 178
Temperance, 178
Walter, 86
William, 178(2)
HARRISON (SLAVE)
Fitt, 179
Tom, 179
Venus, 179

HARROLSON
E. S., 148
HARRY
Wilmoth J., 33
HARTSFIELD
Sarah Adline, 50
HATTON
Howard M., 57
HAWK
Mahulda, 23
Mary, 23
Thurmon, 23
HAYNES
Danny Walker, 88

Kate Brent, 88
Noel Baxter, 88
Scheryl Haynes, 88
Wilmer Brent, 88(2)
Wilmer Carlisle, 88(2)
HEARN
Asa, 133
Elizabeth, 133(2)
Jacob, 133
Jonathan, 133
Judah, 133
Lott, 133
Lucinda Amanda, 133
Mary P., 133
Rhoda Ann Letha, 133
Samuel, 133(2)
Seth, 133
Travis M., 133
William, 133(2)
Zebed, 133
HEIDT
Almirey Clementiney B., 102
Ann Margaret, 102
Bethhena 102
D. S. B. Crocket, 102
Eli Augustus Baldwin, 102
Elizabeth, 102
Gideon Jackson, 102(2)
James Hamilton, 102
John, 102
John William, 102
Sarah Ann 67

Sarah T. Bethena, 102
Wily Hampton, 102
HEIFNER
Frand Pierce, 162
Frank Pierce, 162(2), 163
Lillie Adaline, 162
Martha Clyde, 162
Mary Leonard, 162
Sallie Clyde, 162
Sallie O. Greer, 163
Willa Virginius, 162
HEMPHILL
Elizabeth, 153
HENIS
Henry C., 120
HENLY
Jane Elizabeth Darsey, 188
HENRY
Richard, Jr., 132
Stella Viola, Edgd
HERNDON
Clara, 98
HESSE
Toledo, 85
HESTER
Mollie, 69
HILL
A. A., 31
Abraham Thomas, 44
Adam, 48(2), 49
Albert Meriwether, 45
Alexander Franklin, 45, 46
Ann, 48

Annie, 48
B. F., Sr., 31
Benjamin F., 31
Benjamin F., Jr., 31(2)
Benjamin Franklin, 32
Benjamin Franklin Jr. 32
Burwell O., 44
Burwell Obadiah 45
Capt, 49
Catherine, 45(2)
Champion Travis, 48
Charles Henry, 48, 49
David Ralalend, 31
Edwin, 49
Ella May, 31
Frank Pickins, 49
Georgia Ella Reeves, 31, 32
Hiram Warner, 45(3)
J. Nancy, 31
James, 48(2), 49
James A., 50
James Adam, 48
Joe Baker, 31(2)
Joe Jorden, 31
John, 48(4), 49(4)
John Calvin, 48
Joseph A., 48
Julia Thorpe, 31
Laurence, 49
Mae, 31
Margaret, 48, 49
Martha, 44, 45(2)
Martha Catharine, 44
Mary, 45(2)
Mary Jane, 45
Mary Lizzie, 31
Mary Louisa, 49
Miriam Antionette, 31
Miriam Audrey, 31(2)
Molly, 48(2), 49
Nancy, 48, 49(2)
Nettie A., 32
Peggy, 49
Robert, 48(2), 49(2)
Robert Johnson, 45
Robert Lewis, 48
Samuel, 48, 49
Sarah, 44, 45, 48(3), 49(2)
Sarah A., 49

Sarah Annie, 48
Stella Ora, 31
Stella Viola, 31
T., 49(2)
W. T., 50
William, 48, 49(2)
William Trayler, 48
William, Jr., 48(2)
William, Sr., 48(3)
HILLIARD
Sallie, 78
HODGES
Allie Thomas, 52(2)
HOLBROOK
William Michael Spillane, 183
HOLLAND
Emily Ann, 30
Ervine Walter, 30

Harry Hall, 30
Hettie, 30
Hetty, 29
Hetty James, 30
Hetty Jane, 29
James C., 29,
  30(2)
James Thomas, 29
Jesse Day, 29, 30
Mary H., 30
Mary Hannah
  Brewington, 30
Orlando Stinson, 29
Orlena, 30
Sarah Elizabeth,
  30(2)
HOLLINGSWORTH
Columbus
  Jefferson, 182
Elminy M., 59(2)
Mary Margaret
  Cowan, 183
Robert, 59
Sarah, 69
HOLLINSWORTH
Sarah, 68
HOLLOWAY
Joseph William,
  11
Lewis, 9(2)
HOLMES
Narcissa Jane,
  102
William, 87
HOOK
Athaliah I., 124
HOOKS
Curtis, 154
Nancy, 154
Sarah Frances,
  155
HOOPER
James Clarence,
  Jr., 10
Louise Grady, 10
Margaret West, 10
Oscar Lee, 9, 10
Wandsleigh
  Rudisill, 10
HOOTEN
Littleton, 5
Marthan, 5
William, 5
HORNSBY
Cora Arva, 54
Dora Mary, 54
Effie Clyde, 54
Ezzard Arthur, 54
Frances Lee, 54
Jessie Maude, 54
Sarah, 54
Thomas Jefferson,
  54(2)
HORTON
John L., Rev.,
  118
HOWARD
Lucy Elizabeth,
  120
HOWELL
America, 3(2)
Benjamin, 3
David, 3
Sarah, 3
Wealthy, 3
HUDSON
B. A., 41
HUIE
J. W., Rev., 192
HUMPHREYS
Loula Agnes, 191
HUNT
Constantia, 188, 189
Eugeneous Beamon,
  121

M. L., 121
Martha Ann
 Malissa, 121
Mary Laurah, 121
Rhoda Ann, 121
Rhoda Luvenia,
 121
Richard H.,
 121(2)
Robert Turman,
 121
Thomas, 189
HURRY
Elvie, 43
HUSKE
J. C., Rev., 54

INROUGHTEE
Clayburn, 132(2)
Nancy, 132
IRVINTON
J. W., 15
JACKSON
B. A., Rev., 191
Ella, 15
Eugene B., 99
Minnie Frances,
 33
Nathaniel, 36
William, 109
JAMES
Hyman, 109
Stella Viola,
 Edgd
JAMIESON
Walter, 6
JARVIS
Margaret R., 68
JELKS
Martha E. A., 149
JENCKES
Ebenezar, 175
JENCKS

Julia, 176
JENKINS
Jane, 158
John J., Rev., 4
JEWETT
Mattie Kitty, 57
JOHN COLEMAN 72
Richard, Jr., 132
JOHNSON
A. C., 85
Ambrose, 159
Caleb, 169
E. C., 123
Elizabeth T., 38
G. W. R., 123
George W. W., 123
Henry Colquitt,
 180
James M., 123
John A., 123
John A. N., 123
John Leonard, 38
John M. M., 123
Joseph, 12
L. E. J., 123
Landrum E. J.,
 124
Lenna L., 187
Lenna Lee, 187(2)
Loduski C., 123
Lois, 187
Martha C., 97
Mary, 169, 170
Mary A. M., 123
Mary Ann M., 124
Mary P., 128, 173
Minnie Estelle,
 152
Nancy Mary, 123
Nathan B., 38
Samuel H., 123
W. J., 123
William, 123

William A., 123
JOHNSTON
Catherine, 151
Catherine H., 153
Catherine Hughes,
  153
Elvina B., 173
Elvina C., 173
K. C., 105
Nancy Clark, 153
Richard, 153
William B., 2
JOINER
Lewis, 73
Virginia, 41
JONES
Agnes, 142, 144
F. S. A., 145

Fanney, 27
Fanny, 28
Ida C., 94
Ida Catherine, 94
James, 143
James H., 143
Lewis, 143
Louisa M., 145
Mary, 142
S. A., 145
Samuel A., 144
William, 94(2)
JORDAN
Albert E., 114
Alma M., 109(2)
Annie, 98
Annie B., 97, 169
Beulah E., 97, 98
Drucilla, 108(2)
E. F., 147
Elizabeth, 108
Elizabeth E., 109
Ella May, 109(2)
Ellen H., 114

Emmie M., 97(2)
Hellen G., 114
Henry A., 97(2)
Henry H., 114
Ira T., 114
James B., 97(2)
James W., 108
James Willis, 108
Jessie Will, 109
John A., 97(2),
  98, 173
John Richard, 108
John S., 108
John T., 108
John Thomas, 108
John W., 108(2)
Laura R., 109(2)
Lela, 97
Lizzie E., 108
Lola, 98
Lovicy, 114
Lowery M., 98
M. C., Mrs., 97
Maggie M., 97
Maggie Malissa
  Jordan, 98
Margrett
  Elizabeth, 108
Marion, 108
Marion Augusta,108

Martha C., 98
Mary A., 108
Mary E., 97
Mary Ella, 98
Mary L., 114
Mattie E., 108
McIvina, 108
Melissa A., 114
Melvina
  Elizabeth, 108
Nancy, 108
Narcissa E., 114

Neva M., 109(2)
Newton M., 108, 109
Pearl A., 109(3)
Richard, 108(3)
S., 108
Sallie, 108
Sallie C., 108
Sallie Cahill, 108
Sallie W., 109
Samuel V., 114
Susan E., 109
Susie Ernestine, 109
Thomas George, 114
Warren Q., 114
William, 108
William C., 114
JOYCE
Katharine, 16
JOYNER
Irwin J., 108
JUDSON
Jane Hasseltine 14

KAY
F. M., 78
KEAN
Albert Dozier, 189
KEEN
Robert E., 180
KELLY
Elizabeth, 153
Rebekah, 154
KEMP
Ann Jane, 130
David Edwards, 130
Elizabeth, 130
Elizabeth S., 130
Elizabeth Sherrod, 130
Jane, 130
John, 130(2)
John R., 130
John, Sr., 130
Joseph, 130
Joseph Stephen, 130
Mary E., 130(2)
Moses Harvey, 130
Rhoda, 130
William John, 130
KEMPER
Henry Clay, 7
Oliver, 7
Shepard, 7
KILGORE
A. S., 77
Amanda S., 76
Charles Baxter, 76
J. S., 77
James, Dr., 76, 77
L. J., 77
L. Y., 76
N. M., 77
Nancy M. A., 76
Nora Lenna, 76(2)
T. B., 76
W. B., 77
W. F., 76
KILLGORE
Eliza, 185
KINARD
Mary, 161
Michael, 161
KING
Edward W., 33
KIRK
Rebecca, 113
KNIGHT
John, Rev., 188

KNSWUCK
Matha, 60
KOGER
Mrs., 93
KULE
Louisa, 178

LABOON
Elizabeth Tripp, 152
Joseph, 151, 152
Rachel Mary Ann, 151, 153
LACKEY
Caroline, 18
Charles, 18
Elizabeth, 18(2)
Martha, 18(2)
Mary Ann, 18
Nealy, 18
Neaty, 18(2)
Noah, 18
Pheriby L., 19
William, 18(2), 19(2)
LAMKIN
Marion, 10
LAMPKIN
Lewis, 9
Marion, 8, 9
LANE
B. J., 191
George M., Dr., 192
Jane Alberta Dozier, 192
Mary Frances, 192
R. W., 191
Robert Wilkes, Sr., 192
Robert Willie, 191
William, 138

LANG
Annias, 146
Elizabeth, 146
LASLIE
Rachel Anna, 137
LAWRENCE
John, 33
LEDBETTER
Sarah J., 179, 180
LEE
Polly, 114
William T., 162
LEITS
A. P., 92
D. R. C., 92
J. A., 91
Monroe, 92
Monrow, 92
R. E., 92

LEMASTER
Annie, 164
LENOIR
James Herman, 165
Johnnie, 165
Sallie, 165
LEONORA
Thomas Gastin, 129
LESTER
Donna M., 27
LEWIS
D. H., 49
Dixon H., 49(2)
Hamlin F., 48, 49
Isaac, 145
John Hill, 49
L. D. H., 48
Mary Elmore, 50
Mary H., 49
N., 144
Newton, 144

Samuel P., 145(2)
Sarah A., 48, 49
Sarah Elmore, 49
William James, 145(2)
LINDSEY
Rebecca, 188
LITTLE
A. M., Mrs., 4
Amanda Holland, 4
Elizabeth, 154
F. L., 4
F. M., 4
J. E., 4
J. W., 4
John, Rev., 191
Mary 120
Marry L., 4
LIVINGSTON
James Cooper, 102
Stella Burks, 104
Willard Wise, 102
LONG
Catherine, 161
Jacob, 161
LONGMIRE
Emma R., 35
LOPER
Cordel, 130
Elizabeth, 130
LORENZ
Camilla Agnes, 60
Fred Eugene, 60

Henry, 60
Mary Eugenia, 60
LOVEJOY
Perlina S. A., 68
LOVELLE
Aden, Jr., 43
LOVETT
Charles Candler, 119

David Meriwether, 119
Elizabeth Howard, 119
Robert William, 118, 119(2)
Ruth Candler, 117, 119(2)
LOWE
John Elder, 153(2)
M. G., 188(2)
LUCKY
J. M., 20
John, 21
John F., 20
Mary, 20, 21
Sarah, 21
William, 21
LYLE
Dr., 93
LYLY
Janie Harrington, 16
LYON
William Andrew, 69
MCCALVEY
Margaret, 142
MACCAULEY
Susan, 129
William, 129
MCCLENDON
Frances M., 133
MCCLESKAN
Amanda, 168
MCCLINE
W. H., M. D., 99
MCCONIEI
Milton, 156
MCCONNELL
Joseph, 105
Owen, 9, 11

MCCONNIEL
Sarah Ann, 155
MCCOY
Mary, 114
MCCURRY
Lena May, 85
MCDANIEL
Daniel R., 173
Darling E., 173, 174
Eli C., 173, 174
Elizabeth E., 173
Elvina B., 174
Imand C., 173
Imanda C., 174
James, 173, 174
James W., 173, 174
John J., 173(2)
Mary L., 173
Milda, 173, 174
Sarah S., 173
Sarah S. J., 173
Sarah, Sr., 174
William L., 173, 174
William, Sr., 174
MCDOLE
Jane, 116
MCDONALD
Brazos, 23
George Edward, 21
Treve, 23
MACDONELL
Nancy Collier, 56
R. W., 56
Robert Walker, 56, 57
Tochie, 56
MCDUFFIE
Annie Clifford, 47, 82
M. L., 47

Mann, 46
Manning, 81
R. L., 47
MCGAUGHEY
Mary C., 153
MCGEHEE
Eliza, 26
MCKEE
Catherine, 134
MACKENZIE
Alexander, 112
MCKENZIE
Mary Ann, 113

MCKINLEY
Ann Maria, 29
MCLENDON
Seaborn, 73
MCLUCAS
Daniel, 89
Daniel, Rev., 62
MCMICHAEL
Pollard Brown, 129
William Edward, 188
William, Rev., 182
MCMILLAN
Robert House, 168
MCMURRAY
Penelope, 87
Sarah Jane, 134(2)
MCNAIR
Amanda, 21(2)
MCNEAL
Sarah, 134
MCWHORTER
Bell, 59
Judy, 59
Sara Elizabeth, 59

William A., Jr.,
  58
MADDUX
  N. R., 147
MAGEE
  Mariah Josephine,
  15
MAGILL
  Helen, 120
MAHAN
  L. Lee, 60
  N. D., 62
MAJORS
  Anderson, 137
  Daniel, 137
  David, 136,
  137(2)
  Elizabeth F., 137
Majors (continued)
  John, 137
  Jonathan T., 137
  Louisa, 137
  Malissa, 137
  Martha, 137
  Mary, 136
  Rachel, 137
  Sarah, 136
  Sarah A., 137

  Susan, 137
  Thomas, 136(2)
  Thomas Clements,
  137
  William, 137
  Winnefred, 137
MALONE
  Ives R., 50
MANLY
  Eva Aycock, 18
MARCH
  William George,
  168
MARK

Catherine, 164
MARKLEY
  Willa V., 163
MARKS
  Andria, 164
  Andy, 164
  Elizabeth, 164(2)
  George, 164
  Mary Jane, 164(2)
  Nancy, 164
MARLIN
  Mollie, 52
MARLOR
  Annabel, 49
MAROT
  Nancy, 48
MARTIN
  Ada, 138
  Alice T., 137
  Catherine
    Aquilla, 137
  Charles, 137
  Charles, Rev.,
  138
  Coley Truitt, 138
  Daniel Laslie,
  137
  E. W., 46
  Edmund Wellborn,
  44, 46
  Elizabeth, 137
  Esther Hogan, 137
  G. W., 142
  Ida, 52, 138
  James, 137, 139
  James Arthur, 138
  James Marion, 138
  James, Sr., 138
  John, 138
  John Eubanks, 138
  Lula Bond, 79

  Lula Bonds, 81

M. D., Rev., 44
Mary Anna, 54
Mary Jane, 137
Mary Lydia, 138
Rachel Anna, 137
Sarah Hill, 46
Welborn J., 137
MASON
Kittie, 97
MATHEW
Mary, 51
MATHEWS
Dorothy, 185
Iris, 185
LaVern, 185
Olivia, 185
Thelma, 185
Theodosia E., 122
MATHIS
Henry Edward, 10
James, 42
James E., 41, 44
Marion R., 10
Sarah Catherin, 42
Walter Rylander, 10
MATTHEWS
Elizabeth, 186
MAXWELL
Berry, 187
MAY
Corrie, 169
Mary, 1, 2
MAYES
A. T., 4
John, 74
L., 4
Lou, 4
W. L., 4
MEGEHEE
Betty, 158
Elizabeth, 157
Elizabeth Louisa, 157
Georgia, 157

Georgia Ann, 158
Georgian, 157
Ida Isebell, 157
James Lee, 157
James, 157(2), 158(2)

James R. Lee, 158
Jane, 157
Jasper, 157
John, 157(4), 158(2)
John M., 157
Martha, 157
Mary Jane, 157
Mary L., 157
Mary Lovler, 157
Michael, 157(2), 158(2)
Michael, Sr., 158
Nancy, 157
Robert, 157(2)
Sarah, 157
Virginia, 157
William, 157(3)
MEREDITH
Frances, 79
MERIDETH
Frances, 80(2)
MERIWETHER
Thomas, 189
MERK
Elizabeth, 164
Henry, 164
William E., 164
METTS
Elefair, 159
Martha Elizabeth, 159
Wright, 159(2)
MICHAEL
Ada Jane Harper, 152
Anderson Green,

151, 152
Angeline Collins, 29
David, 151
David Franklin, 152
Elizabeth Catherine, 151
John Anderson, 152
Joseph LaBoon, 152
Mary Emma, 152
Sarah, 152
MIDDLE
Cate Price, 39
MIDDLEBROOKS
Claire, 118
MIDDLETHON
Ann E., 120

William III, 120
William Royall IV, 120
MIDDLETON
William Royal, Jr., 118
MIKEL
Anderson Green, 153
David, 152, 153(2)
Elizabeth, 153
Jacob, 153
James K., 153
John W., 153
Martha Ann, 153
Samuel H., 153
William D., 153
MILAM
Beaulah, 91
MILBORN
Milton, 169

MILBURNE
Milton, 169
MILL
Alexander Franklin, 44
M. C., 44
MILLER
Ann, 134
MILLS
Eliza, 59
Isaac Peter, III, 59
Julia A., 154
Julia G., 58
Julia Goodall, 58
Julia Helen, 59
Larry Taylor, 59
Pete, 57, 58(3),59
Pete, Jr., 58
Pete, Sr., 58
Sara, 58(2)
Sara Brinson, 58
Sarah, 58
MINOR
Virginia, 173
MITCHELL
Caroline L., 46, 81
Caroline Lovedy, 47, 81
Claude L., 150(3)
Elizabeth J., 110
Georgia V., 150
Georgia Virginia, 150
J. R., 164
John J., 110
Joseph Lafac, 109
M. E., 46, 81
Mary E., 151
Mary Eliza, 47, 81
Mary L. B., 109

Norman, 47, 82
Stephen, 47, 81
Susan Cook, 25
Thomas Olanan, 109
W. W., 109
Willis Jackson, 150
MIXTON
Rev., 4
MIZE
Alice, 78
MONTGOMERY
Nancy D., 133
MOON
High, Rev., 116
Lillie Belle, 84
Moses Edward, 152(2)
Mrs., 84
MOORE
George W., 171
Mary, 134
Nannie, 69
MORELAND
Annie M. Strickland, 166
Littleton, 11
Margaret, 166
Marshall, 165, 166
Martha A. S. McCollane, 11
Mary, 165
Rpbert, 166
Sallie Green, 165
T., 12
MORGAN
Amarintha Barwick, 12
Ann, 40(2), 42(2)

Ann Eliza, 41, 44

Annah Lee, 74
Annie E., 44
Annie Virginia, 42, 43
Asa, 71
Asa Ware, 73, 74
Caludia Sophronia, 74
Catherine, 40
Diasy Lucile, 43
E. A., 41
Edward Cobb, 40
Elihu, 71
Elisabeth, 40, 42
Elisha K., 161
Eliza, 44
Eliza Ann, 41
Eunice, 42(2)
Flora, 41(2), 42, 44
George, 40
George C., 40, 42
George Cadogan, 40, 41(2)
Georgia V., 182
Grace E., 41, 44
Grace Elisabeth, 40
Henrietta, 188
Henry, 40, 42
Henry C., 71, 73
Hiram, 71, 73
Hiram Augustus, 73
Incy, 71
Incy Lavonia, 73
James Abner, 73
James Asa, 74
John, 40(2)
John Hampden, 44
John Terrantine, 73
Laura, 44
Laura Ethel, 41,

43
Luke John, 71
M. J., 44
Mariah Sophronia, 73
Martha Ann Elisa Jane, 74
Martha Katharine Frances, 73
Mary, 71

Mary Anny, 73
Mary Elisabeth, 40
Mary Jane, 40, 41
Mary Jane Deborah, 74
Mary Ruth, 41, 43
Nancy H., 41(2), 42, 44
Nancy Hurry, 40
Rebecca, 114
Richard, 40
Richard Price, 40(5), 42
Roland, 71
Ruby Allen, 41
Rubye Allene, 43
Ruth, 44
Sally, 73
Sally Ware, 73
Sarah, 40
Sarah Ann Elizabeth, 73
Sarah Elizabeth, 74
Sarah Price, 40(2)
Septium, 40
Susan Asha, 73
Susannah, 71, 73
Sydney, 40, 42
T. H., 40(2), 41(2), 42, 44
T. H., Jr., 41, 43
Thomas H., 41, 44
Thomas Hurry, 40
Thomas Hurry, Sr., 42
Thomas Jefferson, 73, 74
Virginia M., 43
Willia Belle, 43
William, 40, 71, 73
William Ashburner, 40
William Augustus, 74
William Frederick, 40, 42
William Henry, 40, 42, 73
William Sydney, 40
William, Jr., 71, 73
Willie, 44
Willie Belle, 41
Young Frederick Allen, 74
MORLAND
Martha A. S., 11
MORRISON
Daniel Manson, 62
John, 50
MORROW
America Peacock, 4
MORTON
J. F., 87
Sarah Antoinett, 54
William Thomas, 7
MOSELEY

Mary E., 123
Peter, 145
Rufus D., 145
Rufus Darling, 144
MOSS
John S., 6
MOUK
Esther
  Deleisseline, 13
MOZO
Bailey, 2
George, 2
George D., 2
George Edna, 2
Henry Bailey, 2
MURPHEY
Cornelia L., 151
Levenia, 21
MURPHY
Martha A. S., 12
Mary P., 151
T. K., 11
MURRAY
Eloise, 7
Florence, 7
George Clay, 7(2)
Lucile Murray, 7
MURRY
Patricia, 58
MYRICK
John A., 11

NANCE
Cisaley, 123
NAPIER
Mary A., 24
NASH
Marget, 174
NEESE
L. P., Rev., 191
NETT
Claborn, 34
NEW

L. Myrtle, 92
M. S., 92
M. T., 92(2)
R. B., 93
T. M., 91, 92
NEWSOM
Annie Ruth, 112
David A., 112
David Daniel, 112
Elizabeth Lucy,
  112
Maggie Bell, 112
Margaret, 112
Meta Eta, 112
NEWSOME
Augustua R., 165
Augustus R., 164
Elizabeth
  Lavinia, 165
Joe S., 165
Lizzie, 166
Obedience
  Victoria, 165
Victoria O., 164
NEWTON
John, 9
NEYLE
Mary Bryan, 177
NICHOLAS
Alexis, 6
NICHOLSON
Bertha Lillian,
  163(2)
C. R., 163
D. M., 163(2)
Elizabeth S.,
  163(2)
Elizabeth Sophia
  Spann, 163
Ellona Mildred,
  163(2)
Eula May, 163(2)
James J., 163

Jesse R., 163
Jessie Remous, 163
L., 163
L. M., 163(2)
L. R., 163
Luther, 163
Mamie Ivera, 163
Martha Jane John, 163(2)
Martin L., 163
Mary, 149
Melson, 163
N. N., 163(2)
Vernard Nathaniel, 163
W. J., 163
William Louther, 163

NUCKOLS
James, Jr., 136

OGBURN
Frances Elizabeth, 28
Francis Elizabeth, 27
Polly, 28

OGLESBY
Cecelia, 22
Sarah, 22

OLIPHANT
Elizabeth, 129

OLIVER
Ada E., 7
Ada Estelle Shepard, 7
Amelia Kimbrough, 6
Edith Allen, 7(3)
Emily Waller, 31
F. M., 6
Florence Ann, 6
Florence McCarty 6
H. K., 6
J. M., Mrs., 7
James M., 7(2)
James McCarty, 6(3), 7(2)
James McCarty III, 6
James McCarty, Jr., 6, 7
Kathleen A., 7
Kathlen Ada, 7
Louisa Esten, 7
Louise E., 7
Lucile E., 7
Lucille Estelle, 7
Mary Stone, 7(2)
Mary Winfrey, 16, 17
Matilda Allen, 7
Matilda Louisa Allen, 6, 7
McCarty, 6
McCarty, Rev., 6
Olivia Susanna, 6
Samuel John, 6
Susanna, 6
T. P., M. D., 40(2)
Woodson, 7
Woodson Allen, 6

ORR
A. J., 128
A. J., Rev., 172
Ealsey, 65

OSBORN
Leah King, 8(2)

OSBORNE
Hampton, 16

OVERBY
Ann Elizabeth, 148

Basil Hallum, 148
Benjamin, 149
Benjamin
  Mitchell, 148
John Bayliss
  Earl, 148
Meshack, 149
Nicholas, 148,
  149
Nicholas G., 148
Nimrod, 149
Nimrod W., 148
Obidiah, 149
Peter, 149
OWENS
Abner, 124
Ary Ann, 33
Charlotte E. L.,123
Charlotty Lucy

Elizabeth, 124(2)
Elizabeth
  Candler, 120
F. L., 127
Floman M. P., 124
Gideon, 124
J. M., 123
Jane, 124(2)
John M., 123
Lucy Beall, 120,
  121
M. J., 124
Toll, 124
Tolliver, 124(2)
W. D., 121
William D., 120,
  121
William Davis,
  120
William Davis,
  Jr., 121
OZBURN
Lilla Belle

Tolbert, 116
Ruth Tolbert, 116
Samuel Alonza,
  116

PALMER
Sarah Ann, 155
PANELS
Rev., 188
PARKER
Cloe Amanda, 33
David C., 33
Jacob, 133
James, 33
John Floyd, 32
Louisa Virginia, 33
Martha Frances 33

Mary, 133
Mary Adney, 32
Nancy Ann E., 33
Patsey, 34
Patterson A., 32
Rhoda, 133
Sarah L., 33
W. P., 32
William R., 32
Williams P., 33

PARTON
M., 188
PATRICK
M. J., 164
PATTERSON
Charles B., 27
Charles R., 27
Ida F., 27
Moriah P. Tondee,
  175
Robert M., 134
S. E., 193
Solomon V., 4
PATTON

Nancy, 49(2)
PAYNE
  Emily E., 105(2)
PEACOCK
  Benjah, 3
  Dellemar Clayton, 3
  Edna Zimmerman, 3
  Gideon James, 25
  Ginsy, 3
  Howell, 3
  James Bryson, 3
  Jasper R., 4
  John Tyler, 4
  Laura Rebecca, 4
  Letitia T. R., 4
  Margaret M., 4
  Marietta McQueen, 4
  Patience Pertee, 4
  Polly Virginia, 4
  R. M. O., 3
  Rebecca Melvina, 3
  Robert, 3(2), 4
  Sara Ann, 4
  Simon, 3
  Simon Morris, 3
  Spicy Ann, 3
  Ulala, 4
  Zilpha, 3
PEEPLES
  Bennie Green, 193
  Elizabeth, 193
  Reuben P., 193
PENLAND
  Bennie, 120
  Marian, 120
PENNINGTON
  Anna, 133
PEOPLES
  Rawlin, 188
PERKINS
  Abraham, 67, 68
  Ann, 67
  Chase, 67, 68(2)
  Comfort, 67
  Esther, 67
  Frederick T., 67
  Hannah, 67, 68
  Hannah H., 68
  J. B. O., 68
  John, 67
  John B., 67(2)
  John P., 67
  Jona., 68
  Jonathan, 67(4)
  Juliann, 67
  Leila, 165
  Lydia D., 67
  Mary, 67, 68
  Mary B., 67
  Matthew, 67(2), 68
  Meribah, 67
  Phebe, 67
  Prodate, 67
  Ruth, 67
  Salley M., 67
  Sarah M., 67
  Susannah, 68
  Thomas N., 68
PERSON
  G. W., Rev., 192
PETREE
  John Charles, 168
  Nancy Eveline Edwards, 168
  Willburn, 168
  William Theodore, 168
PETTY
  Fred W., 4
PHAROAH
  Elizabeth W., 20
  Elizabeth Wallis, 21
PHILLIPS
  James Turner, 134
  John Alexander James, 149(2)

Mary, 134
Sarah, 134
William, 156
PINSON
Ellen, 44

PITTS
Chaney, 33
Sarah, 33
PLEDGER
Nancy Adeline, 84(2)
PLOWDEN
Robert Ried, 9,10
POLLARD
Mary, 45
POOL
Elizabeth, 123
POOLE
Burney Steed, 181
POPE
Caroline, 144
Dick, 144
Elick Zander, 144
Elizabeth, 144
F. W., 16, 18
Frances Jame, 144
Frances Marion, 144
James, 17
James Fernanandi, 18
James Lewis, 144
Jesse, 144, 145
Jesse Wright, 144
Jessie Rando, 144(2)
John, 144
John Oliver, 144
Joseph C., 145
Joseph Cunagm, 144
L. S. A., 144
Lydia Shadyan, 144
Martha, 144
Martha Ann, 144, 145
Mary E., 150
Mary Gray, 18
Nancy, 144
Pinkney H., 145
Pinkney Hill, 144
Robert Jabez, 144
Robt. J., 145
S. A. E., 150
Stephen, 144
T. F. W., 18
William, 144
William Allen, 144
0
PORTER
Ann, 124(2)
Ann M., 126
Anthony, 124
Caty, 124(2)
D. W., 124
Douglas W., 124
Douglas Watson, 124
James M., 124
James Madison, 124, 126
John, 124
John W., 124, 126
Margaret, 124(2)
Nancy, 124
Oliver, 124(2), 126
Oliver, Jr., 124
Peggy, 124(2)
Polly, 124
William, 124, 126
POWELL
Asha, 73
Henry, 73(2)

Polly, 73
POWERS
　Elizabeth, 189
　George, 188
　Jane Margaret
　　Gilmore, 188
　John, 189
　Mary C., 188
　Mary Meriwether,
　　189
　Nicholas, 188,
　　189
　Nicholas H., Dr.,
　　188
　Nicholas, Rev., 189
　Sarah, 175(2)
PRICE
　Cate, 39
　David, 39
　Edwina, 170
　Elisabeth, 39(2)
　Richard, 39(3)
　Sarah, 39
　Sarah Wandsleigh,
　　8, 9, 10
　William, 8, 9
PRUETT
　Laurence N., 106(2)
PUTETT

　John, 127

QUILLIAN
　Dr., 191

RABUN
　Matilda Ellis, 21
RAINEY
　Lucy, 86
RAMSEY
　George Edward, 69
RAWLS
　Charlotte

　Raiford, 70
　Corella, 70
　Francis Collier,
　　69
　Francis Collier,
　　Jr., 70
　Morgan, 175, 176
　Selinva V., 176
RAY
　Elvira, 160
REAGAN
　Saleta, 142
REDWINE
　Robbie, 10
REEVES
　W. N., 143
REID
　J. W., Rev., 188
REMINGTON
　Aborn, 8
　Lall Rook, 9
　Lalla Rock, 11
　Lallah Rock, 8
　William Aborn, 9
RENFROE
　Hanna, 85
REVILL
　Harrison, 33
　Nancy, 33
REYNOLDS
　F. F., Rev., 192
　Owen, 52
　Priscilla Goods, 53
RHODES
　Fannie, 142(2)
RICE
　Parker, Rev., 4
　William, 95
RICHARDS
　Aline L., 89
　Cate, 39
　Jessie Bull, 90
RICHARDSON

George Landrum, 85
Leona Booth Chapman, 85
RICK
Theodosis A. S., 181
RIDDELL
William Hugh, 52
RIED
Henry, 10
RIETMAN
Carl A., Dr., 60
RIGHAM
Eugenia, 120
RILEY
Anna Mae, 60
Georgia Ella, 160
Sarah Ann, 160
RIPLEY
Mary Irene, 118
ROBERTS
Abner, 137
Benjamin M., 179
Caroline A., 179
George Edward, 70
Leila, 69, 70
Mary, 70
Oliver, 70
Oliver Toon, 70
Patsy, 179
Rabun Brantly, 69, 70
Ralph, 70
William H., 179
ROBERTSON
Maurice Linden, 7
ROCHESTER
Henry, 22
Marcella, 22
Thomas Horace, 22(2)
Victoria, 22

ROE
Susan Elizabeth, 104

ROGERS
Aggustus Lovely, 168

ROLLINS
Gail Fitzgerald, 99
Harry, 99
Harry Brent, 99
Harry Brent, Jr., 99
James Richard, 99
Michael Richard, 99
Ruth Brent, 99
ROOF
E. F. K., Rev., 41
ROOS
Charles, 165
Helen, 166
Mary Bennett, 165
R. C., 165
Robert C., 166
ROSE
A. M. M. S., 124
Charlotta Cross, 124
Charlotte, 124
Charlotty, 124
Eliza Ann Amanda, 123
Eliza E., 123, 124
Elizabeth Lee, 124
Emily C., 123, 124
Fleming C., 123
Francis Barto, 124
G. W. W., 123, 124
George W. W., 123
George, Sr., 124

J. A., 124
J. M., 123
James M., 123
James M. A., 123, 124
John A., 123, 124
John M. M., 124
John T., 123
Lucy, 124
M. J., 124
Marcus DeLaFayette, 123(2), 124
Martha S. A., 124
Nancy M. W., 124

Nancy Mary, 123
Nancy Mary Jane, 124
Permelia E., 123
Samuel H., 123, 124
Sarah E. P., 124(2)
Tamer, 124
W. M., 124
William, 123(2), 124(2)
William H., 123
William, Sr., 124
ROSENCRNTZ
William, 112
ROSS
Annie Rebecca, 91
ROSSETTER
Sophia F., 3
ROUTIN
James R., 14
ROWELL
John Alllan, 55
John Alln, 54
ROWLAND
B., 112

Isaac B., 112, 113
John Thurston, 112
T. A., 112
ROWLANDS
Mrs., 113
RUDISILL
Dorothy Annie Clare West, 9, 10
James, 9
James Clarence, 8, 9(2), 10
Louise Grady, 9
RYALS
Jessie Lora Bond, 80
Joseph, 146
Penelope, 146(2)

ST. CLOUD
Martha Ines, 69
Victor Ernest, 69

SANBORN
Chase, 68
Hannah H., 68
SANDERS
Emly Elizabeth, 91
I. M., 93
Isiah, 94
Isiah M., 93
Vinie, 94
SANDERSON
W. R., Rev., 60(2)
SANFORD
Katherine, 54
SANFORN
Benaiah, 68
Chase P., 68

Hannah, 68
SATTERWHITE
  Mourning, 33
SAWYER
  David H., 162
  Edna, 23
SAYER
  W. R., 78
SCAIPE
  Charner Poole, 68
  Fletcher Terry, 69
  James M., 68
  Jessie Terry, 68
  Margaret R., 68
  Mary Crosby, 68
  Mary M., 68
  Nancy M. Mc., 68
  Perlina S. A., 68
  Vealento M. J., 68
  William, 68
SCAIPE
  Adam, 69
  Charner Poole, 69
  Charner Augustus, 69
  Edith Olivia, 69
  James Madison, 69
  Margaret Alice, 69
  Martha Elizabeth, 69
  Robert Hollingsworth, 69
  Roland Lee, 69
  Ruth, 69

  William Isaiah, 69
SCARBOROUGH
  N. A., 180
SCHAFFER
  Eliza, 161
SCHMIDT
  Rev., 60

SCHUMPERT
  Amos, 161
  Catherana, 161
  Elisha K., 161
  Elizabeth, 161
  Frederick, 161(2)
  Jacob, 161
  John Frederick, 161
  Magdena, 161
  Mary, 161
  Peter, 161(2)
  Rhoda, 161
  Sarah, 161
  William K., 161
SCOTT
  R. E., 107
  Ruth A., 49
SEABY
  F. R., Rev., 191
SEATON
  W. S., 173
SEAY
  Lucy C., 148
SEE
  Barbary Virginia, 71
  David Tillman, 71
  Ernestine Elizabeth, 71
  Fredinand, 71
  George Winfield, 71
  Hartmell Harris, 71
  John, 71
  John W., 71
  Joshua L., 71
  Lavina S., 71
  Levi Pharoah, 71
  Mary Ann, 71
  Sarah Barthella, 71

Washington, 71
SEE
John 72
SEYMORE
J. Luther, 85
SHANNON

Margaret E., 18
SHEALY
Andrew, 42
Andrew E., 44
Grace Elizabeth, 42
SHEFFIELD
Ada Lee, 181
Audrey Mary, 181(2)
Burney Steed, 181
D. A., 181
Elizabeth, 130
J. S., 180, 181(3)
J. S., Jr., 181
Lillian Lucile, 181
Reuben, 181(2)
Serod, 130
T. A., 181
W. R., 181
William R., 181
SHELFER
Julia F., 187
SHELL
Mary E. L., 174
SHELY
Andrew E., 41
SHEPARD
Ada E., 6
M. M. Stone, 7
O. T., 7
Roger S., 58
SHEPPERD
Sarah A. C., 11

SHERMAN
Martha, 184
SHORTER
Eli, Judge, 26
SHREVE
Richard Price, 39
SIMMONS
Stephen, 142
SIMPSON
G. A., Rev., 193
Kate Orten 193
Stella Viola, 193
SIMSON
Ann, 175
SINGLETON
Elizabeth Jane, 170
Ida, 57
Joe, 57
SKINNER
Mary E., 42
T. H., 42
SMITH
Carrie McLean, 191
Charles C., 192
David Dickson, 64
Edward, 191
Elenor, 5
Elisabeth Jane, 40
Elisha, 5
Elishie, 5
Eliza Ann, 40, 41, 42
Eliza C., 3
Elizabet J., 168
Elizabeth, 114
Elizabeth Jane, 41
Elsie Magnolia, 5
George C., 109
Gertrude, 97

H. E., 142
H. J., 5(2)
Hyrom J., 5
Hyrom Jackson, 5
Ida Belle Price,
 170
Ida Camille
 Dozier, 191
James Robert, 41,
 44
Jane, 41
Jepthey, 64
Jesse, 41
John Edward, Jr.,
 191
Joseph, 87
Joseph Henderson,
 5
Lovell Clay, 5
M. E., 5, 87
Malissa, 101
Martha Dickson,
 64
Mary E., 86
Mary F., 71
Nancy, 64
O. J., 30
Orlena J., 30
Preston, 69
Robert Lee, 7
Sandford
 Anderson, 5
Sarah E., 8
Savannah Roseann, 5
Sylvester, 5
Theo, 109
SNEED
Wilson W., Rev.,
 118(2)
SNELGROVE
Fatima, 134
Manah Wesley, 134
SNOW

Charles Thurston,
 152(2)
SPILLANE
Elizabeth Page,
 183
William Michael,
 182
SPROULL
John T., 101
STAFFORD
Rebecca E., 171
STAPLES
Martha S., 188
STEED
Rev., 190
STELLE
Samson S., 174
STEPHENS
A. C., 91
Alfred Columbus,
 91, 92
B., 92
C., 92
Celia Elizabeth,
 92
Celia Elizabeth
 Cook, 94
D. E., 92
D. V., 92
E. E., 91
Elizabeth C., 93
Emily Elizabeth,
 92
Emily Elizabeth
 Sanders, 94
Emley E., 93
G. B., 91, 92(2),
 93
Greenberry, 91
J. H., 92

J. M., 91(3), 93
Julius Green, 91,

92
L. Octavio, 92
M. A., 91
M. E. T. J., 91, 93
M. F., 91, 93
Melvinnie, 92
Melvinnie M., 93
Minnie A., 91, 93
P. M., 92
R. A., 91, 93
R. L., 92
Reuben Columbus, 93
Robert Luther, 93
Simeon Monroe, 92
Simeon Sylvester, 92
Simon Silvester, 91
W. C., 92
W. T., 91, 92
William Henry Grady, 93

STEPHENSON
Florence, 120
STEVENS
Allen, 126
C. A., 126
Elizabeth, 126
Haley, 126
J. R., 126
Jasper, 126
Joseph, 126
Martha, 126(2)
Newton, 126
Obediah, 126
Thomas, 126
W. C., 126
W. W., 126
Walton, 126
STEWART
Sarah, 38
STONE
Louisa Darsey, 187
Martha, 161
Mary Ann, 8
Michael D., 8
Sarah Elizabeth, 8(2)
Washington W., 186

William D., 8
STOW
Addie, 70
Anthony, 70
Brantly, 70
Edward, 69, 70(2)
Edward, Jr., 70
Fredonia, 70
Fredoria, 70
James Anthony, 70
Kate, 70
Lelia, 70
Lilia, 69
Lillie, 70(2)
Mary Lizzie, 70
Naomi, 70
Rabun, 70(2)
Rabun Susan, 70
Ruth, 70
Walter, 70
STRIBLING
Garnett Bee Bee, 10
Garnett Bob Bee, Dr., 9
George Thomas, 8(2), 10
George Young, 10
Henry Eugene, 9, 10
Lilliam Grady, 9

Lillian Grady, 10
Mona Louise, 10
Myrtle Annie, 9,
  10
Nian Marie, 10
William Stones,
  10
STRICKLAND
Ann Jane, 164,
  165, 166
Annie, 165
Annie Mariah, 165
Benjamin, 165
Elizaaabeth
  Dillon, 165
Elizabeth, 164,
  165
Elizabeth B., 166
Elizabeth D.,
  164, 166
James, 164(2),
  165(2), 166(2)
James Bennett,
  165, 166
James F., 166(2)
James Franklin,
  165
Jane, 165
Jas., 166
Jennie, 164, 166
Joel S., 73
Mary, 165
Mary Eliza, 166
Mary Elizabeth,
  165
Obedience V., 166
Obedience
  Victoria, 165
Peter Larkin,
  165, 166
Sarah L., 164
Sarah Louisa, 165
Stephen A. D.,
  165
Stephen Arnold
  Douglas, 166
Talight Jane, 165
Victoria O., 164
Wilizabeth B.,
  165
William, 165
William B., 165,
  166
Wm. Benjamine,
  166
STUDDARD
Leona Bertha, 24
STURGIS
A., 187
Alfred, 186
Georgia Caroline
  McDuffie, 187
M., 187
Mary Ann, 187
SULLIVAN
Andrew Jackson,
  131
Daniel, 131
Dennis, 131
Elizabeth
  (Betsy), 131
Ferriby, 131
George W., 131
James, 131
John, 131
John William, 131
Mary Ann, 131
Polly, 131

Simeon, 131
Susan, 131
SULLIVANT
Mary Ann, 146
Thomas C., 146
SUMMERLIN
Rachel C., 122

SUMMERLO
  Winifred Frances
    Barwick, 12
SUTTON
  Mary, 186
SWINEY
  M. J., 91
SWINN
  Leslie L., 16
SWITTENBERG
  Catherine, 161

TAGNER
  James Ogletre, 45
TALIAFERRO
  Mary M., 188
TALLIFERRO
  Ben, 25(3)
TALLY
  Philip, 122
TALTON
  John Holmes, 102
TANNER
  Elizabeth, 33
  Ellona Mildred
    N., 163
  Green Whiddon,
    163
  Joseph, 142
TANNON
  R. Price, 39
TATE
  Minor, 25
TATOM
  Abner, 139
  Absalom, 139
  Barnett, 139
  Cynthia, 139
  Elizabeth Ann,
    139
  James, 139
  John, 139
  John, Sr., 139

  Nancy, 139
  William, 139
TAYLOR
  Inez, 57
  James Bennett,
    165
  Jennie Belle, 165
  Mary Caroline, 18
  Mary Strickland,
    165
  Willie Charleton,
    165
  Zacary, 164
  Zachary, 165
TEABRANT
  Bennie, 120
TEASLEY
  Alfert, 155
  E. C., 156
  James W. A., 97
  Mamie, 156
  Mary F., 155
TELFORD
  Harvy, 9
  Iris, 9
  John Newton, 8,
    10
  Lilliam Iris, 10
TERRELL
  Catherine Hill,
    46
  E. B., Dr., 45
THARP
  James Madison,
    102
THOMAS
  Alie Asenath, 51
  Annacaona
    Hantippe, 51
  Bessie Neyle, 177
  Bryan Morel,
    177(2)
  C. A. A., 51

Carolina J. A.,
  51
Caroline J. A.,
  50, 51(3), 52
Catharine
  Drayton, 177
Edith Carson, 177
Eliza Neyle, 177
Elizabeth Neyle,
  177
Frank, 51
Frank A., 52
Franklin
  Alexander, 51
Franklin Andrew, 51

J. S., 177
James Wilson,
  51(2)
John F., 96
John G., Jr., 177
John Greenberry,
  177(2)
John Sherwood,
  177
John T., 177
Joseph H., 51
Martha Gadsden,
  177
Mary Ann, 51
Mary Jane Warner,
  44
Mary New, 177
Milton Guyton, 51
Nancy Catharine,
  51
Sarah, 51
Sarah S., 51
Thomas F.
  Drayton, 177
Virginia, 18
Virginia M.
  Joiner, 44

W. C., 51, 52(2)
William, 11
William C.,
  51(3), 52
William G., 50
William Moses, 51
THOMPSON
  A. Eli, 41
  Amos Eli, 42,
    44(2)
  Annie E., 42
  Asa, Sr., 25
  George E., 21
  John, 132
  Robert Dismukes,
    132
  Sarah, 132
THORNTON
  C. F., 184, 185
  Elizabeth A.,
    184, 185
  James J., 185
  M. A., 184, 185
  N. J., 184
  R. F., 184
  T. A., rev., 84
THRASH
  Martha Ann, 33
THRASHER
  Asenath, 148
  Martha Caroline,
    162
THREADGILL
  George A., 149
  James R., 149
  Rebecca, 149
  Thomas Jelks,
    149(2)
  William, 149(2)
THURMAN
  Amanda Lee, 97(2)
  David Russell, 97
  Edna May, 97

Enoch Lewis, 97
Lillian Ruth, 97
Maude Irene, 97
Otis, 60
Ray Vaughn, 97
Roy Atticus, 97
Sarah Lucile, 97
TINDALL
Lieusinday E., 127, 172
Thomas B., 128, 173
TOLAR
Ella Bell, 50
Lorrsell, 50
Sarah A., 50
TOLMAN
Ebeneer, 41
Eunice, 41
TONDEE
Maria P., 176
TOWE
Anne, 8
TOWNS
George, 114
Margaret Jane Campbell, 114
TRACY
Edward D., 113
Rebecca Caroline, 113
TRAVIS
Amos, 17
TRAWICK
Georgia M., 147
TRAYLOR
Sarah, 49
TRIBBLE
A. K., Rev., 94
TRIPP
Elizabeth, 151
TRUITT
Ally T., 150

Martha, 138
TURK
A. A., 76, 77
A. S., 76
Addison, 74
Cyntha Jane, 75
Era, 74
Isabel Elisabeth, 75
Isabel Elizabeth, 74
Isabella Elizabeth, 76
J. T., 76
James, 75
James Hall, 75
Jane, 74, 75, 76
John, 75
John N., 74(2), 76
John Newton, 74, 75
Luesa Adaline, 75
Lula Jane, 74
Margaret, 74
Margaret Hall, 75
Margaret Manerva, 75
Mary, 75
Mary E., 74
Mary Elisabeth, 74
Mary Malinda, 75
Nora L., 76
Pliney A., 76
Pliney Addison, 75
Robert Lee, 74
Sarah Lititia, 75
T. N., 76
Vincent A., 76
William, 74, 75(4), 76

William Harvy,
  75, 76
TURNER
Ethel, 57(2), 84
J. B., Rev., 192
J. D., Rev., 83
James, 84
James B., Rev. 188

James R., Rev., 188
Nancy, 144
Nancy M., 73
V. A., 149
TURNIPSEED
L. O., 92
M. E. T. J., 92
O. H., 91
T. Octavio, 92
TURPIN
Mary Emily, 60
Ruth Annie, 60(2)
TYER
Nell Florence, 2

UPSHAW
Amey, 100
Amy, 100
Ann, 100
Catherine, 100
George, 100
James, 100
John, 99, 100(2)
Leroy, 100
Middleton, 100
Sarah, 100
Thomas, 100

VAN DYKE
R. J., Rev., 50
VICKERY
Emma, 82, 83
J. P., Rev., 83
James Parker, 82

Susie Shiflet, 83
VIDEAU
Rossie, 83
VILLA
John Charles, 168
VILLA V.
John C., 168
John Charles, 168
John Francis, 168
VINES
Thomas Gastin, 129

WADE

Henry J., 27
Jack, 55
WALDEN
Anne, 132
Elijah, 132
Lewis, 132
Mary, 132
Owen, 132
Samuel, 132
William, 132
WALDING
Fannie, 132
Richard, 132
Sarah, 132(2)
WALDRON
Mary M. D., **16**
WALKER
Absley K., 154
Allen, 154
Ann L., 154
Clarissa L. J.,
  154
David, 36
Dorset, 154
E. A., 147
Elizabeth Hobb,
  154
Emma Geraldine,
  83

Fanna May, 154
Forrest, 83
Freeman F., 154
Harriet Olivia, 154
Henry Buleker, 154
Henry Davis, 37
Henry Wilson, 155
James, 36
James Forest, 83
John, 147, 154(2)
John Daniel, 154
John Edgar, 83
John Ivy, 154
Joseph Franklin, 154
Kinchen W., 154
L. P., 52
Lonnie W., 83
Lucky Medlock, 37
MacNorman, 83
Martha G., 154
Marttha, 37
Mary, 95(2), 154
Nancy, 36, 154
Rebecca, 147
Samuel, 37
Susan T., 154
Susie Margaret, 83
Thomas, 36
Thomas Inman, 83
Trecey E., 154
Virgin Green, 154
William B., 36
William H., 154
Wilson D., 154

WALL
Clarisa Grogan, 96
Clarissa, 94
Clarissa B., 96
E. G., 94
Eliza A., 94, 96
Elizabeth L., 96
John C., 94, 96
Jonathan, 96
Mary A., 94, 96(2)
Robert E., 94
Robert T., 96
Sarah A., 96
T. A., 94
Thomas A., 96
Thomason Amanda, 95
Wilbern, 96
Wilburn, 95
William, 96

WALLACE
Arthur Bates, 53(2)
Emma, 53(2)
Frank P., 7
Lendred, 53
Leola, 53
Mamie, 21
May, 53
S. L., 52, 53(2)

WALLER
Charles R., 30, 31, 131(2)
Daniel, 30, 131
Elizabeth, 30(2), 31, 131(2)
Emily, 31, 131
Handy, 30, 131
Helen, 51
John, 31(2), 131
John, Sr., 30
Nathaniel, 31
Nathaniel E., 30
Nathaniel L., 131
Sarah Brown, 31
William, 30, 131

WANSLEY
Reuben T., 156
WARDEN
Everd, 169(2)
WARDLAKE
Eliza A., 96
WARE
Peter, 71
Sally, 71
Susannah, 71
WARNER
Charles Howard, 46
Eliza Wann, 46
Hiram, 46(3)
Jane Marion, 46
Miranda, 46
Obadiah, 46
Rodolphus, 46
Sarah Watts, 46
Theron, 46
William Henry, 46
WARREN
Annie Dodd, 116
C. C., 120
Catherine C., 117
Catherine Candler, 117(2), 118(2), 119(2)
Glenn Dodd, 119
James Kimbrough, 120
Lucinda, 124
Mary R., 120
Mary Ripley, 118, 119
Norris Walton, 180
Samuel Ozburn, 117(2)
Thomas Ripley, 119
W. C. III, 120
William C., 117(2)
William C. III, 119
William Chester, 116
William Chester II, 118
William Chester III, 117, 118, 119
William Chester IV, 118
William Chester, Jr., 116
WARTHEN
Macon, 154
WASHBURN
Elisabeth A., 141
Michael A., 141
William K., 141
WATKINS
Ben, 126
Charly, 126
Daniel, 26(2)
Elizabeth, 126
James, 26
John, 26
Martha, 26, 126
Mary, 26(2)
Milly, 126
Nancy, 126
Olive, 126
Rose, 126
Rose, Sr., 126
Sarah, 25(2), 26(2)
Susan, 26
Susanna, 26
William, 126
WATSON
A. P., 164
Andrew, 165
Andrew F., Jr., 166

Andrew Pickens, 165
Andrew Pickens, Jr., 165
Elizabeth, 165
Harry Perkins, 166
John Brunson, 137
Lelia, 166
Margaret, 124
Mary M., 165
Strickland, 166
WATTS
Caroline M., 176
Ebiline, 134
James G., 175
WAY
Leland F., Dr., 9
Leland, Dr., 10
WEATHERLY
Eugene, Dr., 97
WEAVER
Benton, 41, 42
Flora, 42
Thomas J., 133
William Benton, 42, 44
William D., 133
WEBB
Eugene, 43(2)
Ruby, 43(2)
T. C., 41
Virginia, 43
Wiley Eugene, 41, 43
WEED
David, 40, 41(2), 42(2)
Eliza Ann, 40, 41
Julia A., 41
Julia Ann, 40(2)
Sarah C., 44
Sarah Catherin, 40
Sarah Catherine, 41
WELCH
Rachel, 161
WELLBORN
Asbury Cleveland, 182, 183
Frances Letitia Cowan, 183
WENTHAN
Katy, 21(2)
WESLEY
John, Rev., 143
Sousan R., 168
WEST
Alfred, 9(2)
Andrew J., 10
Andrew Jackson, 8
Andrew Lewis, 9, 10
Anie Grady, 9
Annie Grady, 8, 10
Edith, 11
Edith Woodfin, 9
Garnett Lee, 8, 9, 11
Harriet Morgan, 8
Harriett Morgan, 8, 10
Henry Haines, 10
Henry Sammones, 8
Henry Sammons, 9(2)
Henry Samones, 10
J. C., Rev., 84
John B., 8(2)
John C., 10
John Calhoun, 8, 9
Lou Kansas, 8(2), 9, 10

Lucy Leah, 9, 10
Marion Francis,
  9, 10
Mary Haines, 9
Maud King, 9
Maude King, 11
Norma Bell, 9
Norman Bell, 10
S. C., Rev., 83
Thelma Remington,
  9, 11
Wandsleigh, 9
Wandsleigh Price,
  10
WHATLEY
Mary, 134
WHEAT
Marcus, 186(2)
Maryann, 187
WHELCHEL
Lizzie, 15
WHITE
Ann Drewsils, 49
George W., 49
George Was., 49
George
  Washington, 49
James F., 156
Margaret, 48
Pinkney, 49(2)
Samuel, M. DD.,
  40
WIATT
Thomas, 34
WILIFORD
Annie, 47, 82
Annie Bell, 47,
  82(16)
Carrie May, 47(2), 82

Dan, 47
Edna, 47
J. H., 46, 81, 82

James, 47
James A., 82
James Archabald,
  47, 82
James H., 47, 82
John Thomas, 47
Joseph F., 47, 82
L. H., 47
Wilie Ed, 47
WILKES
Ida, 191
Ida Cunningham,
  191
WILLIAM .
John Charles, 168
WILLIAMS
A. D., 57
A. M., 56(2), 57
Albert McCoy, 56,
  57, Sara
Arthur Dudley, 57
Carrie, 57
E. T., 57
Francina, 56(2)
H. J., 57
Hannah Guillan,
  57
Henry J., 57
Howard J., 57, 58
Howard James,
  57(2), 58
Inez, 58
Inez Taylor, 58
Jackie Tochie, 56
James L., 188
John, 56
John B., 173
John H., 33
John W., 57
Julia Dora, 58
Julia Goodall,
  58(2)
Kitty, 57

L. L., 56
Leonara Cickett
  Wills, 56
Lucins Elijah, 57
Lucius E., 57,
  58(5)
Lucius Elijah,
  57, 58
Marie, 16
Mariha Jewitt, 57
Mary Jane, 44
N. C., 58
N. E., 56, 57
Nancy Callie, 57
Sallie G., 58
Sarah, 56
Sarah Frances
  Eliza, 57
Sarah Goodall, 58
T. M., 41, 42, 44
Theodore
  Middleton, 44(3)
Tochie, 57
W. D., 56(2),
  57(2), 58(2)
William, 44
William Brown, 56
William C., 188
William D., 56,
  57(2), 58(2)
William Dismuke,
  56(2), 57(2)
WILLINGHAM
Sarah J., 96
WILLS
Martha, 173
WILLSON
Mary J., 106
WILSON
Ann, 146
N. H., 87
Rachel Jane, 160
WIMBERLY

Amelia E., 6
WINGATE
Frances, 142
WINN
Mary, 56
WOLF
Adolphus C., 122
Elizaer
  Catherine, 122
Hannah, 122
Hannah E., 122
Hannah Elizabeth,
  122
J. C., 121
John C., 122
Joseph, 121, 122
Joseph H., 122
M. L., 122
Mary Jane, 122(2)
Mary L., 122

Nonie Ora, 122(2)
Permelia Emeline,
  122
Rachel C., 122
Servitus Alvie,
  122(2)
Theodosia E., 122
William G., 122
William Goren,
  122
WOLTZ
Elizabeth, 6
WOOD
Fred, 85
WOODS
Eliza, 130
Nancy, 174
WOODSON
Lucy, 26
WRAY
W. A., 85
WRIGHT

Abraham, 73
Alva Pearce, 7
Alva Pierce, 7
Ann, 73, 139
Burl J. T., 86
Deborah, 73
E. W., 87
Elicif C., 87
Elicif COrdelia, 86
Elisan William, 86
George Absalom, 73
I. J. G., 87
Jane, 87
John Lowen, 86
Louis, 144
Louise Oliver, 7
Mary Adeline Elizabeth, 86
Mary Ann, 87(2)
Mertie F., 87
Mertis Francina, 86
Winfred Jett, 86
Young Frederick, 73

John Philip, 69

YARBROUGH
Dr., 191

YONG
Edward Ellis, 25
YOUNG
Eliza C. Cobb, 155
George H., 26
George V., 155
Lucy Watkins, 16
ZACHY
Ann Elizabeth, 56
ZIEGLER

Other books by Jeannette Holland Austin:

1860 Paulding County, Georgia Census

Alabama Bible Records

DeKalb County, Georgia Probate Records

*Fayette County, Georgia Probate Records: Volume II
Annual Returns, Inventories, Sales, Bonds, 1845-1897*

Georgia Bible Records, Supplement, 1772-1940

Georgia Obituaries, 1740-1935

Georgia Obituaries, 1905-1910

Jackson County, Georgia Tombstones
Jeannette Holland Austin and Dorothy Holland Herring

Masters of the Low Country: A History of the Georgia Colony

North Carolina–South Carolina Bible Records

The Georgians Database: Genealogical Notes

Virginia Bible Records

www.ingramcontent.com/pod-product-compliance
Lightning Source LLC
Chambersburg PA
CBHW071702160426
43195CB00012B/1553